LIVING THE NIGHTMARE

Escape from Kuwait

Karen Kirk Huffman

ISBN: 1-886225-34-6

Cover Art by Angie Johnson Art Productions

Library of Congress Catologuing-in-Publication Data

Huffman, Karen Kirk, 1937-1996.
    Living the nightmare : escape from Kuwait / Karen Kirk Huffman.
        p.   cm.
    ISBN 1-886225-34-6 (alk. paper)
    1. Ali. 2. Dina. 3. Persian Gulf War, 1991-
-Personal narratives, Kuwaiti.   I. Title.
DS79.74.H84 1998   98-47559
956.7044'2—dc21   CIP

DAGEFORDE
Publishing, inc.

Dageforde Publishing, Inc
122 South 29th Street
Lincoln, Nebraska 68510
Phone: (402) 475-1123 Fax: (402) 475-1176
Visit our web site at: http://www.dageforde.com
email: info@dageforde.com

Printed in the United States of America
10 9 8 7 6 5 4 3 2 1

This book is dedicated to the people of Kuwait
for their defiance of Saddam Hussein and their resiliency
in enduring his military occupation and destruction,
of their homeland. And most importantly, to those brave
souls who gave their lives in the name of freedom.

FOREWORD

Sometimes I wonder if there is anyone in the world who can really understand how we Kuwaitis felt when we woke up one morning to find ourselves living in an occupied country. The words "outraged," "helpless," "frightened," or "shocked" might come to mind, but even though those are good words, they are not adequate to describe the impact the invasion had on us.

We are a peaceful people. War was a foreign word to us. We had never experienced war until we were suddenly thrust into its jaws. In just a few hours, and through no fault of our own, except that of having the poor judgment to trust Saddam Hussein, we were an occupied country. We had lost something that we had always taken for granted, but what we now know is the most precious thing in our lives: our freedom.

Until you have lived such an experience, you will never be able to know what losing your freedom means. Suddenly you find yourself in a world where there is no sunshine. There are only dark, cloudy days. It is a vicious world. A cruel world. A criminal world.

Many of us died during the seven months we were forced to live in that world, some horribly. But, by the grace of Allah, many more of us survived. It is we, the survivors, who are bound by the ghosts of the dead to tell their stories to the world. It is we, who must warn the world that as long as there is one man like Saddam Hussein alive, and in power, the freedom of no nation will ever be safe.

It is my hope that this book will do both—honor Kuwait's martyrs, and bring further dishonor to the man who murdered them.

—Ali A.

A BRIEF HISTORY OF KUWAIT

The State of Kuwait is located in the upper, northwestern tip of the Arabian Gulf. Shaped like a triangle, it borders Iraq on the north and Saudi Arabia on the west. Its southern edge shares a border with Saudi Arabia while the waters of the Arabian Gulf provide its eastern boundary.

The distance between the northern tip of Kuwait and its southern border is 124 miles, while the distance between the eastern and western boundaries is about 106 miles. The topography is mainly flat desert interspersed with shallow depressions and low hills.

There are two main seasons: the long, hot summer, which brings intense sandstorms and humid temperatures averaging 120 degrees; and the winter season, which is usually short but cold (lows in the 40s) with limited rainfall.

The country of Kuwait began as a small village, chosen as a base by hunters sometime in the seventeenth century. They named it "Kout," and it soon became a converging point for many of the indigent Utub tribes who were forced out of the interior of the Arabian Peninsula by drought, famine, and hostile tribes.

In the early 1700s the clan that was to become the ruling dynasty of Kuwait, the Al-Sabahs, immigrated to the area. Their rule began in 1752 when Sheik Sabah the First was elected to represent the coastal settlers in their dealings with the Ottoman Turks, rulers of the area at the time. The family has continued an uninterrupted reign since.

The area became known as Kuwait in about 1765. At that time the village that was to become a country had a population of about 10,000.

The nomadic hunting culture of the new settlers quickly changed to one shaped around pearl-diving, fishing and trading, yet their economic status changed little from what it had been in the interior. They remained an impoverished people who had simply exchanged their tents for mud huts.

In 1899, Kuwait, seeking protection from the Turks, requested to become a British protectorate. Britain accepted the responsibility and the agreement drafted between the two countries endured with few changes until June 19, 1961, when Kuwait was granted full independence. The country was accepted as an official member of the Arab League on July 20 of that same year.

The first move after the declaration of independence was to hold general elections to establish the first National Assembly, whose initial task was drafting a permanent constitution. The first session of the assembly was held in January of 1962. The constitution was signed on November 11, 1962, and on May 14, 1963, Kuwait became a member of the United Nations.

Today, even though the state of Kuwait is one of the smallest in the world, it is one of the richest and most beautiful in the Arabian Gulf area.

Its native population is estimated at just over 750,000; however with the addition of foreigners who live and work in the country, the total head count jumps to just over two million. Arabs form the biggest percentage of Kuwait's population equation while non-Arabs are dominated by Asians. A large number of Palestinians (nearly a quarter of a million) settled in the country after they lost their homeland to Israel.

Oil exploration began in 1923, with the first drop of crude being pumped from the Burgeon oil fields in 1936. World War II delayed commercial exports of petroleum until 1946. When exportation began, Kuwait suddenly found itself a wealthy nation. Taking a different path than some neighboring Arab states who also had become oil rich, Kuwait's rulers chose to put Kuwait's oil money into developing the country and its people, instead of building a huge military force.

Thus beauty began to emerge in a country where only the bleakness of an untamed desert had been seen for centuries.

Thousands of multi-story business buildings rose out of the wasteland. Thousands of large, comfortable homes and apartments and hundreds of schools and shopping centers were built. Some of the most well-equipped, professionally-staffed hospitals in the world were constructed, providing free medical care for all of the country's residents.

The seafront was developed into one of the most beautiful in the Middle East. Foliage was planted, and electric plants, sanitation facilities and water systems were installed. Experiments in agriculture began. Salaries went up in both government and private sectors, while food and consumer goods prices remained low.

Top-notch security was instigated. People took late night walks anywhere in the country with no fear of being accosted. Murder and theft occurred only rarely. The country cultivated a good relationship with most other countries in the world, in addition to its Arab brothers.

Education became one of Kuwait's top priorities. In 1956, the country adopted a free education plan that divided studies into four categories: kindergarten, primary, intermediary, and secondary, with the last three categories lasting four years each (the kindergarten program is for two years). In addition to the state-run schools, there also are some 100 private schools in the country.

In 1966, the educational plan was extended to include university education with the opening of Kuwait University. Today, education expense ranks second (public works is first) in expenditures in the government's annual budgets.

Scientific research has become another priority in Kuwait. To achieve progress in science, the government established two major organizations to promote scientific research: the Kuwait Institute for Scientific Research, which opened in 1971; and the Kuwait Foundation for the Advancement of Science.

In just a few years, this country that had once been a tiny piece of destitute, desolate desert became a cultured, peaceful, prosperous oasis. But, unfortunately, it also became an object of envy and desire for one of its neighbors.

INTRODUCTION

This book was inspired by actual incidents that occurred in Kuwait during the Iraqi invasion and occupation. The majority of the stories you are about to read were supplied by an American woman and her Kuwaiti husband who were living in Kuwait at the time of the invasion. Their families and friends also have contributed accounts of personal experiences during those dark days.

All of those who have related their stories are "average" Kuwaitis. Despite the image most Americans have of the citizens of Kuwait, they are not all wealthy. The country is wealthy, as are the members of the "establishment," but the vast majority of Kuwaitis are not. They are, as this book will show, people engaged in making a living as librarians, mechanics, bank tellers, businessmen, engineers, utility plant workers—common, ordinary people, by any American standard.

In most cases, first names of the Kuwaiti characters are real; the absence of surnames is for a good reason. Fear is still very much alive in the country. These people live on Iraq's doorstep. They do not yet feel safe from the long arm of Saddam Hussein. Christian and surnames of the American characters are real.

Readers will notice that what the Western world calls the "Persian" Gulf is called the "Arabian" Gulf throughout this book. The latter name is preferable in the Middle East, and out of respect for those telling the stories, it is used here.

And, last, but not least, the use of Arabic words has been kept at a minimum so as not to distract from the story. Arabic words are used only when there is no true English substitute.

CHAPTER 1

At 1:00 on the morning of August 2, 1990, Fuad, a twenty-four-year-old soldier from Rumaithiya, Kuwait, was standing guard duty at Al-Salem Army Base in northern Kuwait. It was a boring job and Fuad was having trouble staying awake. Propping his rifle against a truck, he stretched his long, lanky body, trying to shake the sleepiness from it.

The night had seemed quieter than usual, almost ominously so. He had not even heard the stirring of desert creatures in their perpetual search for food in the cold darkness. For some reason, the stillness gave Fuad an uneasy feeling.

He yawned, rubbing his bearded face briskly. He would be happy when his shift ended and he could crawl into a warm bed. Pulling his jacket collar snugly around his neck, he leaned back against the truck and reached in his pocket for a cigarette.

"Damned habit," he growled aloud. As he struck a match he remembered how many times he had promised himself he would quit smoking. "Tomorrow," he had told himself, every day for nearly a year.

As he stood shivering and drawing in deep puffs of smoke, his ears picked up a slight noise. He strained to listen, and in the distance, toward the Iraqi border, he heard a faint rumbling. The noise gradually grew in intensity and Fuad decided it sounded like tanks and other armored vehicles. The sound puzzled him. He knew there were no Kuwaiti maneuvers underway or he would have been involved in them. Dropping the cigarette, he reached for his field phone to summon the on-duty officer.

A few minutes later the officer, a captain, appeared at Fuad's post. He, too, heard the low rumble and looking through his binoculars, he confirmed to Fuad that the rumble was coming from tanks—tanks that were flying Saudi Arabian flags. *Strange*, both men thought. *Why would Saudi vehicles be coming into Kuwait from the north?* The captain decided to summon the base commander.

By the time the commander arrived at Fuad's post, the oncoming parade was visible without field glasses. The commander's brow furrowed in concentration. He couldn't remember having been notified of any training exercises. The Saudis surely wouldn't train on Kuwaiti soil without notifying the proper authorities. Shaking his head, the commander walked back to his office and ordered an alert to be sounded, but instructed his men not to fire at the approaching entourage.

As the vehicles moved swiftly toward the base, Fuad could see they were accompanied by truckloads of foot soldiers. Peering more intensely through his binoculars, he noticed that not all of the vehicles bore Saudi flags. Some were flying the Iraqi flag.

Fuad shivered again, but this time it wasn't from the cold night air. At almost the same instant that he saw the Iraqi flags, the oncoming vehicles opened fire. Fuad fell to the ground clutching his rifle. The awful truth struck him like a sledgehammer. *Kuwait was being invaded!*

Within minutes of the first Iraqi shots, the commander ordered his men to return fire but the meager weapons in the Kuwaiti arsenal were no match for the weaponry coming at them. The defense of the base was over almost as quickly as it had begun.

Kuwaiti soldiers began fleeing for their lives. Running as fast as his shaking legs would carry him, Fuad glanced over his shoulder to see the captain following a few paces behind. As they sprinted across the desert a missile from one of the Iraqi tanks exploded some twenty feet to the left of them, knocking both men to the ground.

Fuad instantly jumped back up and turned around, looking for the captain. He was sitting on the ground, a look of surprise on his face as he watched blood and intestines pour out of his belly.

Fuad took a step toward his superior, but the officer toppled over, dead. Fuad turned around and continued his terrified dash for safety.

Without warning and with calculated deadliness, the siege of Kuwait had begun.

■ ■ ■

Personnel at Ahmad al-Jaber Air Force Base, which was located south of the army base, did not receive notification about the Iraqi rampage into Kuwait until two hours after the invaders had crossed the border. When the news came, several pilots rushed to their planes and roared off the runways in an anxious attempt to intercept the Iraqi planes and bombard the enemy's ground forces.

Nasir, a thirty-year-old captain from Kuwait City, was one of the first Kuwaiti pilots to climb into his missile-loaded Skyhawk. A mixture of hatred and excitement gripped him as, with a blast of hot exhaust, he streaked into the moonless night sky.

A light haze of clouds hung over Nasir's cockpit and through them, he could see a few stars. *Flight instructors would consider this perfect weather for a training attack*, he thought. A chill went down his spine as he remembered that, this time, he *wasn't* on a training mission. *This was the real thing.* His country had been invaded. This was what all the years of instruction and discipline had been aimed at—defending his country. In all his years in the air force, he had never believed he would have to fly his plane against a real enemy. Now, that was exactly what he was doing.

Within minutes of becoming airborne, Nasir's radar picked up movement from a large number of vehicles on the ground near the town of Al-Jar. He had no way of knowing it, but it was the tank division that had overrun the army base. Nasir sighted in on the target and pushed his missile release mechanism. A feeling of exhilaration and power came over him as he watched the missiles explode amongst the Iraqis.

"Die you sons-of-bitches!" he shouted. "You've come to Kuwait to die!"

Suddenly, as Nasir banked the plane to head back to Ahmad al-Jaber, he felt a *thump* and looked out his window to see fire spurting from the right wing of the Skyhawk. He'd taken a hit. Then he felt pain in his arm and glanced down to see blood trickling down his right hand. His shoulder felt as if it were on fire.

"God help me," he muttered as he continued his turn back towards the base, "I have to get back and reload!" He could feel himself growing weaker and weaker with each passing minute. He didn't feel so full of power now. "Please, don't let me pass out," he prayed as he neared the landing strip.

Nasir managed to set the plane down, but then discovered that the escape ladder had been shot away. Gritting his teeth against the pain, he jumped to the runway, landing in a crumpled heap. In the distance, an ambulance siren shrieked, and soon Nasir felt himself being lifted from the ground.

"I killed them!" he shouted at an ambulance attendant. "I killed those bastards...those dogs!"

Then Nasir floated away on a cloud of agony as the medics picked him up and put him on a stretcher.

■ ■ ■

Hesham yawned and stretched his six-foot-two frame as he walked out of a rear door at Kuwait International Airport. He didn't like working nights but his boss had given him little choice in the matter. He'd told the twenty-six-year-old Hesham, low man on the flag crew in seniority, that he had to work the shift until a replacement could be found for a worker who had quit without notice two weeks earlier. Hesham was hoping the replacement would be hired quickly. He much preferred being in his warm bed in Rumaithiya at 3:00 in the morning.

A British airliner had just landed and Hesham coached the pilot to a gate. His job done, the Kuwaiti decided to go back inside the terminal, but as he turned around he noticed that the runway lights were going off. Changing direction, he headed for the observation tower to ask what the problem was. The thought that a hijacked plane had asked to land crossed his mind. Maybe a bit of excitement for a change, Hesham grinned. When he reached the tower, one of the controllers told Hesham that tower personnel had simply been ordered to douse the lights immediately.

"I wonder why," Hesham mused.

The controller threw up his hands and shrugged his shoulders. "Your guess is as good as mine," he answered.

As Hesham turned to leave the tower, he overheard a conversation between a Kuwait Airways pilot and another controller. The pilot was asking for landing instructions for his flight, which had originated in Thailand. The controller told the pilot he couldn't land at Kuwait International, but had to fly on to the next closest airport, which was at Bahrain, instead. The pilot was complaining that he was low on fuel, but the controller still insisted he couldn't turn the runway lights on. Listening to the conversation, Hesham began to get a very uncomfortable feeling. A plane in possible fuel trouble would not be waved off just to prevent a hijacked plane from landing along with it. Something quite serious had prompted the orders to the tower, he feared.

Leaving the tower, he headed toward the terminal, but he'd only taken a few steps when he heard the roar of a plane. Glancing up he could see the lights of the aircraft streaking toward him. He tensed, fearing that it might be the Kuwaiti jetliner trying to land in the dark, despite the order to continue to Bahrain. Rooted to the pavement by a feeling of impending danger, Hesham watched as the plane's lights continued their glide toward the airport. Suddenly they swooped downward and an explosion split the night air. The concussion knocked him to the ground.

My God, he thought, *the plane has crashed*. But as the words were forming in his mind, he looked up to the sky again and saw the lights of the aircraft racing toward the horizon. A few minutes later he heard the ear-splitting screams of three more planes followed by more explosions. Then he heard shouting. Picking himself up, he ran toward the terminal. People were pouring out of the building as if they were being chased by the devil. He asked a worried-looking security guard what had happened.

"I don't know for sure," the guard answered, "but somebody said the runways have been bombed."

"*Bombed*?" Hesham laughed. "Who the hell would *bomb* the runways?"

He turned and ran toward the landing strips. A cloud of smoke billowed up from the area. Hesham shook his head. *A plane at some other gate must have exploded*. Then he remembered the planes in the sky. Turning toward the terminal, he heard the whine of jet engines again. Hesham watched as the observation tower and the airport's radar units disappeared in a blinding flash of light.

"The sons-of-bitches!" he shrieked in disbelief. "Somebody *is* bombing us!"

This time he saw a flag on the side of one of the planes. It was an Iraqi flag. Now Hesham knew who the sons-of-bitches were. With fear in his heart, he turned and ran toward his car. If the Iraqis *were* invading Kuwait, he wanted to get to Rumaithiya and his family before they did.

■ ■ ■

They came from the north. Under the cover of darkness, 100,000 of Saddam Hussein's million-man army spread like a malignancy over the length and breadth of Kuwait.

There were units from Iraq's elite Republican Guard, armed with the newest and best weapons in the country's extensive arsenal, and regular army troops, shabbily dressed and equipped with weapons of lesser quality.

Britain had carved the Kuwaiti-Iraqi border in the desert sand at the end of World War I after the collapse of the Ottoman Turk Empire, which had sided with Germany during the war. Iraqi leaders had screamed "foul" since then, claiming that Kuwait was an inherent part of Iraq, but nobody had listened. Now Saddam would *make* the world listen. By force he would take control of land that, in his mind, was rightfully his.

Few Iraqi soldiers who came to Kuwait wanted to be there, trudging towards an unknown destiny. It had only been two years since an eight-year conflict with Iran had ended. Now their superior officers were telling them the Kuwaitis had "invited" them into their country to help overthrow their current government. That was a clever lie devised by Saddam to confuse Kuwait and the rest of the world, and to glorify himself in the eyes of his own people. Iraqis would see him as the benevolent protector of Kuwaitis who wanted their rulers ousted.

Most of the soldiers didn't believe anything the officers said. Officers were always telling lies, but no matter what they thought, they knew they had no choice but to follow orders. If they refused, they would be shot—or worse yet, their families would be executed. So they rolled through the border station at Al-Abdaly, crushed the Al-Salem Army Base, thundered past the Ar-Rawdhatain Oil Fields, then continued south to Al-Jahra, Kuwait City, Ahmadi, and the oil fields in the south and west.

Thousands of them were killed by the out-numbered, more lightly-equipped Kuwaiti defenders who fought bravely to turn the invaders away. Thousands more walked over their bodies to continue the relentless march.

Someone once said, "Beware the fury of a patient man." Saddam had coveted Kuwait patiently since 1979, when he had become president of Iraq. For ten years his spies had helped prepare for the unleashing of his fury. Iraqis worked in nearly every employment sector in Kuwait, from white-collar jobs in the ministry departments, to janitors at military bases, to car washers who wandered through suburban streets begging for work. An unusually large number of Iraqis were stationed at the Iraqi Embassy in Kuwait City. Just a month before the attack, a group of oil ministers from Baghdad had been given tours of Kuwait's three main oil refineries, ostensibly to gather information to update their own refineries. The maps of the refineries and oil fields that the trusting Kuwaitis gave them would be of great benefit to Saddam in the coming weeks. The invaders had knowledge of every military base, city, street, commercial building, and house in Kuwait because of the information gathered by these spies.

Saddam was a master of trickery and treachery. And he had picked a perfect time to put his scheme into play. An estimated 200,000 of the country's residents, including military personnel (the military contingent totaled only a little over 20,000 at full strength) were out of the country on their annual vacations. Saddam knew he could control his weaker neighbor in a matter of hours.

CHAPTER 2

The gray predawn haze shrouding Kuwait's small gulf coast city of Rumaithiya began its gradual surrender to stabs of piercing sunlight as Ali rolled over on the mattress. Slowly and deliberately he stretched his muscular, five-foot-nine body as he opened one eye to squint at the clock on the bedside table. It read 5:15.

A look of puzzlement crossed Ali's dark, handsome face. Why had he woke up? He'd barely fallen back to sleep after answering the *azan* (the Muslim call to prayer) and now he was awake again. After the first *azan* of the day, he always slept until the alarm sounded at 6:00.

Lying there, the thirty-three-year-old Kuwaiti sleepily listened for sounds in the family compound where he and his American wife, Dina, and their five children lived with his parents, three brothers, and their families. It is common in Muslim families for a married son and his family to live with his parents. As had all of his neighbors, Ali's father had built a three-story, fifty-room house containing separate apartments for all of his sons. Only the oldest did not live there.

Ali could not hear any signs of activity in the other apartments. Nothing in the compound had woke him. *Must have been a dream*, he decided. Suddenly a loud "boom" penetrated his semi-conscious mind, bringing him straight up in bed. That was it! That's what had shaken him from a sound sleep.

"Good Lord," Dina mumbled as she, too, sat up. "What was that?" Her large, dark brown eyes roamed around the room, searching for the cause of the noise.

Ali threw off the covers and swung his feet to the floor. "I don't know," he answered, standing up and heading for the bedroom window. "A sonic boom, I guess. Kuwaiti fighter planes must be in training."

He peered out the window at the glistening new day and shivered, noticing his hands felt clammy. *Odd*, he thought. The feeling that had come over him was as strange as the sound of the *booms* in the early morning stillness.

Turning toward the hallway that led to the bathroom, he said, "I'm going to get ready for work." Even though this was Thursday, a non-working day for many people in Kuwait (Thursday and Friday are the Arab world's Saturday and Sunday), Ali was among those Kuwaitis who worked a six-day week. He had just changed jobs in May, leaving the privately owned National Bank of Kuwait City to take a position in a government library in the town of Qadisiya, a few minutes north of Rumaithiya.

Dina groaned and sank back down on her pillow. The one thing she'd never liked about the speed of light was that it arrived at her bedroom window too early in the morning.

At that moment, her three oldest sons, nine-year-old Jassim, four-year-old Zade, and three-year-old Yacoub, along with their six-year-old sister, Nadia, burst into the bedroom.

"Mamma, Mamma!" Jassim shouted. "What was that noise?"

"It scared me awake!" Zade shrieked.

"Me, too! Me, too!" Yacoub and Nadia piped up.

Dina laughed and rolled over, pushing her long, brown hair out of her eyes. Patting the bed as an invitation for all of them to jump onto it with her, she answered, "Kuwaiti fighter planes in training, your father said. Now see what you've done? You made so much noise, you woke up baby Husain."

As Dina slid her slender, five-foot-five body out of bed and picked up the squalling baby, another *boom*, louder than the previous ones, rattled the room. It brought Ali out of the bathroom to the living room window where he was joined by Dina. The air pulsed with the sound of planes. As they looked toward the sky, they saw two fighter jets streak directly over the compound. The color drained from Ali's face as he recognized an Iraqi flag painted on the side of each jet.

Glancing at her husband out of the corner of her eye, Dina asked, "Those are our jets, right?"

"I told you they were," Ali answered, turning away from her. She'd be able to tell he was lying if she saw his face. *What could this possibly mean*, he wondered as he began dressing hurriedly. He wanted to leave the apartment before Dina or the children could ask him any more questions.

■ ■ ■

After watching his friend, Nasir, and several other Kuwaiti pilots streak down the runways at Ahmad al-Jaber Air Base at three a.m., Ali's cousin, Major Abdul-Samad—a short, stocky man with a perpetual and beguiling smile—returned to the communications section in the basement of one of the buildings. Since base officials had become aware of the invasion, the major, who was the on-duty officer in his section, had been manning a telephone, summoning off-duty personnel back to the base.

As dawn approached, air-raid sirens began shrieking a warning and almost simultaneously, the cement floor in the underground room quivered under Abdul-Samad's feet as Iraqi bombs began to explode. The major and several other men ran up the stairs, where they watched Iraqi planes as they bombed the runways. Although the men had been expecting the base to be hit for nearly two hours, the scene that unfolded before their eyes seemed unreal...a dream...a terrible, frightening dream. Horrified, they watched as planes and buildings disintegrated. War had reared its ugly head and was bringing death down upon them. Almost as one, the men turned around and descended the steps to the communications room, unable to continue watching the destruction.

Abdul-Samad wiped tears from his eyes and sweat from his shaking hands before he reached for a list of phone numbers. As he began dialing, he knew his efforts were futile. No matter how many men he called back to the base, it wouldn't be enough to stop the Iraqis.

■ ■ ■

As soon as Ali left the apartment for work, Dina put the baby back in his crib with a bottle. Husain's black eyes sparkled as he rewarded his mother for his breakfast with a cherubic smile that spread across his round, chubby face. She bent down and gave her eight-month-old a kiss on the forehead and then hustled off to settle the other four children at the breakfast table.

That done, she padded into the living room on bare feet (shoes are not worn in Muslim homes) and turned on the television. There was no picture from either of the Kuwaiti stations. Only the sound of Kuwaiti national songs could be heard, along with the sporadic *booms* that continued in the distance.

"That's funny," she mumbled to herself as she stared at the blank television screen.

She jumped when the phone rang. Picking it up, she heard a hysterical voice on the other end.

"We're surrounded by Iraqi soldiers!" the voice screeched. Dina recognized it as Ali's youngest sister, Nassima, who lived with her husband Mohammed and their four children in Ahmadi, about twenty-five minutes south of Rumaithiya. The invaders, after storming into Kuwait City just before daybreak, stayed to the west of the smaller towns along the coast, as they headed southwest for the vast expanses of the Maqwa, Burgan, and Ahmadi oil fields near Ahmadi.

"Nassima!" Dina screamed back. "Nassima, settle down! I can't understand you!"

"We've been invaded by Iraq!" Nassima sobbed. "They have been bombing Ahmadi since 2:30. Oh, Dina, I'm sure they're also in Rumaithiya, or soon will be. Go buy food, now!"

The line went dead. Staring at the receiver, Dina dropped it back into its cradle. *What was the matter with her sister-in-law? Had she gone crazy? If there had been an invasion, there would have been some warning...the air raid sirens would have sounded.*

Turning around, Dina caught a glimpse of herself in a mirror above the television. A stranger with a horribly white face stared back at her. Her stomach churned with shock. Racing for the bathroom, she threw up. *This has to be a terrible dream*, she thought. But she knew Nassima's voice had sounded far too real for the phone call to have been a dream. Her entire body throbbed to the savage beat of fear. *My God,* her brain screamed. *Did I come to Kuwait seven years ago to make my home and raise a family just to see them die in a war?*

With trembling hands, she splashed water on her face, left the bathroom and headed for the kitchen to check the children. They were still dawdling over their cereal. "Finish your breakfast!" she commanded harshly. "I'll be right back."

The four gave each other puzzled looks as their mother dashed out of the door and headed for the other third-floor apartment. Ali's second youngest brother, Mahmoud, a theatre lighting engineer, his wife, Huda, and their two sons shared the top floor of the building with Ali and Dina. Red, the second oldest brother, a night security guard at Kuwait International, his wife and four sons, and Ahmad, the youngest brother, a Ministry of Finance employee and the only unmarried son in the family, shared the second floor of the structure.

As she pounded on her brother-in-law's door, Dina could hear his radio blasting national songs. Mahmoud, a tall, good-looking man with striking Arabic features, opened his door. Dina gasped when she gazed up into his face and saw the same ashen hue that she had seen in her mirror. His usually strong, sure face had melted into a maze of apprehension and bewilderment. She did not have to ask if what Nassima said was true. The answer was in his eyes. As he took her hand and led her into the apartment, she began to cry.

"We are being invaded," she sobbed. "How did you know?'

"When I heard the *booms*," Mahmoud answered, "I was sure they were bombs—then I saw Iraqi planes fly overhead...."

"Iraqi planes!" Dina gasped. "Ali said those were *our* planes!"

"He's wrong. I saw Iraqi flags on them. I don't want to frighten you, Dina, but the Iraqis are in now, and there's no way out for us."

Panic seized her and she began screaming. "Food...we have to buy food...Ali has gone to work. You must go buy as much food as you can...milk for Husain!"

Her voice trailed off as she rushed out of Mahmoud's apartment and into her own. Grabbing what money she could find to help buy the supplies, she scurried back to his door, shoved the money into his hands, then turned and flew headlong down the stairs to Ali's parents' quarters on the first floor and basement levels of the house. Behind her she could hear Husain howling in his crib.

She burst into her in-laws' living room, tears streaming down her face. "Nassima called me. Ahmadi is surrounded by Iraqi soldiers, and they are on their way to Rumaithiya!" she shouted when she saw Ali's father, Eidan.

"Yes," Eidan said calmly. "Nassima also called me. There is something unusual happening, but everything will be taken care of in a few hours."

"But Haji (a Muslim term of respect given to a father who has been to the holy city of Mecca) Eidan, Mahmoud also said he is sure the Iraqis are attacking us."

Eidan, a man of average height and build, was an old-fashioned, aristocratic-looking Arab. Unlike many modern-day Kuwaitis, such as his sons, who occasionally wore western-style clothes, Eidan was always dressed in the traditional Arab garb of *distasha* (a long white robe), *gutra* (a shoulder-length white head covering) and *agal* (a black band that holds the gutra in place). He had been reading since he answered the azan. After his recent retirement from the money-exchanging business, the sixty-year-old had indulged his hobbies of religion, world politics, and history and was constantly studying one subject or the other. Eidan had heard the *booms* and seen the planes fly over the compound, but he was not accepting the idea of an invasion. *Some silly war games,* he'd guessed.

"Come, sit down and calm yourself," he said, leading Dina to a chair. She was shaking so badly she thought she'd collapse before she reached it.

"The Iraqis, Haji Eidan! If it's the Iraqis, they could be here in a few hours. We could all be dead in a few hours!"

"Don't worry," Eidan soothed. "Everything will be all right." War had not come to Kuwait since the ancient days. There certainly was no reason to believe that it was here now.

His quiet calm helped Dina control her tears, but her heart was still pounding with fright and her mind was a jumble of thoughts. *What should I do? How can I keep my babies safe?*

Suddenly, she remembered Husain's cries. "I have to go back to the children," she said, jumping up from the chair and heading for the door.

Her father-in-law called after her. "Be calm, have faith. All will be well soon."

Back in her apartment, an irrational thought came to Dina's mind. *Damn, I just cleaned yesterday! If they bomb us, the apartment will be all dusty again!*

"What the hell's the matter with you," she scolded herself. "Think straight! Bombs…if they do bomb us, we'll be safer in the basement. That's right, Dina. Now you're making sense!"

She headed for the bedroom, picked up the sobbing baby, then started pulling suitcases from the closet. She could taste her fear as she began stuffing clothes into the bags. She had heard of the atrocities civilians had been subjected to during the Iran-Iraq War. Details of the horrors stabbed into her brain. *Were those awful things going to happen to her family and friends?* She turned around when she heard a quivering voice behind her. There stood the children staring at her.

"What's the matter, Mamma?" Jassim asked, his limpid, black eyes now clouded with worry. "We heard you screaming, and you've been crying."

Dina knelt in front of them. She had to get a grip on herself for their sake. Forcing the panic from her voice, she gathered them close and said, "Yes, Mamma's been crying. There is a problem in our country, but Haji Eidan said it will be over in a few hours."

Jassim's eyes grew bigger and he ran a hand through his black hair, a habit he had when he was nervous, but he said nothing. Tears began to roll down Nadia's pretty, olive-skinned face and Dina brushed her daughter's dark, curly hair off her forehead and wiped her eyes. Zade and Yacoub, too young to understand what their mother had said, turned back toward their room to play.

"Come," Dina said to Jassim and Nadia, "help me pack some things."

"Oh, good," the tearful Nadia said, "we're going to America!" The only time they ever used suitcases was for a trip to America or England.

"No, sweetheart," Dina forced a smile. "We're just moving downstairs for a few days."

"But why?" Nadia persisted.

"We'll talk later," Dina said.

What would she talk about? Tell my children the Iraqis were blowing their country apart? Tell them they might be dead tomorrow?

"Stop it," she shouted at herself. "You're only making things worse thinking like that. Haji Eidan said everything would be all right, remember?"

Quickly she ushered Jassim and Nadia into the bedroom the four children shared. Zade and Yacoub were having a merry time jumping on the beds. Dina screamed at them to quit. Two round, dark faces looked up at her in surprise. Their mother rarely yelled at them. *What was the matter with her this morning?* She ordered all of the children to get dressed. When they were done, she handed each child a suitcase and told them to fill it with clothes and their favorite toys and games. They hustled to their tasks obediently.

"Mamma," Jassim said quietly as he handed her an armload of shirts and trousers. "Those aren't *sonic booms* are they?" Before Dina could answer him, he added, "They're bombs."

Dina swallowed hard, forcing down more tears. Her fourth grader was much wiser than his years. Taking the clothes from him and putting them in the suitcase, she said, "Yes, Jassim, I think they might be."

Will my son live to celebrate his tenth birthday in three months? Will Husain see his first birthday? God, she prayed silently, *help me control myself! Please let Haji Eidan be right. Please let it be over soon. Please let Jassim have the biggest birthday party he's ever had!* Her mind was an invisible Ping-Pong ball, bouncing back and forth between fear and faith.

After they had the suitcases full, Dina instructed the children to go into her bedroom and stay there while she took several bags downstairs. Mahmoud was just coming out of his apartment on his way for the supplies as she clanked past his door.

When he saw the suitcases, he asked, "Where the hell do you think you're going? America? I told you there's no way out!"

Dina ignored him and continued toward the stairs. As she thumped down the steps, Ali's mother, Bedreah, appeared at her apartment door in her nightclothes to see what the noise was about. She'd been awakened when her daughter-in-law burst into her apartment earlier, but did not want to face her at that time.

Bedreah had grasped the truth of the situation as soon as she heard the *booms*. Her face showed no fear or consternation, even though she knew the next few hours and days would take all the strength she could muster. She also knew when she glanced at her daughter-in-law's face as she rushed by, that she was aware of what was happening.

"Wait," Bedreah called, "where are you going?"

"I decided the children would be safer in the basement."

"Yes," Bedreah nodded, "that is a wise decision."

As soon as the bags were deposited in the basement, Dina ran back to her apartment and began rummaging around, looking for birth certificates, passports, any piece of paper she thought might be important to them later. *Why?* her mind asked. *Mahmoud said there was no way out!*

It took nearly an hour to find all the papers for the seven of them. After they were rounded up, she gathered up the children and the rest of the bags and headed for the stairs again.

■ ■ ■

When Ali walked out of the house that morning and headed for his car, he spied a neighbor across the street.

"Jaber," Ali called out, "what's happening?"

Jaber shrugged his shoulders. "I don't know."

"Do you think the Iraqis…?" Ali's question trailed off.

Jaber shrugged again, "I don't know," he repeated, "but I plan to find out." Both men got into their cars and headed in different directions.

By the time he had driven a few blocks, Ali sensed that something was terribly wrong. People were driving like maniacs and wrecked cars littered the streets. No one was stopping to help anyone. Drivers were screaming at each other. This wasn't normal in Kuwait. The sight of the two airplanes outside his bedroom window kept flashing through his mind. *There couldn't have been Iraqi flags on them,* he told himself.

He'd turned on his radio as soon as he'd started the car. All he could find on the Kuwaiti stations was the sound of national songs. Now a thought struck him and he turned the dial in search of an Iraqi station.

The Iraqi announcer's voice thundered in Ali's ears as he urged all military reservists in Iraq to report for duty.

"The people of Kuwait have asked Iraq to help them overthrow their government," the fanatical-sounding voice screeched.

Ali shook his head. *What the hell is he talking about? We don't need any help. We're doing fine. Why should we need anyone interfering with our country—our politics?*

There had been demands to restore the parliament, which had been dismantled in 1986 because of political upheaval, but the demands had been set forth in a peaceful manner. Ali doubted that the people working on the parliamentary issue would ask Iraq to help in their cause, especially if it would mean bloodshed in their own country. *Would they?*

His head was swimming. Nothing was making any sense.

Was this a repeat of a 1961 Iraqi threat? That year, after Britain had granted Kuwait its independence, Iraq had amassed troops along the Kuwaiti border, intending to use force to take over the country. The troops quickly dispersed when British forces came to Kuwait's aid. Saddam surely wasn't invading now, knowing Britain would come to its friend's aid again!

Then Ali thought about all the threats and rhetoric Saddam had been hurling at Kuwait in recent weeks. In early July Saddam had called on Kuwait to lower its oil production, charging that it was overproducing in order to ruin Iraq's economy. Iraq also had accused Kuwait of stealing Iraqi oil from the Rumaila oil fields and brought up the old subject of ports. Saddam demanded a multi-year lease for Kuwait's Warba and Bubiyan Islands. He wanted those islands badly, not only for their oil production, but because of the gulf accessibility he would gain with them. In addition, the Iraqi dictator also had threatened to establish a puppet government in Kuwait.

Yesterday, Ali remembered, the Iraqis had walked out of a meeting in Jiddah, Saudi Arabia, that Egyptian President Hosni Mubarak had arranged between Iraq and Kuwait in an attempt to ease tensions between the two countries. The Iraqi officials left after accusing the Kuwaiti representatives of not being "serious" during the discussions. Even after the walkout, the Kuwaitis thought the dictator was bluffing. They had lived for years under his bluffs and threats, but he had said publicly that he wouldn't invade his neighbors. The Kuwaitis believed him. Was Saddam invading the country for his own selfish reasons and against promises that he wouldn't?

Ali's heart began pounding. His chest felt tight and he found breathing difficult. His throat was dry and it threatened to clamp shut. He wondered if he was going to have a heart attack. *Jesus Christ*, part of his mind thought, *here we are…this is a real war! For whatever reason, it is war! Another part kept whispering, no, no…Kuwait is Iraq's ally, Kuwait supported Iraq in the Iran-Iraq War!*

What is war? he asked himself. No Kuwaiti of his or his father's generation had ever experienced it. Bombing, destruction, killing. Ali's eyes filled with tears as he thought of Dina, the children, his parents, brothers, sisters…how would they accept war? *Would they survive it?*

His mind faded back to when he'd first met Dina. In 1978 he'd gone to America for his college education. He'd initially enrolled in Southeastern Oklahoma State University, but left there after only one semester and went to a smaller college, this one in Bellevue, Nebraska, near Omaha. He'd met Dina at the school library in March of 1979. She was three years younger than he, and he thought she was the most beautiful girl he'd ever seen. Being of Italian descent, her dark eyes and hair made him think she looked slightly Arabic. He'd made up his mind the first time he saw her that he was going to make her his wife, and he did in 1980. He had brought her, Jassim and Nadia, to Kuwait to live in 1983, after he received his bachelor's degree in business administration. *Have I brought them here only to see their lives end in a war?*

"Allahu akbar!" (God is great), the Iraqi announcer shouted, bringing Ali back to the present. Each word sank into his heart like a cold knife. He slammed his fist on the steering wheel. *Is God really great if He is allowing this to happen?*

■ ■ ■

As he exited Al-Fahaheel Expressway, the main highway into Qadisiya, Ali was forced to stop at a red light. Studying the faces of other drivers around him, he saw fright and confusion. Glancing into the rearview mirror, he saw the same thing in his own face. Suddenly he noticed there were cars on the other side of the intersection in the wrong lane—his lane. It dawned on him that the traffic going away from Qadisiya toward Rumaithiya had been unusually heavy all along his route. Glancing to the left, toward Kuwait City, he knew the reason for the southerly flow of cars and trucks. A huge cloud of black smoke hung over the city. People were evacuating the city!

The traffic light turned green. To his surprise, Ali's foot wouldn't work on the accelerator. His legs were numb. Maneuvering in the seat to bring his hips into the action, he squirmed into a position that created enough pressure on the gas pedal so the car would move forward. He threaded through oncoming traffic and turned as quickly as possible onto side streets that would eventually lead him to the library.

There were no lights on in the building when he pulled into a parking stall. Ali's heart sank. The janitor was always the first one in the building every morning and the lights were always on. This was another sign pointing toward the fact that all was not well in Kuwait on this morning. *Maybe he just didn't turn on any lights*, Ali hoped.

Getting out of the car and testing his legs to see if they would hold him (the numbness had left as quickly as it had come) he walked up the library steps and shoved his key into the lock. As the tumblers clicked, he pushed the door open and yelled, "Ben!" There was no answer from the janitor.

Walking down the hall toward his office he felt as if someone was watching him. The hairs on the back of his neck prickled.

"Ben, where the hell are you?" he called again. Still no answer. There were only the sounds of a ticking clock and the persistent rumble, roar, and "boom" around the city.

He sank into the chair behind his desk and flipped the radio on. Still only Kuwaiti national songs. He tuned in a different Iraqi station. This announcer echoed the first announcer's words.

"Kuwait is saved! The request to help free the people of Kuwait is being honored. We've come to help you in your struggle against the Al-Sabah family...Iraqi troops will defend the revolution and the Kuwaiti people...."

Ali reached for the phone. Dialing one of the larger libraries in Kuwait City, he prayed someone would answer in a calm, normal voice. He put the receiver down after the tenth ring. He dialed another library in the city. No answer there, either.

The *booms* entered his consciousness again. Each one seemed closer than the last. He began to realize the "booms" he was hearing were explosions. His untrained ear had not known the sound of bombs, so it had identified the noise as something he'd heard before—the sound a jet plane makes when it breaks the sound barrier. *These are not sonic booms!*

He glanced at his watch, picked up the phone again, but immediately dropped it. *What the hell am I doing here?* he thought. Grabbing his keys off the desk he walked quickly toward the front door, went out, slammed and locked it. Getting into the car, he headed for a nearby supermarket. *If this is for real, I need to buy as many food supplies as possible.*

He went to a bank machine first and made a withdrawal, then walked into the store and grabbed a cart. He shoved it aimlessly up and down the aisles, pulling canned goods and staples off the shelves and frozen foods from the freezers. When the first cart was filled he went for a second, then a third. After he repeated his rampage throughout the store with the other two carts, he shoved all of them to the front of the store. Then as an afterthought, he took a fourth and rushed to the rear of the store, where he asked an employee to fill it with bottled water. As he lined the carts up at a checkout stand he noticed there were some fifty people, similarly loaded with supplies, in front of him. Directly in front of him was a young, well-dressed woman. He decided to strike up a conversation with her to see if she knew what was happening.

"You don't know?" she asked in surprise. Then she told him that her brother, who was in the army, had phoned her house early that morning to tell her Iraq had invaded Kuwait.

"My brother said they swarmed over the border like ants."

The only thing Ali could think of to say was, "You've got to be kidding!"

The woman looked at him and shook her head. "My God, what's wrong with you people? You are the third person I've told this story to, and no one has believed me. Believe this!" she shouted. "My brother saw them! My brother ran for his life from them because that was all he and the other soldiers could do! There were thousands of Iraqis for only a handful of soldiers to stop!"

Seeing the passion in the woman's eyes, Ali believed. The thin thread of denial he had been trying to hold onto was now broken.

■ ■ ■

While Dina herded the children down the stairs she tried not to think about what was happening in Kuwait, but her mind wouldn't cooperate. Unbidden thoughts whirled through her brain.

Dina had grown to love Kuwait and its people as much as she loved her native country. Kuwait was a generous and peaceful nation. Its people were a gentle and kind people. They did not deserve to be trampled into the ground by an aggressor nation. Of course she had been uneasy and frightened when Ali had first begun talking about taking her to Kuwait to live. She had never been more than a hundred miles from her home in Papillion, Nebraska! Moving halfway around the world was a terrifying thought for a twenty-three-year-old with two babies. She had been torn between the prospect of leaving everything familiar to go to a strange country to live among strange people; and refusing to go, which would make Ali miserable for the rest of his life. She knew how much he missed his family.

Even though the decision to move to Kuwait had been born in agony, she had soon realized it had been the right one. With Ali's family's help, she had quickly learned to be completely happy and content in her adopted country, and was no longer a stranger among strange people. Kuwait had become her home in every sense of the word. She had kept her American citizenship, but now considered herself a Kuwaiti citizen, too.

She had never had reason to regret or question that decision—until now. Now she was wishing she could turn back the hands of time and find herself waking up from this nightmare in the safety of her old bedroom in Papillion.

CHAPTER 3

The checkers worked like friends, and Ali was soon piling his purchases into the car. He filled the back seat, then the front, and finally the trunk. He had spent nearly $500.

Sliding into the car, he turned on the ignition and pulled back onto the expressway. As he drove, his mind filled with thoughts. *All these years we've lived and built our lives, married, had babies. Now Saddam has come to take our lives away from us.*

As a child, Ali had been to Iraq a couple of times. He'd never liked the country. It was filthy and the people were desperately poor. Unlike Kuwait's leaders, who had channeled their country's oil wealth to human resources, Iraq's leaders had used its country's oil money for military purposes, depriving the vast majority of its people of even the basic comforts of life.

Ali knew when these people arrived in Kuwait and saw this clean, luxurious country, they would tear it apart. Dismantle it. Take everything back to their country. Kill and maim in the process.

As he neared his usual Rumaithiya exit off the expressway, Fifth Ring Road, Ali saw a Kuwaiti police officer with a machine gun blocking the road. "Go! go!" the officer yelled, waving Ali on. "You cannot use this exit!"

Puzzled, Ali drove on to the next exit. It also was blocked, as was the next. The bitter bile of panic was beginning to well up in his throat. *Were the Iraqis already in Rumaithiya? Was there fighting in his town—on his street?*

Ali continued down the expressway at breakneck speed, praying the next exit wouldn't be blocked. It wasn't.

Racing through the streets of Rumaithiya, he saw or heard nothing that would indicate the Iraqis were in the town. With a sigh of relief, he pulled into the yard of the family compound at 9:00. Mahmoud was just getting out of his supply-laden car. The two brothers studied each other's faces. Each seemed to be asking the other, *Why is this happening?* As they began unloading the cars, their father came out the front door.

"Well," Eidan said to Ali, "you're back from working already. What's happening?"

Ali told his father what he had heard on the radio, in the supermarket, and what he had seen on the way to the library and back home.

"Kuwait has been invaded," Ali concluded.

"No, I don't think so," Eidan shook his head. "Kuwait is an independent country. It is a member of the United Nations and the Arab League. Nobody could just invade us like that."

Ali thought, *he's right. It shouldn't be that simple, but Saddam is a barbarian with no respect for international rules or laws.*

To his father he said, "Wake up! You have to accept the fact that Iraq has invaded us!"

Eidan just kept shaking his head and saying, "No, Ali, you are wrong."

Ali decided not to argue. The truth would strike his father soon enough.

After the cars were unloaded and the supplies stacked in the basement, Ali headed upstairs to his apartment. He met Dina and the children on their way to the basement, each dragging a suitcase. He could see that Dina had been crying. She was pale as a ghost. She knew.

Trying to be casual, he asked, "What are you doing?"

"I'm moving the children downstairs, where they will be safer."

Not wanting to say anything that might upset her further, Ali took the suitcase from her hand, leaving her holding Husain. Then he noticed how badly she was shaking so he rescued the baby, too, before he fell out of his mother's quivering arms.

When they all reached the basement, Ali asked his wife if she had called the American Embassy.

"Why?"

"To see if they know what's going on!" Ali nearly shouted. "Go do it, now!"

Dina reached for the phone and dialed the embassy. A clerk answered on the first ring. Ali heard Dina ask if anyone could tell her what was happening, and then she put the receiver back into the cradle.

"What did they say?"

"They said, 'you know as much as we do', and hung up," Dina answered. Tears were filling her eyes again, but she forced herself to fight them off. She didn't want to upset the children more than they already were.

"Go ahead and unpack," Ali said gently. "Then try phoning your parents. They surely know in America what's happened here. They will be worried until they know you are safe."

Safe? Dina wanted to scream. *Sure I'm safe! There are only a few thousand Iraqis with guns and bombs heading for my house. If that's safe, I'll grow a beard and call myself Mohammed!*

But she held her tongue and began the job of settling the children into one of the *derwanias* (similar to a family room).

■ ■ ■

Ali interrupted his younger brother. "Do you believe this is a revolution?"

Hesham and the others gathered in the yard shook their heads negatively.

"There were only Iraqis coming at us at the base, said Fuad, who had made it safely back to Rumaithiya from the army base during the night. If they were coming to help us in a revolution, why would they fly Saudi flags on their vehicles? The bastards are lying!"

Abass, a husky, bespectacled oil refinery employee who was about Ali's age and height, spoke up and reminded the group there had been no rumors in the country that would lead anyone to believe there was an underground movement to overthrow the Kuwaiti government, even by those seeking reinstatement of Parliament.

Ali nodded in agreement with his friend. "That's true, and you know this country, there would be no way a revolution could be planned without some word of it leaking out."

The rest of the group agreed with Ali's statement. They also agreed the best way to hear the real story about what was happening in their country would be to listen to foreign news broadcasts.

■ ■ ■

At 2:30 A.M., the day after the invasion, Major Abdul-Samad was awakened from a fitful sleep by a "buzzing" sound. His first thought was that Iraqi tanks had arrived at the air base. But when he rose from his cot and looked out the window of his barracks, he saw several Kuwaiti planes that had been spared destruction by Iraqi bombs, climbing into the night sky. Their pilots were taking them to safety in Saudi Arabia.

Ali's cousin silently cheered the brave pilots. As a flight engineer, the thirty-three-year-old Kuwaiti was not capable of flying a plane out of the country himself, but had he been able

Living the Nightmare

Ali headed back up the stairs and encountered his mother coming out of her apartment. She was dressed to go out and her face betrayed no fear, but Ali could tell she knew what the situation was.

Bedreah, a sturdily-built woman of average height, married Eidan at the age of 11 and bore the first of her eight children, son Saleh, at age thirteen. Not as "traditional" an Arab as her husband, she more-or-less adopted the middle road when clothing style changes began to come about in the Middle East. Although a devout Muslim, she didn't wear the ultrareligious black cape and head scarf that leaves only the eyes uncovered, but she also didn't choose the Western style of dress as many Kuwaiti women did. Instead, her wardrobe consisted of colorful, but conservative dresses that covered the arms to the wrists and the legs to the ankles. She always wore an *abiya* (a black head scarf that covers only the hair) when she left the house or when she had guests.

Bedreah's life revolved around her husband and children, and she was the indomitable force in the house. She ruled the family with a firm, fair, and always steady hand. It would be unthinkable for her to show any fear or concern in front of her family. She had always been in complete control and she had decided that morning that, no matter what, she would maintain her control in this crisis to help allay her children's fears.

"You're not leaving the house," Ali said in surprise.

"Of course," Bedreah called over her shoulder, "I must go for supplies." Then she disappeared through the front door with her driver, Everest, in tow. Both Bedreah and Eidan had failing eyesight and were unable to drive, so for nearly twenty-five years they had employed two men from India as drivers.

Knowing it would do no good to argue with his headstrong mother, Ali turned around and exited the house through the back door. He found his father, Mahmoud and Ahmad, his youngest brother, standing in the yard with two neighbors. Hesham was one of them. He was telling the men about the bombing at the airport.

Eidan's face grew pale as he listened to the story. His second son, Reda, would normally have been at work at the airport, but he and his family were in England on their annual vacation. Eidan didn't want to think about what could have happened to his son had he been on duty.

All of a sudden there was a roar above the men's heads. Looking up, they saw a group of about fifteen helicopters. Ali could see Iraqi flags on each one. The others thought they were Kuwaiti helicopters.

"See, those are ours!" Eidan shouted triumphantly. The old man's faith in the security of his country and its stature in the world was unshakable.

"Stop kidding yourselves!" Ali screamed. "Look at those Iraqi flags!"

As they stood watching the aircraft, a chill went down Ali's spine. *Those helicopters are messengers of death,* he thought. *They are on a mission of murder. We're not used to this,* his brain screamed. Kuwaitis are novices at seeing violent death at the hands of another. Murder was a rare occurrence in the country. Ali wondered how he, and his countrymen, were going to digest it on a daily basis.

■ ■ ■

The helicopters were, indeed, on a mission of murder. They were headed for Bayan Palace, the Islamic conference center in the town of Bayan, a few minutes' drive from Rumaithiya. The palace, which was being used as a temporary office for the emir, Sheik Jaber al-Ahmad al-Sabah, had been under siege for several hours, which was why the expressway exits Ali had attempted to use were blocked off. The entire al-Sabah family was on Saddam's "hit list" and if the emir could be captured, he would be the grandest prize of all.

Taking the palace had not been as easy a task as the Iraqi officers in charge of the job had thought it would be. Even when faced with the additional troops brought in by the helicopters, units of the Kuwaiti National Guard (which is charged with protecting the emir) stationed at the palace continued to put up fierce resistance. Hundreds of Iraqi soldiers died in the gunfire that hailed down on them from defenders positioned in the palace's high towers. Embarrassed and incensed by their lack of quick success, the Iraqi officers finally summoned tanks for assistance, and as soon as they moved in, the battle was over.

When the Iraqis entered the palace, they didn't find the emir. They didn't find him either when they attacked his home, Dasman Palace. His cousin, Sheik Sa'ad al-Abdullah al-Salem al-Sabah, the crown prince, and prime ministers had gotten to the emir first and hustled him off to safety in Saudi Arabia. However, the emir's younger brother, Sheik Fahad al-Ahmed al-Sabah, was at Dasman Palace when the Iraqis arrived. He was killed while helping defend the west gate of his brother's home.

The Kuwaiti National Guard sustained the highest casualties of any fighting unit in Kuwait during the invasion, with most of the fatalities coming from the Bayan and Dasman Palace fighting.

■ ■ ■

More neighbors joined the men gathered around Hesham in Ali's yard and the discussion of the situation continued. Periodically, one or another would walk to the front of the compound to look for signs of Iraqi vehicles on one of the town's main streets, Naser al-Mubarak.

Ali glanced at his watch sometime after the helicopters passed overhead and noticed his mother and Everest had been gone nearly two hours. *It shouldn't take them that long to go to the local supermarket and back.* He expressed his concern to the others.

Ahmad volunteered to go look for her. He came back a short time later to report that the nearest supermarket, the one Bedreah usually shopped at, was closed. Then Mahmoud decided to search for his mother, returning an hour later after finding no trace of Bedreah or Everest at any of the markets in Rumaithiya—they were all closed.

Two more hours went by and the family began to think the worst. Had Bedreah and her driver somehow crossed paths with Iraqi soldiers? Had a bomb struck the car? Explosions had continued throughout the morning.

Then, as the men were trying to decide what to do, Bedreah walked in the front door, her arms loaded with packages. Everest trailed behind her, his arms also full. She had not given up on her search of an open market after she had found those in Rumaithiya closed. Everest had driven her to a nearby town where they found one still open, but most of its stock had been sadly depleted. Bedreah was depressed because she had come back with the car only half full.

■ ■ ■

While Ali was worrying about his mother, worry also was plaguing one of his friends at the National Bank of Kuwait in Kuwait City. Ali's former coworker Mubarek was looking down the barrel of an Iraqi machine gun.

The thirty-two-year-old bookkeeper's usually happy, friendly face was now masked with fear. He had been one of only a few bank employees who had reported for work that morning. His wife had begged him not to leave their house in Al-Salmiya. She didn't like the *booms* she was hearing, or what she was seeing on Kuwait television, which was nothing. He wished now that he'd listened to her.

The bank employees were lined up in front of the teller windows. *We must look like ducks in a shooting gallery,* Mubarek thought. He'd taken his family to an amusement park recently, and they had shot at some of those toy ducks. Now he wondered if the Iraqi soldiers were going to do the same thing to all of the people in the bank.

An Iraqi officer walked into the building, looked at the line of "ducks," and grinned.

"Why are you trembling?" he asked one of the women. She started crying. The officer scowled and moved down the line.

When he came to Mubarek, he asked, "What are you doing here? You no longer work here. This is now an Iraqi bank!"

Then the officer turned to his men and shouted, "Get them out of here!"

The employees needed no further invitation. They all scrambled for the door. Behind them they could hear the Iraqis laughing.

Mubarek glanced over his shoulder on his way out. The soldiers were hastily stuffing money from the cash drawers into their pockets. He would find out later that every bank in Kuwait had been similarly looted. The thieves, however, were sorely disappointed a few days later when the Iraqi government devalued the Kuwaiti dinar to match its own, which was ten times lower in value. The bank raiders were only one-tenth as rich as they thought they would be.

■ ■ ■

None of Ali's family had eaten since breakfast, so when Bedreah arrived home from the market she immediately began fixing a meal for all of them. Her efforts were useless. No one could eat.

The phone rang constantly with reports from family and friends in other areas of Kuwait. No one had good news to relay. Ali's Aunt Miriam, the mother of Air Force Major Abdul-Samad, was especially agitated over the situation. There had been no word yet that the air force base had fallen, but she feared it would only be a matter of time before her son was either dead or in the hands of the Iraqis.

Throughout the afternoon, the men stayed glued to the local radio and television stations. About every half hour an announcer would break into the national songs repertoire with a plea to the men, "Report to the nearest military unit. Your country is calling you." Ali and his brothers shook their heads. They were reluctant to answer the call, not knowing what the real situation was in the country. They would not help overthrow their own government. They also thought that maybe the pleas were being broadcast by an Iraqi invader, and even possibly a Kuwaiti dissident, as a way to round up reservists and other military personnel who were not on duty that day. There were also calls for help directed at Kuwait's Arab brothers and at the Western world. Yet, sadly, there was little information about what was happening inside the country.

Hearing the pleas for help, Eidan admitted something was drastically wrong. However, he still wouldn't call the situation an "invasion," and continued to assure everyone that the crisis would be over "in a matter of hours."

Then the Kuwaiti radio and television stations fell silent. The next day, all of Kuwait would learn that the Iraqis had taken over the information ministry, where the state-run stations were housed. Kuwaitis would wind up hearing most of the invasion news through the British Broadcasting Company (BBC) and Voice of America radio stations.

While the men listened to the broadcasts, the women concentrated on putting the newly-purchased food supplies away. Food was hidden in every closet, drawer, nook, and cranny in the house. Bedreah was determined that if Iraqi soldiers came to steal food from her house, they wouldn't get it all.

During the afternoon, Ali discovered that Dina had not called her family. He kept urging her to do so, but she continued to ignore his pleas. She didn't want to contact them. She knew they would beg her to board the next plane out of Kuwait. She didn't want to tell them, as Mahmoud had so succinctly put it, "there's no way out."

■ ■ ■

Dina's family was frantic to find out information about her.

Her parents, Richard and Camille Menard, brother Dino, and sister Gina had left their home in Papillion, a small city on the southwest edge of Omaha, and moved to California shortly after Dina and Ali went to Kuwait. Richard and Camille had divorced in 1986 and both had remarried. Camille and Dino remained in California, but Richard returned to Omaha. Gina also went back to Nebraska, where she enrolled as a student at the University of Nebraska in Lincoln and became a wife and mother.

At her home in Grover City, Camille, a small woman with classic Italian beauty, took out her rosary as soon as she heard about the invasion. Then she started dialing Dina's phone number. No one answered. Camille was scared to death that her daughter was already dead. She had come close to losing her son in 1981, when he was critically injured in a motorcycle accident. That accident had not only nearly destroyed Dino's life, it had almost destroyed her own. She felt she would never be able to live if she lost one of her children. Not only was Camille frightened, she also was angry. She had been devastated when she found out that Dina and Ali were planning to make their home in Kuwait after his graduation from college. Nothing had been said before the wedding about them going there to live. She fought the move vigorously, fearing for the safety of her daughter and grandchildren in a part of the world she knew little about but considered to be unstable and dangerous. Now her fears had come true.

Dina's father, whom she affectionately called "Poppy," and his new wife Pat were vacationing with friends at a remote cabin in the Colorado mountains when they heard the news on the radio. Richard immediately left the cabin in search of a phone. It didn't do him any good to find one, because he couldn't get through to Kuwait, either.

Gina had no better luck trying to reach her sister that day from her home in Lincoln. The circuits were always busy.

All three would find out the next day that they would never be successful in contacting Dina by phone. The international telephone lines into Kuwait went down on August 3.

■ ■ ■

At 5:00 that evening, Ali answered a knock at the front door to find Faisal, a grim-faced neighbor from across the street, standing in the entryway.

"Ali, they are on the beach!" The beach was only two miles from the family compound.

The beach! Ali shook his head sadly. That was Dina and the children's favorite place to go. Every Wednesday after work, he usually took them out to eat at one of the many American fast-food restaurants in the area. Then they would go to the beach. The children loved to collect seashells and wade in the beautiful blue waters of the gulf. Now the Iraqis controlled their beach.

Ali was surprised that it had taken the Iraqis that long to get to Rumaithiya. It was only about fifteen minutes from Kuwait City, and he knew they had taken that city early in the morning. He did not know the invaders had initially bypassed the northern coastal towns in their hurried march to the southern oil fields.

Sinking down on a chair in his mother's first-floor kitchen, Ali recalled the last time they had been at the beach— just last week. He had taken his camcorder to film the children frolicking in the sand. He and Dina had been videotaping movies of the more attractive areas in the country and sending them back to America in an attempt to encourage Dina's family and friends to make a trip to Kuwait. Although Ali, Dina, and the children had been back to America a couple of times since 1983, none of her family or friends had ever come to Kuwait. For one reason, Ali couldn't convince them that life in Kuwait was safe, and not much different from that in the United States. Kuwait offered modern hotels, supermarkets, shopping malls, hospitals, movie theaters, swimming pools—almost anything there was in America could be found in Kuwait. But Dina's family continued to be hesitant, expressing concern about the instability of the Middle East. Dina's father had even made Ali promise when they'd moved to Kuwait that he would put Dina and the children on a plane at the first sign of trouble.

Well, trouble was here now and there was no way he could get them out of the country. Slowly he rose from the chair and headed for the basement, where the rest of the family was gathered. He had to tell them the Iraqis had arrived in Rumaithiya.

■ ■ ■

After Eidan heard Ali repeat Faisal's news, the old man insisted on seeing if it was the truth. He still would not believe the Iraqis were taking over the country. Ali agreed to drive his father to the beach so that he could see for himself that their neighbor was not inventing stories. Ali knew the trip might be dangerous, but he also knew that he had to make his father face the truth. The two men got into Ali's car and drove northward along the beach road to the town of Al-Salmiya. All along the way, they wove their way around Iraqi tanks and personnel carriers.

"See, Dad?" Ali said. "Will you believe now that we've been invaded?"

Eidan frowned and shrugged. "Yes," he said, "I can see there are Iraqis in Kuwait, but I feel in my heart that they will be gone tomorrow. Kuwait's friends will make sure of that."

Ali hoped his father was right, but in his heart, he knew it would take more than a day to get Saddam out of a country he had wanted so badly for so long.

■ ■ ■

At Mubarak Hospital in Al-Jabriya, a government hospital a few minutes to the northwest of Rumaithiya, a maintenance engineer named Abo-Ahmad was moving tiredly through the building towards the front lobby. He and his wife, Um-Ahmad, a nurse, had been at the hospital for nearly twelve hours. Now at 8:30 P.M., he and every other hospital employee was exhausted.

The two had left their home in Rumaithiya that morning, taking their usual route along Al-Fahaheel Expressway. They were aware there was an invasion underway and had been hesitant to leave their home, but they knew they would be needed at the hospital. As they neared Bayan, they were waved down by a Kuwaiti police officer who told them the Iraqis were on the palace grounds and advised them to find an alternate route to Al-Jabriya. They slowly worked their way to the hospital along side streets, and when they reached it they knew they were in for a long day. Emergency vehicles, sirens screaming, converged on the medical center with both wounded civilians and Kuwaiti and Iraqi soldiers. Adding to the confusion was a tremendous influx of Kuwaitis who came to the hospital to volunteer their help in caring for the casualties.

Abo-Ahmad was recruited to help carry the injured to treatment rooms where doctors and nurses were hindered in their work by Iraqi officers, who insisted on being in the rooms to assure their men received proper care. The officers threatened to shoot anyone who did not treat an Iraqi with the same care as a Kuwaiti. When he wasn't carrying people to treatment or to their beds after treatment, Abo-Ahmad was carrying bodies to the hospital's morgue. When the morgue became full, he stacked the dead outside the door.

Now, as he sank down into a chair in the lobby for a brief rest, he watched as a high-ranking Iraqi officer stormed into the hospital and demanded that all of the medical center's emergency vehicles be turned over to him.

"These vehicles are now Iraqi vehicles to be used to transport our wounded to our own hospitals!" he shouted at several doctors who were also taking a brief respite in the lobby.

One of the doctors argued with the officer, pleading that some vehicles be left for hospital use. "Go see how many Iraqi soldiers have been transported to this hospital by those ambulances!" the doctor challenged the officer.

The officer finally agreed to send a couple of his men to see if the doctor was telling the truth, and when they returned to report the hospital was full of Iraqi wounded, the officer agreed to leave two ambulances.

After the Iraqis left, Abo-Ahmad sighed and closed his eyes. He wished he could keep them closed forever to blot out the horror and fear he had witnessed in just a few short hours of the invasion, and that he knew he would see much more of in the coming days.

■ ■ ■

The first night of occupation fell over Rumaithiya. The men in Ali's family dragged mattresses from the upper floors to the basement and the women began placing them around the rooms. Dina, with Bedreah's help, had convinced the other family members that they also should move downstairs.

The children thought it was a great adventure. They were allowed to watch all the video movies and play all the video games they wanted. *Anything*, their mothers thought, so they wouldn't ask questions they couldn't answer.

The family settled down for a restless night, with explosions and sporadic machine gun fire penetrating the darkness. Dina sobbed quietly in Ali's arms. She only knew of war through movies and books. Her generation had never experienced it. What was she to expect? How would this end? How could she protect her children? She hadn't let them out of her sight all day, and didn't intend to until they returned to a normal life. Would they return to a normal life? Kuwait's military was so weak compared to Iraq's. They couldn't possibly turn away the invaders. Would America rescue them? If it did, would the Iraqis have a special vendetta against American citizens in Kuwait?

All of these questions tortured her mind. Would she go insane before it was over? As the tears trickled down her cheeks, she remembered something she'd read long ago: "There is no distance on this earth as far away as yesterday." She couldn't remember who had written those words, but whoever it was knew what he was talking about. To keep her sanity today and tomorrow, Dina knew she would have to hold on to all of her yesterdays. Her happy yesterdays seemed very far away that night.

CHAPTER 4

As the sun peeked over the horizon on August 3, the sound of a baby crying woke Dina. She had finally sobbed herself into a restless doze and now she had difficulty figuring out where she was. The baby let out another *yowl* and suddenly she remembered. Husain was lying on his mattress next to hers on the floor of one of Ali's parents' *derwanias*. The Iraqis had chased her family out of their beds yesterday.

Ali stirred beside her, got up, and went to fetch a bottle for his son. Dina picked up the baby and carried him to a table, where a stack of diapers was piled. As she finished changing him, Ali returned with the bottle. They both sat down on the makeshift bed, watching Husain suck on his breakfast.

Dina's face was as white as the sheets she had slept on, and her eyes were red and puffy. "What now?" she asked.

"I don't know, honey," Ali answered. It broke his heart to see the unhappiness and fear in her eyes. "We'll see what the situation is today—maybe it's over now."

Dina doubted that very much. Explosions still erupted around them.

The older children stirred on their mattresses and Dina could hear the sounds of family members arising in other parts of the basement. Everyone except Eidan had slept downstairs. He would not be forced out of his bed.

Dina and Ali stood up and headed for Bedreah's basement kitchen. No need to dress this morning. Dina had not allowed them to undress last night in case they had to leave the house in a hurry. The children followed them. Dina put on a kettle for tea and began pulling bowls and cereal from the cupboards. All four of the youngsters were very quiet. Their eyes followed their mother while she set the table. Not one of them asked why they weren't eating in their own apartment. One by one, the other family members began coming into the kitchen. Everyone was quiet, wondering what had happened during the night and what the day would bring. Ali, Mahmoud, Ahmad, and their cousin, Hameed, brother of Abdul-Samad and of Mahmoud's wife, Huda (first cousins are allowed to marry in Kuwait), went into another room and turned on the radio and television. The eighteen-year-old Hameed had been sent by his mother, Miriam, to his aunt Bedreah's house after Miriam had determined that the concentration of Iraqis in Rumaithiya was much smaller at that point in the invasion than it was in her town of Al-Sulaibikhat, on the north edge of Kuwait City. Finding nothing on the local stations, Ali flipped through several Iraqi stations where they heard the same thing they had the day before: Iraq was helping its Kuwaiti friends in their revolution against the Al-Sabahs.

"Bullshit," Ali said. "No matter how much they talk, they are not going to convince me there's any revolution in this country." Ali had done much thinking during the night and was convinced the Iraqi radio announcers had been lying about that country being asked to come into Kuwait. The other three agreed with Ali, but reminded him there was no proof to the contrary.

Then Ali suddenly thought about BBC Radio. Maybe they would learn more from England. He turned the dial and caught the BBC announcer as he was naming countries throughout the world that had been outraged by the invasion news. Not only did they hear the names of neighbors they expected would support them against Iraq, like Saudi Arabia, Egypt, and Syria, but also named were the United States, Great Britain and France. The men cheered when they heard the names of these powerful nations. The BBC announcer added that the United Nations was meeting to consider action to condemn Iraq. The four heard that Iraq was not only in control of most of the military bases in Kuwait, but also the airport, television and radio stations, all governmental buildings, and the royal palace. It was through this broadcast they learned that the emir was safe in Saudi Arabia and that Kuwait was under a round-the-clock curfew. Since Ali had heard the announcer use only the word *invasion,* and not *revolution,* the broadcast helped confirm his decision that Iraq had not been "invited" into the country.

"This is an attempt by Saddam to grab our oil," Ali insisted. "I know in my heart that's what it is!" He jumped up from the sofa, stormed past the kitchen, and started up the stairs, both brothers and Hameed on his heels.

"You are *not* going outside," Bedreah called from the kitchen doorway. "All of you stay in this house!" Bedreah would accumulate many gray hairs over the next few months trying to keep her sons and nephew out of harm's way.

They ignored her, climbed the stairs, banged through the back door, and headed across the street to the house of a neighbor named Abass. Abass's family's compound had quickly become the neighborhood rallying point after the invasion. Hesham and several other neighbors were standing in the yard when the four arrived. Ali asked Hesham if he had heard any news that morning.

"Only what's on the Iraqi stations," Hesham said.

"We've just been listening to BBC and they're calling this an 'invasion,' not a 'revolution,'" the tall, powerfully-built Ahmad said excitedly. "The Iraqis are in control of about everything in the country, including the royal palace."

to, he knew in his soul that he would be headed for Saudi Arabia right now.

Everyone knew it was only a matter of time before the Iraqis took over the base. Had they not bypassed Ahmad al-Jaber to rush to the oil fields in the south, the Iraqi flag would already be flying over their heads.

Abdul-Samad, a devout Muslim, said his prayers and returned to his cot. He slept for several hours before he was awakened by the wailing of air-raid sirens. The Iraqis were dropping bombs again. He wondered what they were targeting now. After the runways had been bombed the day before, the Iraqis had left, but they had returned in the afternoon to bomb the building housing the base's ammunition supply.

When Abdul-Samad thought about that raid he cursed. Spies had told the Iraqis which building housed the ammunition. Only the day before the invasion, the last of the weapons in the arsenal had been moved from one building to another. The Iraqis did not bomb the old building—they bombed the new building. They knew the ammunition had been moved. *The bastards had eliminated the base's ability to put up a viable defense*, Abdul-Samad thought. *But their aim wasn't good enough to entirely demolish the runways.* At least a handful of planes had escaped and would be able to return later to exact revenge on the invaders.

The major stayed on his cot despite the roar of the explosions. He had made up his mind after the first Iraqi raid that he was not going to take cover in an underground bunker. If it was God's will that he survive the Iraqi attacks, he would survive them above ground.

He looked around the barracks. Everyone was awake, but few were running for cover. The barracks were unusually crowded. Most of the off-duty personnel who had been reached yesterday had come to the base, and as the fighting continued throughout the day, many servicemen from other areas had retreated to Ahmad al-Jaber. Even civilian policemen and security guards had come to the base for refuge and with the hope of helping to defend it against the Iraqis.

After the bombing stopped, some men left to go eat breakfast, but Abdul-Samad remained in his quarters until noon, when it was time to go to the mosque for prayers. After the prayers ended, the base commander told the men that Iraqi tanks were very near. He ordered them to surrender without resistance. Their guns were to be left in the mosque. *This is it*, Abdul-Samad thought to himself. *Soon we will all either be dead or prisoners.*

By one o'clock the entire base was surrounded by enemy tanks and soldiers. Not a shot was fired. Slowly the Kuwaitis began walking toward the Iraqis. Abdul-Samad felt the strangling sensation of sheer terror. Would the Iraqis open fire and massacre everyone? If they did begin to shoot, there was no hope. The Kuwaitis were not only unarmed, they were terribly outnumbered. He imagined he could see the face of death in the nearest Iraqi. He knew that his fate, and that of every other Kuwaiti on the base, was truly in the hands of God.

The Iraqi officers ordered the Kuwaitis to line up. A shudder racked Abdul-Samad's body as he thought of a story he had heard from the Iran-Iraq War. The Iraqis had captured several hundred Iranians, lined them up on the pretext of passing out water to them, and then opened fire on the defenseless men. The Kuwaiti prisoners were ordered to sit on the ground in the merciless sun. Then the Iraqis moved through the lines and began asking questions.

"Is there anyone here of Iraqi origin?" an officer shouted. Several men Abdul-Samad knew were not Iraqi stood up and the officer, without even checking the men's papers, said, "Go home."

"Who among you are civilians?" the officer continued. Several men in training suits and *distashas* rose from the ground and, once again, without verification, the officer said, "Go home."

"Are any of you pilots?" the officer barked. This time no one moved. Everyone feared he would be executed for the raids the few pilots like Nasir had made on the Iraqis yesterday.

"Do you harbor American pilots at this base?" the officer continued. No one answered this time, either.

Finally, the officer exhausted his weak line of questioning and walked away. It was the middle of the afternoon and the prisoners were beginning to suffer badly from the sun and lack of water. Some of them began to beg for water.

"Please bring us water...we are Arabs like you...we are Muslims like you...." But their pleas were ignored.

Before long, the Iraqi officer returned. He ordered the Kuwaiti officers to stand and then told them to march to several trucks parked a short distance away. Abdul-Samad hesitated. He had removed his military insignia from his shirt so the Iraqis would not know he was an officer, but then decided he would go with his fellow officers. It was impossible to know if he would be any safer as an enlisted man, anyway.

He walked to a truck that was being worked on by an Iraqi soldier. An officer was instructing the soldier on the repair of the engine and the soldier was arguing with him. Suddenly the officer took out his gun and shot the soldier in the head. Abdul-Samad could hardly believe his eyes. *What kind of an officer would shoot his own man,* he wondered. *My God, he thought, we have been captured by animals!*

While the Kuwaitis waited to see what their fate would be, they began to notice several trucks parked at different buildings on the base. They watched as every piece of furniture and equipment in the buildings was loaded on the trucks in preparation for transportation to Iraq. They also saw soldiers looting the food supplies in the base canteen and officers' club. The Iraqis were shoving food into their mouths as fast as their hands could get it there. They are starved, Abdul-Samad thought to himself. I am hungry. I have not eaten since yesterday evening, but those men are starving! Again Abdul-

Samad wondered what kind of men the Iraqi officers were, not to provide adequate food for their men.

The trucks left the base and a murmur went through the group in Abdul-Samad's truck. He looked out the back of the vehicle and couldn't believe the number of tanks he saw surrounding the base. *There must be hundreds,* he thought. If we had fired one shot we would have been annihilated.

After they had driven on the road outside the base confines for several minutes, the trucks pulled up in front of a fenced-in fire station. The men were ordered out of the truck and to the basement of the station. Again, they were questioned—mostly stupid questions like before, Abdul-Samad decided. Then they were told to go back outside and sit down on the sand.

After about an hour of waiting, the Iraqi officer began calling out some 50 names of men who were then led off to waiting trucks. The Iraqis ignored the thunder of questions from the Kuwaitis about where the men were being taken. Many of the prisoners bowed their heads in prayer, fearful for the men's lives.

Cries for water began to penetrate the camp once again and finally a guard pointed to a nearby metal tank and told the prisoners to go get a drink. Abdul-Samad nearly retched when he looked at the water. It was filthy dirty, red-colored and very hot from sitting in the sun. But their thirst was so terrible, the men drank from the stagnant-smelling mess anyway.

The men had only been at the fire station a few hours when civilians, in defiance of the Iraqi curfew, began surging through the gate. Word had spread quickly that the base had been captured. Mothers, fathers, wives, and children were looking for their loved ones. Some families had brought *distashas* and *qutras* with them, and several prisoners, including the wounded Nasir, walked out the gate with his family after he donned the white robe and headdress. *The Iraqis really are stupid,* Abdul-Samad decided. *Prisoners are escaping in broad daylight, right under their noses!* Others were able to gain freedom by bribing the guards with money or expensive watches. Abdul-Samad had no expensive watch, and only a few dinars in his pocket. Hardly enough to bribe his way out.

Several of those who left promised to return with food and water. Some did—others were too afraid of being recaptured.

One of those who returned was a Kuwaiti sergeant. He came back the next day with a van full of bread, bottled water, and rice. When he left, he took with him a long list of telephone numbers so that he could call families and tell them their men were safe. Abdul-Samad was torn about whether to give the sergeant his wife's telephone number, but then decided he'd better not. He did not want her to take the risk of coming to find him, and he knew that she, and his mother, would do so if they knew where he was.

The first night of captivity came, and the prisoners tried to sleep on the sand or asphalt parking areas of the fire station. As uncomfortable as he was, Abdul-Samad dozed off only to be awakened a few minutes later by a scream from a nearby colleague. The man had been bitten by a black scorpion. After that, it was hard to fall back asleep.

■ ■ ■

Dina, Bedreah, and Mahmoud's slender, pretty wife Huda spent the first morning of the occupation talking about what they could do to ensure the safety of those in the compound. Since there were rumors that the Iraqis were searching homes for weapons and pictures of the royal family, they decided the best approach would be to go through each apartment gathering up things that might incite Iraqi wrath, and then, destroy them. Dina and Bedreah agreed to do the search while Huda remained in the basement with the children, who were playing video games.

The two went first to Dina's apartment and took down the Kuwaiti and American flags—even the hand-drawn ones Jassim had so proudly brought home from school to tack on the wall in the kitchen. They gathered up all magazines, books, and newspapers that had any reference to the Al-Sabah family. All correspondence from Dina's family and friends was thrown into a plastic garbage bag with the other items. This all would be burned. They hid picture albums under clothes in dresser drawers and stripped the apartment of jewelry and other valuables.

Then they searched Mahmoud's, Ahmad's, and Reda's apartments in a similar manner. While in Reda's quarters, Bedreah's iron facade wilted for a few moments. Sitting in her son's chair, she started to cry. She thanked God that Reda and his family were safe, as was her oldest daughter Masuma and her four children, and her middle daughter Khadeja and her family, who also were in England. But her heart ached for the rest of her family who had become prisoners of terror. Bedreah said a quick prayer that she would find a way to free the rest of her family from this nightmare. Then, wiping her tears, she helped Dina finish the task on the upper floors and descended the stairs to her own apartment.

Eidan had come to the basement for his breakfast that morning, but disappeared back into his own quarters shortly thereafter. Now he demanded to know what was going on as he watched Dina and Bedreah rifling through drawers and closets. They explained their task to him and he shook his head.

"I told you this will all be over soon," he growled, but he didn't hinder their mission. At least it gave them something to do other than sit around and worry.

It took them most of the morning, but they felt better when the job was done. When Dina returned to the basement, she took the valuables she'd gathered in her apartment, made a slit in several packages of Pampers, and tucked them inside the diapers. *I should put some of Husain's "poopy" diapers in there too,* she thought. Then some marauding Iraqi soldier would get a sweet-smelling handful if he started rummaging through the package looking for papers or valuables.

Dina had always had an uninhibited sense of humor. It was one of her personality traits that Ali loved. While they were courting she not only had helped him polish up his weak skills in the English language, she also had helped her too-shy and reserved Arabic boyfriend lighten up. Ali had found life much more enjoyable after he met Dina.

Now, even in fear, her sense of humor had surfaced. However, it disappeared a short time later when she learned the international phone lines were dead. She had finally found the nerve to call her "Poppy" and now she couldn't reach him.

■ ■ ■

Ali turned BBC Radio on again when he, his brothers, and Hameed returned from Abass's house. An announcer was rehashing details of the invasion when another announcer interrupted the programming to report that the U.N. Security Council had taken official action to condemn Iraq's invasion of Kuwait. Iraq had been ordered to withdraw, immediately and unconditionally. All of them were excited about the news, but none more than Eidan.

"See!" Eidan shouted. "I told you this would be over in a few days. Iraq would not dare defy a United Nations dictum!"

Poor Eidan!

■ ■ ■

By the second day of the invasion, the Iraqis had taken a deadly hold on their neighbor. There had been no time for officials to set off sirens to warn the civilian population of the pestilence that was pouring into their country. Hundreds of bodies littered Kuwait City streets. Some who lie dead or dying were Iraqis, some were Kuwaiti soldiers who fought a brave, but futile battle, and some were Kuwaiti civilians. It didn't matter to the Iraqis who they killed.

One of the fiercest and bloodiest battles was fought at the Ministry of Defense. Some 300 Kuwaiti soldiers with light arms attempted to defend the ministry against thousands of Iraqi troops with tanks. After a brief battle, the Kuwaiti officers realized there was no way to repulse the invaders. Surrounded by fearful odds, they surrendered in hopes of saving their men. Yet, surrender meant nothing to this group of Iraqis. Unlike what happened at the air force base, after these invaders gathered up the Kuwaiti weapons, the defenders were shot.

Then the Iraqis took over the national guard headquarters, police academy, and military academy, which were all located in one area of Kuwait City called *"Gewan."* However, military and police installations weren't the only targets. The Iraqis also stormed civilian-operated facilities like the Ministry of Health complex in the town of Al-Shuwaikh. There they put aside their guns long enough to go on a raping spree in the nurses' dormitories.

■ ■ ■

Later in the day, Dina and the women also decided that not only would the family remain together in the basement for the time being, all of the cooking in the compound would be done together. They would use the one electric stove in the house, which happened to be in the basement, to prepare meals as long as electricity was still available. If the power plant went down, they would be forced to use bottled gas. Mahmoud and Bedreah had managed to bring back several bottles of gas from the foray to the stores; however, the women knew it wasn't enough for an extended period of time.

Conservation was to be the key for survival, they agreed. Even though food was in abundance at the moment, they had no idea how long it was going to have to last. Therefore, frozen food would be used first in case electric service ended; canned food would be eaten last. Not even a bite of bread or a drop of milk would be thrown away. As best they could, they would ration the food—cooking only what would be required for a satisfying meal. Water would be as important as food, and they agreed that anything capable of holding water would be kept filled to the brim in case the Iraqis shut off the water supply.

In Kuwait, the main meal of the day is served around two in the afternoon, after the men in the family finish their work day. Because of the heat, workers go to work earlier than they do in America, so they are home earlier. The work day for all government sectors and many private sectors is six hours, rather than the eight hours Americans usually work. Even though the men would not be going to work for a while, the women agreed the meal schedule would remain the same.

Dina knew that eating all of their meals with the rest of the family would be a bit difficult for her, Ali and the children to get used to. Since she had arrived in Kuwait, she had become a good Mid-Eastern cook, thanks to Bedreah's tutoring, and usually served a Mid-Eastern dish for the main meal, but the lighter meal in the evening consisted of American or Italian food. She knew they would get hungry for something other than rice and chicken or lamb-based dishes, which are the Kuwaiti mainstay, but she also knew she had to be practical, so she didn't lodge any objections to the plan.

During the afternoon the women also gathered more clothing, toys, and games from Mahmoud's and Ali's apartments and Huda and Dina concentrated on arranging the basement so that each of the families would have more privacy. They were thankful the children seemed to be satisfied with the video games and movies, but they wondered how long it would be before they would become bored and start to pester their mothers to go outside or back to their own quarters. Dina and Huda knew they couldn't let them do either.

■ ■ ■

After the evening meal, Ali, Mahmoud, Ahmad, and Hameed went back outside to discuss the U.N. action with neighbors who had gathered on several benches outside the wall surrounding Abass's house. All agreed the resolution was good news; however, they were concerned about how much more damage the Iraqis would do before they left Kuwait. Many of the neighbors had friends or relatives in Kuwait City who had phoned them with reports of looting and wanton vandalism in the city. Everyone doubted Iraq would leave Kuwait without punishing it further.

The men agreed that until they found out what retaliation the U.N. censorship might bring from the Iraqis, and in view of the total curfew that was in effect, they should all stay close to home for a few days, listening for developments on radio and television.

When the group broke up, Ahmad went back inside his house, but Ali, Mahmoud and Hameed went to the front of the compound to see if there was any Iraqi activity on the main road, which was accessible by one of the inner streets (similar to alleys) that connected the homes in the neighborhood. If there were Iraqis on Naser Al-Mubarak Street, the enemy could also be in the neighborhood.

They could easily watch the street without being seen through an opening in the brick wall that surrounded the compound. All of the houses in the neighborhood were built in the same fashion: multistory buildings surrounded by brick walls.

Ali's watch read nine o'clock when they sat down on the top step near the entryway, which was bordered by an oasis of flowers and shrubs. It was almost dark. Surely they would be safe for a few minutes while they watched to see if there were any Iraqi vehicles on the streets.

They had only been on their vigil a few minutes when Ali heard a *zing, ping* near his left ear. He paled as it dawned on him that a bullet had just struck the wall behind him.

"Get down!" Ali shouted as he dove off the step, pulling his brother, who was sitting beside him, down with him.

Mahmoud, who was now lying in the flower bed with Ali, and Hameed, who was still sitting on the step, looked at Ali in bewilderment. They had been talking and had heard nothing.

Spitting dirt out of his mouth, Mahmoud snorted angrily, "What's the matter with you?"

"Goddamn it, there are bullets flying around!" Ali shrieked.

Hameed, a short, wiry youth, slithered quickly down the steps and crawled under a bush. They remained stretched out in the sand for several minutes, listening to the sound of rifle fire. When it stopped, they made a mad dash for the front door.

After the door was locked behind them, they stood shaking with fear. *Would they be followed into the house by Iraqi soldiers?* Not wanting to go to the basement where the rest of the family was, they sat in silence in Bedreah's dark dining room for some thirty minutes before they decided they had not been seen by the soldiers or whoever had been firing the guns. On the way to the basement, they agreed they would not say anything to anyone about the incident. No sense in alarming anyone needlessly, Ali thought.

Later that night, lying sleepless on his mattress, Ali wondered *how much more bullet-dodging there would be in the next few days* (or weeks…or months…his mind whirled) *while Iraq was complying with the U.N. order to get out.*

■ ■ ■

While Ali, Mahmoud, and Hameed were dodging stray bullets in Rumaithiya, three oil-rig workers were dodging dead bodies in an attempt to make their way home to Ahmadi. Omar, Mansoor, and Naif were on a Kuwait Oil Company rig north of Kuwait City when the Iraqis crossed the border. Fearing an invasion was underway, they called the general superintendent of the drilling department, Ali's brother-in-law Mohammed, at his home in Ahmadi at two that morning to ask what they should do. Mohammed advised they hide until after the Iraqis passed and then try to drive home.

They found a secure hiding place, where, for all that night and the next day, the three watched as thousands of Iraqis marched by them.

At nightfall on the second day, the climbed into Omar's car and headed south toward Ahmadi. Driving was difficult because of the Iraqi bodies and burned-out vehicles that littered the roads. Nasir and his fellow pilots had taken a toll on the invaders.

The intermittent *thump, thump* sound the car made when it passed over the bodies soon grated on Omar's nerves. He pulled to the side of the road and refused to drive farther. Mansoor took over the wheel and the men reached Ahmadi safely at midnight. When Mansoor phoned Mohammed to tell him the three were home, he told his supervisor that God had been watching over them on their trip from the oil field. The men had seen and heard gunfire and explosions all along their route, but somehow had managed to stay out of the Iraqis' way. He also told Mohammed it would be a long time before Omar would be ready to go back to the oil rig. The experience left him in a deep state of shock.

CHAPTER 5

The morning of August 4 came and the Iraqis still had not offered the air force prisoners anything to eat. There was still only the stinking red-colored water to drink.

At mid-morning Major Abdul-Samad noticed that one of the sergeants in his immediate group was missing. A few minutes later, the man appeared and sat down close to the Major.

"I found some food in the fire station," the sergeant whispered. He passed the meager collection of wilted vegetables around to the men nearest him. Each took one or two pieces and passed it on. Abdul-Samad thought nothing had ever tasted so delicious.

After he had eaten, the Major dozed in the sunlight for a few minutes before becoming aware that a shadow had moved over him. He opened his eyes to find a Bedouin standing nearby.

The Bedouin peered down at the men a few minutes and then asked, "Are you hungry?"

"Starving!" Abdul-Samad and the others answered.

The Bedouin left and a short time later he was back with a huge sack full of dairy foods. A near-riot developed as Abdul-Samad and other officers began to pass out the supplies.

God curse the Iraqis, the Major thought. *They are nothing but dogs forcing us to become animals, too.*

Later in the day, Abdul-Samad had a chance to escape. He watched as one of the men from the base took a cardboard carton from the fire station and carried it to a van that was sitting outside the fence. The man put the carton into the van and climbed in behind it. He went unnoticed by the guards. Abdul-Samad quickly went into the fire station and picked up a carton. As he neared the van a guard spied him.

Shouldering his gun, the guard asked, "Where do you think you're going, buddy?"

"I am carrying cartons to the van for transportation elsewhere," Abdul-Samad answered.

"No, you're not," the soldier said. "Get back inside the fence!"

The escape attempt was short-lived and would be the only one that Abdul-Samad would have a chance to make.

■ ■ ■

Unlike in Kuwait, news was not hard to come by in America. Dina's family was hearing more about what was happening in Kuwait than was Dina. And it made them even more anxious about her and her family's fate.

Her father Richard, a big, robust, usually calm man, paced the floor of the Colorado mountain cabin like a caged tiger after he came back from trying to call Dina.

While he was in town, he also had called Gina and she had given him U.S. State Department telephone numbers that were being broadcast over the television stations for those who wanted to find out information about family and friends in Kuwait. He tried calling the numbers but couldn't get through.

After a sleepless night, Richard and his wife Pat decided the day after the invasion announcement that they could no longer stay in Colorado. Dina would be unable to reach her father if she tried to call.

Pat and Richard had been married that March and she only knew Dina through telephone conversations with her. But she knew how close the girl was to her father. If Dina could possibly do it, she *would* try to get in touch with her "Poppy." She wouldn't be able to do that if they remained at the cabin.

They drove straight through to Omaha, making the trip in just over ten hours. Richard tried once to get through to Kuwait after they got home and that's when he discovered the international lines were down. Then he sat spellbound in front of television, watching reports from the Middle East until his eyes would no longer stay open. He spent the whole weekend dialing the phone numbers Gina had given him, again with no luck.

Then on Monday he called both Nebraska senators, James J. Exon and Robert Kerrey. The two agreed to try to obtain information through the American Embassy in Kuwait, but they could find out no more about Dina than Richard had.

In California, Dina's mother Camille was having better luck in contacting the U.S. State Department. A department representative took information about Dina from Camille and agreed to cable her through the American Embassy in Kuwait. Dina never received the cable. However, the department did, within the first few days of the invasion, establish a "Kuwaiti Task Force," which with Camille had daily contact. Even though she received no information about her daughter through the task force, the organization provided comfort and support for her.

In Lincoln, Gina was wondering if she would lose her mind before the crisis was over. She and Dina had never been particularly close while they were growing up. The fact that Gina was four years younger than Dina had a lot to do with that, but they had become very close since they reached adulthood. The two didn't look much like sisters, except both had inherited their mother's beauty. While Dina was slender, Gina was even more so. Dina had an olive complexion, while Gina had fairer skin. Gina was a couple of inches shorter than her sister, and while Dina was more even-tempered, Gina was a fireball. Right now, Gina was in the mood to tear the world apart to find out if her sister was still alive.

After running into dead ends in trying to reach Dina by phone and in obtaining information about her from the State Department, Gina decided to try to contact her through the Kuwait Embassy in Washington, D.C. several days after the invasion. She wrote a letter to Sheik Saud Naser al-Sabah, the Kuwait ambassador to the U.S., who had been in the States at the time of the invasion. He, in turn, and unbeknownst to Gina, managed to get a cable through to the American Embassy in Kuwait expressing Dina's family's concerns.

Dina was ecstatic when the embassy telephoned her with the message, and asked if they would cable Gina with a reply. Her message was: "Don't worry. We are fine. We have our faith. It is not the right time to leave." She didn't have the heart to tell her sister there was no plane she could take out of Kuwait. The Iraqis had reopened the airport, but the only flight operating was one to Baghdad.

Gina was both relieved and troubled when she received the unexpected cable a week later. Her sister was apparently still alive, but why was she being so stubborn about leaving Kuwait?

■ ■ ■

On the afternoon of August 4, Ali heard that the round-the-clock curfew had been lifted. Now Kuwaitis would be allowed on the streets of their country from dawn until eleven at night. He waited until the next day before going out into the streets to look for additional supplies.

Ali knew it was essential that he find an outlet for supplies. The neighbors had discovered that one of the men in a nearby neighborhood had panicked the day of the invasion and went to Saudi Arabia, leaving his wife and five children behind with little food and no money. The neighbors all pitched in and took food to the family, depleting their own supplies. Ali felt sure more situations such as that would continue to surface in the days to come and he knew his family and neighbors would respond in the same manner.

Restocking the supplies would be necessary until the Iraqis left. And it would be necessary for Ali to take on the task, Bedreah decided. He was the most even-tempered of the three sons available for the duty. Mahmoud had a gentle, timid personality and would probably collapse out of fear if faced by an Iraqi soldier. The high-spirited Ahmad had a quick temper and would likely fall into deep trouble if he was stopped at a checkpoint.

Ali crossed his fingers and left early in the morning for the neighborhood supermarket. It was closed, so he drove to the next neighborhood. That store also was closed. All of the smaller markets in the thirteen *plots* (neighborhoods) in Rumaithiya were closed, but the larger central store in the town of 20,000 people had reopened. The Iraqis hadn't gotten to it yet; it still had some supplies.

Eventually the invaders cleaned out every grocery store and warehouse, along with the government warehouses where two years' worth of emergency supplies were stored. The goods were transported to Iraq to replace supplies that had been cut off by the U.N. embargo.

However, there were some clever Kuwaitis who saw the handwriting on the wall. They bought up the stock in many of the stores before the Iraqis could get to it, hid it in their basements, and then after the stores were either shut down by force or from lack of food, loaded up the trunks of their cars and started a "flea market" in parking lots. Because of these entrepreneurs, non-perishable food was available for several months after the supermarkets closed.

Ali bought cigarettes, a couple of carts full of canned goods, and a case each of ketchup and Tabasco sauce. He knew all the cigarettes would disappear when the Iraqis found the store. The price of a pack of cigarettes in Iraq was equal to a month's salary for an Iraqi. He bought the ketchup and Tabasco sauce for Mahmoud. His brother ate one or the other on everything. The man would starve to death without them.

While he was paying for his purchases, he noticed that the woman checking out in front of him did not pay for her supplies. Instead of handing the checker cash, the checker handed her a piece of paper to sign. Ali asked the checker about it. The young man told him that the company had ordered the checkers to let Kuwaitis who had been caught with no cash when the invasion came to purchase groceries on credit.

The checker added, "The boss said he would rather let those who have no cash now buy on credit and hope they will pay their bill later than to let the Iraqis steal the food."

Ali decided whoever "the boss" was, he was one helluva guy.

Once the Kuwaiti government-in-exile was organized, it relieved individual merchants and flea market operators of the burden of extending credit. The government issued "coupons" to residents to be used to purchase necessary items on a credit basis. The coupons were distributed by the Kuwaiti resistance, and at the end of the occupation, the Kuwaiti government redeemed them for cash.

■ ■ ■

During the outing, Ali managed to avoid the few Iraqi checkpoints that he had heard had been positioned in the area, but he couldn't avoid seeing the damage the Iraqis had done in just a few short days. Rumaithiya had taken on an eerie look. There were several buildings that had been hit by artillery fire, tank guns, or simply set afire by the invaders. Some stores looked like they had been completely stripped of goods—even toy, plumbing, and clothing stores. When the Iraqis completed their withdrawal, Ali thought, the store owners would have nothing left.

Ali and the other men had seen truckload after truckload of goods being transported up Al-Fahaheel Expressway toward Iraq, but most of those trucks were filled with raw materials: lumber, concrete, and sewer pipes. Obviously, the Iraqis were taking finished goods back to their country by the truckload, too. The looting wasn't just by individual soldiers smashing in store windows, as Kuwait City residents had reported. It was an organized activity. The Iraqis intended to clean out every store in the country, one by one.

As he was returning to the compound, Ali noticed that the usually immaculate, tree-lined streets were now littered with trash and raw garbage. He began to think about what his neighborhood could do to avoid the threat of vermin and disease that would come soon. Garbage pickups had halted the day of the invasion. Most garbage haulers were foreigners who had fled the country, but had they stayed, there still would have been few pickups. The Iraqis took most of the garbage trucks for use in their country. Ali knew that if he and his neighbors were going to get rid of their trash they would have to do it themselves. He decided that when he returned home, he would discuss the problem with them. They would work out some plan to keep the garbage from piling up.

They had already worked out a security plan. Two or three men in each household had been keeping watch from a balcony of their home every night. The watches began at 11:00 P.M., curfew time, when the nightly gatherings at Abass's house ended, and lasted until dawn.

As Ali pulled into his parking space in the compound, he realized he had seen no evidence on his first trip out that the Iraqis were complying with the U.N. resolution to leave the country. A chill fingered its way down his spine as he thought, *Saddam is not going to pull out voluntarily—he will have to be* forced *out.*

■ ■ ■

Toward evening, Ali, Mahmoud, and Hameed went to Abass's yard to talk to the neighbors about the garbage situation and Baghdad's announcement that morning that a new military government had been established to govern Kuwait.

Dina and Bedreah were sitting in the kitchen while Huda entertained the children in the living room. The two young mothers decided they would take turns playing games with the children in the hope of occupying them so they would forget about going outside to play. After only three days of confinement they were already beginning to tire of taped movies and video games.

The telephone rang and Dina picked it up. It was Ahmad's fiancee, Afaf, calling from her parents' home.

"Dina," she said, "I told Ahmad wrong about what to do with the charcoal in order to use it during the chemical attack."

Dina turned pale. "I'm sorry," she said, "I didn't hear what you said."

Afaf repeated, "You need to tell Ahmad the proper way to use the charcoal for the chemical attack tonight." Then she continued to explain that the charcoal needed to be crushed into tiny pieces, heated to release all harmful gases, cooled down, and then put into a light cloth for use as a breathing mask.

Dina wanted to scream at Afaf. *Chemical attack? There's going to be a chemical attack tonight?* But she didn't want to upset Bedreah, so she mustered a smile and said, "Okay, I'll tell him," and hung up the phone. Bedreah knew there was something wrong, but Dina told her she was fine—she just had to go out into the yard and deliver a message to Ahmad from Afaf.

Dina ran up the stairs to the outside door as fast as her legs would carry her.

"Ahmad!" she screeched as she ran toward the men congregated on Abass's benches. "Afaf called about how to use charcoal in a chemical attack. Are we really going to have a chemical attack tonight?"

Ali and Ahmad ran to her and pushed her down on a bench. The wild look in her eyes told them she was in total panic.

"Calm yourself," Ahmad said. "There is a rumor there will be. Mahmoud's friend, Yacoub, called during dinner and passed the rumor on to us. We have already taken care of everything."

"*Taken care?*" Dina shouted. "*Taken care?* How can you *take care* of a chemical attack?"

Ahmad explained that while Ali was out looking for supplies, he, Mahmoud, and Hameed had sealed Mahmoud's apartment from outside air, filled bathtubs in both Mahmoud's and Ali's apartments with water in case someone had to wash chemicals off their body, and gathered up extra clothing, blankets and towels. Charcoal breathing masks were ready for use. Yacoub had also told Ahmad how to make the breathing masks.

After the truth of the invasion had settled in on the family, their greatest fear became that of a chemical attack. They knew Saddam had gassed thousands of people, even some of his own, during the Iraq-Iran War. No one in the house spoke much about it, but it was always on everyone's mind. Now her brother-in-law was telling her tonight might be the night!

Dina jumped up from the bench and screamed, "We will never see another day!" She turned and ran for her house. She had to think of something to protect her children! Ali ran after her, catching her as she neared the back door.

"Dina," he said quietly as he put his arms around her. "Calm down. If you go into the house like this, you will scare everyone to death!"

She sat down on the steps and started to cry. "Ali," she sobbed, "I can't let the children die like this!"

"It is only a rumor, sweetheart," he comforted. "There will be rumors like this every day Iraq is in this country. It does not mean that it's going to happen. All we can do is stay calm and pray that it doesn't."

Dina knew he was right. Prayers were the only thing that could save her babies.

■ ■ ■

"Get up! Come on, you lazy bastards, get on your feet!" an Iraqi guard shouted on the morning of August 5.

Major Abdul-Samad opened his eyes to see the Iraqi standing over him with a gun pointed at his head. Quickly he rose from his bed of sand at the fire station, and as he did, he saw that several dozen soldiers, guns at the ready, had formed a ring around the air force prisoners.

Abdul-Samad looked at the guard and asked, "Where are we going?"

"To Basra," the guard growled.

God Gracious, Abdul-Samad thought, *we are going to Iraq!* Fright filled his heart; he felt like a cornered cat. Glancing around frantically for a possible avenue of escape, it didn't take him long to see there was no way out. Armed guards were everywhere.

Several trucks arrived and the prisoners were herded on board. As the trucks began leaving, Abdul-Samad saw an old woman running toward his truck. Tears were streaming down her face and she was shouting, "My son.... Is my son there with you?" No one in the truck knew her. No one answered her.

The woman began running toward another truck, repeating her tearful cry. The trucks began to pick up speed, and the old woman fell behind. Abdul-Samad looked back to see that she had sunk to the ground in a cloud of dust. She seemed to be looking straight at him, her arms raised as if she were pleading with him to tell her where her son was. *That could be my mother,* the major thought as tears welled up in his eyes.

The trucks soon entered the Sixth Ring Motorway and headed toward Al-Jahra in northern Kuwait. The prisoners grinned at each other when they saw the bombed-out Iraqi tanks and other enemy vehicles that lined the road. They knew they were clear evidence of the damage done by their base's pilots.

As the trucks rolled on toward the border station of Al-Abdaly, Abdul-Samad wondered if he would ever come back to Kuwait and his home in the town of Al-Ferdous. *What is my fate? Will I be killed, or worse yet, will I stay forever a prisoner? What will happen to my country? My family?* While he was in Kuwait, there was at least a chance he would be able to see his family, his three children. *No chance now,* he shook his head. He would soon be in Iraq. When they reached the border they saw that the Iraqis had already removed all Kuwaiti border marks. *It is all one now,* Abdul-Samad sighed, *all one country. God Gracious! Why is this happening?*

The trucks moved through Safwan, Iraq, and the prisoners began crying for water. The cruel sun had beaten down on them for several hours and thirst was becoming unbearable. The trucks stopped and the guards brought water. It tasted so salty Abdul-Samad gagged. He knew instantly that it had come from Basra, which got its drinking water from a river that flows into the gulf. Gulf water backs up into the river, giving it a salty taste. Basra natives are used to the taste, but others found the water less than palatable.

Once again the trucks started up and after another hour's drive they pulled into a prison encampment near Basra.

Prison officials refused to let the trucks unload. The camp was already full to its brim.

Such was the case at several other camps the trucks stopped at as they continued to wind their way deeper and deeper into Iraq. At one camp they were ordered out of the trucks and they thought their journey had ended. While he was waiting to see what would happen next, Abdul-Samad began looking around the camp. Unexpectedly, he saw a group of American, British, and French men, women, and children standing near one of the buildings. *They must be hostages,* Abdul-Samad decided. As he watched, the group boarded a bus. He wondered where they were being taken.

After their bus left, an Iraqi officer began shouting at the prisoners to separate themselves into groups according to rank. Abdul-Samad moved to an area where several other majors were standing. Then they were all ordered back into the trucks.

One of the senior Kuwaiti officers asked a guard where they were being taken and the guard said, "Don't worry…you are going to a luxurious hotel for a bath and rest." Then the Iraqi chortled cruelly.

Again the trucks began their northward trek. Abdul-Samad developed a fierce headache and soon fell asleep. When the trucks stopped, he woke and stood to see if he could identify where they were. That was an easy take, he realized immediately. They were right back at the camp they had just left.

It was now dark and the prisoners pleaded for food and water and to be let off the trucks so they could say their prayers and stretch out on the sand to sleep.

"Tell me who your God is!" one of the Iraqi officers shouted.

"Allah!" the prisoners cried in unison.

"No!" the officer screamed. "It is not Allah—it is Saddam Hussein! Those who will acknowledge your new leader as their God can leave their truck!"

No one moved.

Dawn finally came and the prisoners resumed their pleas for food and water. Within a short time, they were ordered off the trucks and marched to a bathroom. Abdul-Samad was appalled at the horribly filthy accommodations. The toilets were overflowing and the smell of feces and urine made his eyes water. There was no drinking water available.

Back outside, the prisoners were told to sit on the ground. The sand was a welcome relief from the uncomfortable truck bed. Abdul-Samad's headache was still with him and he closed his eyes, wrapped his hands around his knees, and cradled his head in his arms. Within a few minutes, he was roused by shouting. An Iraqi officer was yelling at a young boy who held a large bowl of rice in one hand and a bottle of water in the other. The major watched with interest as a woman walked over to the officer and explained that she had heard the prisoners plead for food and water and had gone to her house to fetch them. Her son had come back with her to help pass them out. The officer told both of them to leave, and then ordered the prisoners to reboard the trucks.

This time the trucks headed for a train station. When they reached it, the prisoners were told they were going to Baghdad.

While Abdul-Samad stood in the boarding line, he heard a commotion a few paces away. An old lady was crying and berating an Iraqi guard.

"God curse you," she screamed. "God damn you. Instead of capturing the Jews, you capture your Kuwaiti cousins...you fail to fight the Jews...you are only brave enough to fight your Arab brothers!"

Obviously not all Iraqis supported Saddam and his policies, Abdul-Samad grinned to himself as he swung on board the train. Shuffling down the aisle listlessly, he heard a familiar voice call out his name. Turning around he saw two men from his hometown seated a few rows back. He had walked right by them and not seen them. They leaped from their seats and rushed to the major, wrapping him in their arms.

"We thought you were dead," one of them said. "When the air base was overrun, we thought you had been killed."

Abdul-Samad explained that the base had been surrendered to avoid bloodshed and told his friends about his imprisonment thus far.

"But you," Abdul-Samad said after he finished his brief story, "what are you two doing here?"

The men explained that they had been arrested for curfew violation the day after the invasion.

"My family," Abdul-Samad said, "are they well?"

"Yes," one of the men, who was also a neighbor, answered. "No one was injured in the invasion. They are just sick with worry over you."

Maybe I should have had the sergeant try to contact them, Abdul-Samad frowned.

The three found seats together where they sat for three hours talking, all the while growing more thirsty and hungry. Finally, at noon, the train began to move. As soon as it was underway, guards came through the cars with water and sandwiches. The water was warm, but clean and free from salt, and the sandwiches were made out of spoiled duck meat, which was covered with rotten tomatoes, but the men were so hungry they ate them anyway.

After he ate, Abdul-Samad's headache began to ease and he dozed, dreaming about his homeland and family. Again he wondered in his dream if he would see either again.

When they arrived in Baghdad the prisoners learned what their final destination would be.

Al-Rasheed prisoner of war camp.

■ ■ ■

After Dina had gained some control over her fear of a possible chemical attack, she had gone into the house to face

Bedreah and Huda. Ali agreed they should be made aware of the rumor, but that the children would not be told. They could not even understand the threat of guns and bombs, let alone a silent death from chemicals.

Bedreah was still in the kitchen. She looked pale and nervous. Dina wondered if someone had already told her the rumor, but when Bedreah saw Dina, she started babbling something about Iraqis being at Nassima and Mohammed's house.

Dina's heart sank. She searched her mother-in-law's eyes. "Are they all right?"

"Shaken," Bedreah answered, "but no one was harmed." Bedreah recited the story Nassima had told her. Two soldiers had come to the door asking for bread and water. They said they had eaten little since the invasion and were very hungry. Afraid to refuse them, Mohammed, who had answered their knock, told them to wait in the courtyard and he would bring them food. He filled a jug with water, grabbed a loaf of bread and a liter of milk from the refrigerator, and took them to the soldiers. He was followed out the door by his six-year-old son, Salem.

When the soldiers saw Salem, they refused to take the milk. "Keep that for your children," one of the soldiers told Mohammed. "I have three children of my own. I would not take milk from a baby."

While the soldiers were eating, they talked to Mohammed and Salem.

"You have a beautiful country," the soldier with the family said. "I would like to come here to work." Then he asked Mohammed if he would get him a visa so he could seek employment in Kuwait.

Mohammed, still not wanting to stir up any trouble, told the soldier, "Sure, I will try."

When the soldiers finished eating, they shook hands with Mohammed and Salem and left.

The soldier who had asked about the visa said, "I will come back later and see if you were able to get the visa."

Mohammed never saw him again. He wonders if he was one of the Iraqis who eventually fell to the guns of the Kuwaiti resistance.

■ ■ ■

The family spent an anxious night waiting for the chemical attack. Dina decided it would be better not to know before one was launched. Thinking about watching her children draw their last breath was more than she could bear. It would be better if the Iraqis would drop a bomb on the house and make death instantaneous.

A chemical attack never developed, but they were routed out of their beds once during the night by a huge explosion. The men herded everyone into Mahmoud's sealed-off quarters where they stayed for an hour before thinking it might be safe to return to their beds.

Ali learned the next day that resistance efforts had begun in earnest in Rumaithiya. The explosion had occurred when the Kuwaiti fighters blew up an Iraqi ammunition truck.

CHAPTER 6

Demonstrations against the Iraqi takeover had begun inside Kuwait the day after the invasion. In the early days, people were not afraid to go out into the streets to voice their opinions.

Late on the day of August 8, a demonstration was staged in the town of Al-Jabriya. Women and children marched peacefully through the streets carrying pictures of the emir and crown prince and signs proclaiming, "We Deny the Invasion and Occupation," or "Saddam Hussein Go Home—You're Not Welcome Here," and other slogans.

About 6:30 P.M., as the group of around 200 moved past the police station, the air suddenly exploded with the sound of rifle and machine gun fire. Most of the demonstrators began screaming and running away from the station where the firing had come from, but a beautiful twenty-year-old woman by the name of Sana'a and about twenty other women continued their march. A few seconds later, more shots rang out. Several women and children were slightly wounded, but nine bullets found their mark in Sana'a's body. One of the Iraqi soldiers, firing from the roof of the station, had obviously taken direct aim at her.

As she fell to the pavement mortally wounded, her mother, who was among the demonstrators, rushed to her fallen daughter and cradled her in her lap. Sana'a's dying words were, "My job is over...." Thus she became one of Kuwait's first female heroes. There would be many to follow in her bloody footsteps.

■ ■ ■

On August 6, the United Nations passed its second resolution. This one ordered a worldwide embargo on trade with Iraq. The United States immediately sent more naval ships (six warships had already been sent to the area) to enforce the resolution, and France and Britain followed suit on August 13.

Saddam showed his disdain for that resolution when, two days later, August 8, he announced the annexation of Kuwait. The dictator ordered that all diplomatic missions in Kuwait terminate work by August 24, and transfer embassy functions to Baghdad.

On August 9, in response to the dictator's action, the United Nations passed its third resolution. This one nullified the annexation. As the U.N. was discussing this resolution, Baghdad announced it was closing its country's borders to foreigners, trapping thousands inside both Iraq and Kuwait.

Saddam was growing angrier every day. Even his Arab brothers weren't giving him any support. So on August 10, he made an attempt to draw the Arab countries to him by calling for a "holy war" on America to topple the "emirs of oil." Rulers from twelve of the twenty Arab League states ignored Saddam, announcing instead that they would send their troops to the side of the Americans in the Arabian desert. Arab sheiks and presidents from Morocco, Egypt, Syria, Saudi Arabia, Bahrain, Qatar, the United Arab Emirates, and Somalia voted to honor the worldwide U.N. trade embargo.

Only Libya voted against the move. Mauritania, Algeria, Tunisia, Sudan, Jordan, and Yemen, plus the Palestinian Liberation Organization, either took no position, abstained, or was absent during the vote. Jordan would later violate the embargo by sending weapons, raw materials, and foodstuffs to Iraq, and the Palestinians eventually threw their support to Saddam, who had promised to give them back their homeland, once things were settled in Kuwait. The Iraqi dictator's answer to his Arab brothers' snub was to order increased terror in his newly annexed territory. On August 11 the first Westerner, a British businessman was shot and killed by an Iraqi soldier as he tried to flee from Kuwait into Saudi Arabia. On August 20, Saddam announced a roundup of all foreign nationals in Iraq and Kuwait "for their own protection." His foreign minister, Tariq Aziz, explained to the world that these "guests" of the Iraqis would be treated well but would be considered "insurance" against an attack on Iraq. Those rounded up were housed as human shields at sites likely to be targets in an armed conflict. Saddam paraded some of his "guests" on Iraqi television in an effort to show how well they were being treated. Nearly all of the hostages were ultimately released, which allowed them to tell stories contradicting Saddam's claims of humaen treatment.

"I wasn't a guest," an El Paso, Texas, man said after he returned home. "I damn near starved to death!"

On August 18, the U.N. Security Council demanded that Iraq allow all foreign hostages to leave. The next day, Saddam offered to do so if the foreign troops that had begun arriving in Saudi Arabia would go home and if the embargo were lifted. His offer was rejected.

The final act by the United Nations in August was the passage of a resolution on the twenty-fifth allowing military action to enforce the economic embargo of Iraq.

■ ■ ■

Farouk liked to hunt. Every night the airport ground guidance crew member grabbed his trusty machine gun and pistol and left his home in Rumaithiya to hunt rats—two-legged rats who had scurried out of Iraq and infested his homeland with the plague of repression.

Tall, gutsy, and outspoken, the twenty-five-year-old was well-known and highly respected in his neighborhood. He was one of the first resistance fighters; one of the few Kuwaitis who owned a gun at the time of the invasion. He was determined to fight for his land, pride, and dignity.

Men and women like Farouk didn't wait for an official resistance effort to be organized. They began killing Iraqis the day of the invasion. Singly and in numbers as few as two and three, they staged daring and sometimes suicidal attacks. Iraq, despite its military might, was unable to stop these attacks.

At first it was easy for Farouk and the others to kill Iraqis. They could count on bagging two or three every night. In the beginning, the Iraqi soldiers were naive and stupid. They went out into the streets day and night, alone or in small groups. They didn't think they had anything to fear from the Kuwaitis, since their leaders had told them Kuwait asked Iraq to help overthrow its government. They were easy prey, and after they were eliminated, their weapons were taken and given to other Kuwaitis who also wanted to join in the hunt (this was how Farouk acquired his machine gun). For each dead Iraqi, there was one more armed Kuwaiti.

But soon, the Iraqis realized there was much to fear from a Kuwaiti. What their leaders had told them was a lie. Kuwait hadn't asked Iraq into their country. Kuwaitis killed Iraqis every chance they got. The soldiers began banding together for safety. This made hunting a bit more difficult for Farouk, but the challenge was exhilarating. This made the reward—a dead Iraqi—even more coveted.

Even though Farouk was a good hunter, his luck disappeared one night. Two nearby towns, Al-Salmiya and Hawalli, were his usual hunting grounds, but one night in mid-August, Farouk, his eighteen-year-old nephew Facil, and a friend Sauod decided to see what the hunting was like in Al-Jabriya. It wasn't so good. All three were captured.

As they drove into the town that night, they suddenly found themselves in a traffic jam at an Iraqi checkpoint. They knew they would never pass the checkpoint since they had weapons, so they turned onto a side street and drove between two houses where they hid their guns in a pile of garbage. Then they drove a few more blocks before abandoning the car. After walking for several minutes, they spotted a vacant house and broke into it. Five Iraqi soldiers spotted them going into the house and arrested them.

During the questioning at the Al-Jabriya Police Station, Farouk and the others told their interrogators they had gone into the house looking for food, but the Iraqis laughed at them. The interrogators told them they knew they were resistance fighters and demanded to know where their weapons were. The Kuwaitis continued to protest their innocence. After the Iraqis questioned them together for several hours, they separated the three men. The Kuwaitis were then beaten and tortured in an attempt to get them to confess and name other resistance members. The Iraqis' attempts were futile, and the men were thrown into a jail cell.

Three days later, Farouk's sister Narjis, learned from his wife that he and the others were missing. Narjis was a "regular" at the police stations in the area. Her eldest son, Hosam, had been arrested soon after the invasion, and she made regular trips to the stations trying to find him. Now she included her brother, nephew, and Sauod in her searches. Narjis went to several stations before winding up at the one where the three were being held. The Iraqis admitted having the men, but her tearful plea for their release fell on deaf ears. A soldier spit in her face and threw her out of the station.

Narjis went home and called another brother, Mohammed. Mohammed went to the station. The Iraqis beat him and threw him into a cell, but released him the next day.

After Mohammed returned home, Narjis decided to make another rescue attempt. This time she took money, a television set, VCR, and jewelry to bribe the Iraqis. It worked. Greed overshadowed the value of the prisoners and Narjis managed to get all three released.

Farouk, a husky weightlifter and boxer, survived the ordeal in fairly good shape. So did Sauod. Facil was less fortunate. The youngster had been severely beaten and will always carry emotional scars from his brief imprisonment.

Farouk went into hiding after his release. He knew that, even though the Iraqis hadn't found him with a gun at the time of his arrest, he was on their list and would be a prime suspect in the future. He had been in hiding at his wife's parents' home only a short time when a raid on Narjis's home by Iraqi intelligence agents sent him to the streets again. His sister's house had become a meeting place for the fighters. Every man in the house at the time of the raid was arrested and hauled off to jail.

Farouk had missed hunting rats anyway, so the raid served as an excuse for him to pick up his guns again.

■ ■ ■

Ali's luck in avoiding Iraqi checkpoints on his first trip out of the compound didn't hold. More checkpoints were established during the second and third weeks of the occupation. Now he couldn't travel any distance from the house without eventually coming to at least one, usually two or three.

At the beginning of the occupation, the guards at the checkpoints rarely harassed the Kuwaiti civilians. They simply checked the person's civil identification card and driver's license. If they were in order, he was allowed to pass. But eventually, the checks became more thorough. Guards began asking for other proof of citizenship, and sometimes would, for no reason, search the driver and his vehicle.

Stories began to make the rounds of people who had been roughed up at checkpoints. On the other hand, there were people who said Iraqis had apologized to them for being in Kuwait.

Fuad told the men one night that a guard he'd encountered told him he'd been tricked into going to Kuwait. "He told me he thought he was being sent to Kuwait to help the people in a revolution against their government, but he added, 'I see no revolution,'" Fuad said.

Another neighbor reported that his identification card had been taken from him by a guard. The guard told him he could pick it up at the Rumaithiya Police Station later. All of the police stations in Kuwait were now Iraqi headquarters. The neighbor needed the identification but was reluctant to go to the station to retrieve it. He knew the Iraqis were arresting young men traveling alone as suspected resistance fighters. He thought the confiscation of his I.D. might be a ploy to lure him to the station so he could be arrested. It became more apparent as time passed there were some Iraqis who were friendly and some who were deadly. Kuwaitis soon figured out what made the difference. Most of the friendly soldiers were from Saddam's regular army, while the deadly ones were members of his intelligence agency or secret police. But no matter what guard was on duty, a man seemed to be in less danger if he wasn't alone. Men accompanied by their wives and/or children seemed to be less of a target at checkpoints.

■ ■ ■

One night in the middle of August, Ali received a phone call from Essa, a friend who lived several houses away.

"Ali," Essa said. "I just saw a group of very young boys pass my apartment with rifles and shotguns. Now they are hiding in the garden next door. What do you suppose they're up to?"

"How young?"

"No more than seventeen. Some look even younger."

Ali, who had just come home from Abass's house and was getting ready to take up his lookout post on Ahmad's balcony, told Essa he would take a look from the balcony to see what he could make of the situation. "You stay by the phone...I'll call you back in a few minutes," Ali promised.

Ali went out on the balcony with his binoculars, but couldn't see into the garden Essa was talking about, so he went back inside and called Abass, who had a better vantage point to inspect that particular area. Abass reported that he could see nothing either, so Ali called Essa back and said the group must have left.

"Yes," Essa said. "I just saw them go. A civilian car pulled up, the youths talked to the driver for a few minutes, and then they walked off."

Later that night, the neighborhood watchmen heard the roar of gunfire coming from the direction of Salwa, the town just south of Rumaithiya. The next day they learned that the checkpoint between the two towns had been hit by resistance fighters. Ali and the other men concluded that the group Essa had seen were the raiders.

"So young," Essa shook his head. "Just babies, and they are fighting a war."

■ ■ ■

Along with the annexation announcement on August 8, was a statement that members of Iraq's "People's Army" were being sent to Kuwait to assist in the "orderly transition" of the annexation. Some friendly guards at the checkpoints came from this grubby, underfed, reluctant group of "volunteers."

To hasten the process of acquiring bodies for this army, "Uncle Saddam" simply pointed his finger at the streets of Baghdad. "Enlistment" buses were sent out to patrol the streets, and when a male, regardless of age, was spotted, the patrol would grab him, put him on the bus, and tell him he was now part of the People's Army. The Iraqis usually got eighteen to twenty volunteers per gallon on these recruitment runs.

Ahmadi Rambo was a member of this band of soldiers. The old man hadn't even had time to notify his family that he had "volunteered" before he was put on a bus headed for Kuwait. He wound up in the town of Ahmadi where he was given his nickname by residents who came to know him. No one ever learned his real name.

"Rambo" represented many men in Saddam's People's Army. He was so old and so weakened by undernourishment, he didn't have any energy to threaten anyone. He was the direct opposite of what his nickname implied and was the butt of jokes from the other guards. The jokes didn't bother "Rambo." All he wanted to do was sit quietly in a cool place, dreaming about having so much food to eat his belly wouldn't hold it all. He became an institution in Ahmadi. If you were in his line at the checkpoint, you knew you wouldn't be hassled. Some who befriended him wonder what happened to him after the liberation.

■ ■ ■

In hopes of avoiding suspicion that he might be a resistance fighter, Ali began taking one or two of the children with him when he left the compound. He and Dina had a hellish argument over the idea. She was even more protective of the children since the chemical attack scare; the children weren't going to be put in further jeopardy outside the compound. It had taken all of the men in the house to convince her they would be in no more danger than they were at home and that Ali would be safer while they were with him.

Ali had become increasingly worried about Mubarek, his friend and former coworker at the bank. He hadn't been successful in contacting him by telephone since the invasion, so one day, the third week into the occupation, Ali asked Zade and Yacoub, his second and third sons, if they wanted to go to Mubarek's house with him. Both jumped up and down with excitement—neither had been out of the house since the invasion. They hopped into the car with their father and Ali headed towards Al-Salmiya, just a few minutes north of Rumaithiya. The boys chattered excitedly, not seeming to notice the soldiers and military equipment scattered along the streets.

They passed the first checkpoint with no problem, but as they neared a second, one of the five soldiers on duty marched toward their car with a threatening look on his face. When he arrived at the driver's side, he pointed his machine gun at Ali's head and ordered him out of the vehicle.

"Get your ass out right now!" the guard shouted as Ali hung back, afraid to leave the boys in the car alone.

He quickly slid out of the car, and the soldier crawled into the vehicle and started poking around the back seat, on the floorboard, and under the seat. Ali looked at Zade and Yacoub. They stared back at him, their huge black eyes clouded with fright.

"Please don't scare the children," Ali told the soldier.

"Shut up!" the soldier growled.

Once the Iraqi soldier had completed his search of the back seat, he ordered the boys to the back so he could search the front. Then he got out of the car and told Ali to open the trunk. When he was through rummaging through that, he motioned for Ali to get back into the car. Ali did. Zade and Yacoub jumped back into the front seat with him.

Ali was angry over the guard frightening his sons. "You could at least have said something to reassure the children," Ali told the soldier.

"Shut up, or I'll shoot you in front of them!" the soldier hissed.

Ali could have kicked himself. *What had made him say that?* It only put them in more danger. Now Ali was really frightened. If he was going to get a bullet in the head, he certainly didn't want it to be in front of Zade and Yacoub!

"I'm sorry," he apologized to the guard. "Is there anything else?"

"No, just get the hell out of here!" The soldier slung his gun over his shoulder and backed away.

Ali did—just as fast as he dared.

"Dad, that guy had a gun," Zade said. "He said he was going to shoot you!"

"I know, son," Ali answered, "but it's all okay now. We're going home."

"Let's stop at the supermarket for candy," Yacoub piped up.

"You dope!" Zade scowled at his younger brother. "Don't you remember, Dad said the supermarket's closed. We'll have to wait until the Iraqis leave."

Tears came to Ali's eyes. He couldn't even go buy his sons a treat to soothe their fright. *Those bastards,* he cursed under his breath. *They'll pay for this, one way or another.*

A few days later he learned from another friend that Mubarek was alive and well. He had taken his family to his parents' home in a remote section of the country.

■ ■ ■

Ali knew he didn't have a prayer in hiding the incident from Dina. If he didn't tell her, the boys would.

Another wave of hysteria engulfed Dina, just as it had when she learned about the possible chemical attack. She forbade him to take any of the children out again—or to go out himself. He agreed he wouldn't take the children, but he couldn't promise he wouldn't leave again. Someone must continue the search for food.

It was becoming more apparent every day that Saddam would ignore the Security Council's withdrawal order.

■ ■ ■

The checkpoint incident was not the only scare Dina would have that week. Two days later, after supper, Bedreah asked Ali for permission to take Yacoub with her to visit a neighbor, just two houses away. Ali agreed. He didn't see any real danger since they were staying in the neighborhood, and he figured they would be back before Dina even knew they were gone. Bedreah and Yacoub left the house by the back way.

They hadn't been gone more than half an hour when a horrendous explosion shook the neighborhood. The Kuwaiti resistance had ambushed another Iraqi ammunition truck.

Ali rushed up the stairs to the back door. Bedreah was pounding toward him as fast as her legs would go, abiya flapping straight behind her. She hadn't stopped to retrieve her shoes outside the neighbor's door, so she was barefoot and had her grandson by the hand. His little feet never touched the ground during the flight.

When the explosion hit, Dina automatically began gathering the children around her and discovered Yacoub was missing. Then she saw Ali running up the stairs. *Why would he be going upstairs*, she wondered.

Yacoub! It hit her like a bolt of lightning. For some reason, *Yacoub was outside!* She jumped up and ran after her husband, reaching the door at the same time as Bedreah and Yacoub. A horrified screech tore from her throat as she grabbed her son and dashed to the basement, holding the three-year-old so tight he could scarcely breathe.

"Mamma," the frightened youngster said through his tears, "I forgot my shoes!"

Dina sat down, still holding him in her arms, and cried with him.

"That's OK, Yacoub," she said. "We'll buy you another pair."

"I know," the little boy sobbed, "after the Iraqis leave."

The following day, Asedour, Eidan's driver, came into the basement screaming, "They have Ali...the Iraqis have Ali!"

Dina began screaming right along with Asedour. Mahmoud had to slap her face several times to bring her out of her hysteria so she could tell her father-in-law where she kept Ali's papers. Eidan was going to the authorities to find his son.

Ali had told his family that morning that he was going out to find a garage that could do some minor repair work on his car. From what Asedour was saying, Eidan figured Ali had been stopped at one of the checkpoints, and for some reason, arrested.

Eidan took the papers from Dina's trembling hands, grabbed the badly frightened driver by the arm (Dina's outburst had made him even more terrified), and ordered him to take him to where he had last seen Ali.

When they arrived at the checkpoint, Eidan saw his son's car parked off to the side of the road. He marched to the guard standing nearest the car and asked, "Where is my son? I have been told you have taken my son. I am here to trade myself for my son."

The guard started laughing. "I don't have your son," he told Eidan. Then, pointing a finger at Asedour, he asked, "What did that fool tell you?"

"He said that you have my son," Eidan repeated. "There was no one with this man when we confiscated the car," the guard said. "He didn't have the proper papers, and we suspected the vehicle had been stolen."

Eidan turned to Asedour, suddenly remembering the difficulty the Indian driver had in speaking Arabic.

"You said the Iraqis took Ali," Eidan said to Asedour. "Did they take Ali, or did they just take Ali's car?"

"Car," Asedour's face brightened. "Iraqis take Ali's car." In his panic, he hadn't been able to remember the Arabic word for *car*. The driver had become terror stricken because he was sure Eidan would fire him for having lost the car to the Iraqis.

The old man could have choked Asedour, and at the same time, kissed him. Eidan had just had the fright of his life, but his son was safe!

Turning toward the guard, Eidan smiled broadly and said, "This is all a misunderstanding. This is my driver, and these are the papers for the car. Will you release it to me?"

The guard checked the papers, then handed the car keys to Eidan. Asedour drove him back to the compound.

When they arrived, there stood Ali at the front door. He had not thought to tell the family that he had changed his mind about taking the car to the garage and was going to Fuad's house instead, or that he'd given Asedour permission to take the car to visit a friend.

It was the last time he didn't let someone know what his plans were or where he was going.

■ ■ ■

Dina steadily went downhill after those incidents. Her nerves had been rubbed raw. She jumped at every sound and grew even more protective of the children, and yet, she was constantly yelling at them. She felt more like a warden than a mother.

In addition to being frightened, Dina missed her freedom. Unlike most women in Middle Eastern countries, Kuwaiti women were allowed to drive and be out on the streets by themselves. Dina wanted to get into her car and drive to a friend's house for tea, wander around one of the shopping malls, or go to her beloved beach. She had never realized before what the word "freedom" meant. Now she felt like a wild bird that had suddenly found itself in a cage.

Lack of sleep brought dark circles under her hollow eyes, and the sight of food usually turned her stomach. She had already lost ten pounds from her slim frame and would ultimately lose ten more. Ali and Bedreah began a campaign to convince her to take the children and leave the country.

"I won't go unless everyone goes," she told them. "If we're going to die, we'll all die together!"

Dina knew the only way anyone could leave the country was by car, through the desert. The Iraqis, of course, were guarding the Saudi Arabian border. Sometimes they would announce the border was open, and thousands of people would rush for freedom, only to find that by the time they got there, it was closed again.

Stories filtered back to Rumaithiya of people, not only Kuwaitis but many other nationalities, who had left for Saudi territory after the invasion. Some made it—others died. Many of those who survived the trip owed their success to bedouins who guided them through the desert wastelands. In some cases, as people throughout Kuwait were learning about checkpoints, the success of an escape seemed to depend on whether you happened upon a "good" Iraqi guard or a "bad" Iraqi guard.

Dina hated the desert as much as she hated the Iraqis. She decided she would rather see her children shot by an Iraqi soldier in front of her eyes than have them die a slow death from starvation or dehydration after being lost in that horrible wasteland.

Unfortunately, Dina's fears came true for many people who tried to escape. Some who left wound up turning back. Those who aborted their flight to freedom told friends of seeing the bodies of entire families who had perished from lack of food and water after their cars became bogged down in the sand, or of having their food and water stolen and their lives threatened by snarling border guards. Some said they had seen others shot on the spot when guards discovered they were carrying forged papers.

Very early in the occupation, a few Kuwaitis were able to buy their freedom from the Iraqis but after the Kuwaiti dinar was devalued, the chances of purchasing freedom decreased dramatically.

Farouk told his neighbors about a resistance fighter who became lost in the desert while trying to take his family to safety. While driving aimlessly in the scorching heat, the family happened upon several Iraqi soldiers who were in desperate need of water. Two of the soldiers in the group were already dead from thirst. The Kuwaitis gave them water and the Iraqis thanked them by pointing the direction to the Saudi border. The man left some of his remaining food and water with the soldiers, then took his family on to safety. Farouk's friend brought guns back to Kuwait for the resistance and had returned many times to Saudi for more weapons. Each time he returned, he had new stories to tell of death in the desert.

■ ■ ■

During the month of August, a tremendous buildup of military might began in the gulf area. The world's leaders were not only worried about getting Saddam out of Kuwait. They also worried the dictator might try to grab Saudi Arabian oil fields.

Warships in the gulf were put on alert, and deployment of U.S. troops and equipment to Saudi Arabia began on August 8. By the end of the month, there were some thirty ships in the gulf, hundreds of aircraft, and 70,000 U.S. regular army and marine troops on Saudi soil, poised to defend that country from an Iraqi invasion, and if necessary, free Kuwait. Additional regulars were arriving daily, and President Bush decided to activate the reserves, which could provide 200,000 more fighting men and women. Canada, Britain, France, Belgium, the Netherlands, Italy, and Australia also had naval vessels in the area. Britain sent a squadron of planes. Completing the scorecard against Saddam by the end of August were 1,200 ground troops from Bangladesh, 4,000 from Egypt, 1,200 from Morocco, and 2,000 from Syria. The Gulf Cooperation Council—composed of Saudi Arabia, Bahrain, Oman, the United Arab Emirates, and Qatar—had 10,000 fighting men available. Kuwait's crown prince announced Kuwait would "fight and fight and fight, until we drive out the aggressors from our country. We will never submit or surrender to threats of aggression or occupation." The prince added that his government was forming a liberation army to help in military action to free his country.

On August 26, the United Nations offered its first formal attempt to mediate the crisis. U.N. Secretary General Javier Perez de Cuellar traveled to Jordan to meet with Iraqi officials, but after two days of talks, he gave up. Iraqi leaders said they would "eat mud" before yielding to the U.N.'s demands.

As before, Saddam ignored the United Nations, as well as the troop buildup and the prince's warnings, and increased his reign of terror on Westerners. House searches began in an attempt to pick up additional non-Arab foreigners for use as hostages.

■ ■ ■

Ali received a phone call one day in late August telling him that a house in another neighborhood of Rumaithiya had been searched for foreigners. The caller said it would be more than likely that the Iraqis would be in the neighborhood within hours.

Ali tried to comfort Dina by telling her she wouldn't be bothered because she was married to a Kuwaiti. That didn't do much to allay her fears, and then later, Ali found out it wasn't the truth, in at least one case.

Ali and Dina had become close friends with a Kuwaiti man, Ismial, and his English wife, Elaine. Ismial told Ali that another English woman, who also was married to a Kuwaiti, had been picked up in a house search. She had not been heard from since.

Everyone thought that because of her dark hair, eyes, and skin coloring, Dina had a good chance of passing as an Arab if she were confronted. About a month before the invasion she had decided to adopt part of the Muslim dress, so she was now wearing a *hejab* (a light-colored head scarf) and dresses to the wrists and ankles. This made her look even more Arabic. And she had learned to speak the Arabic language very well. But they worried about the Iraqis finding her birth certificate, passport, and other papers that would identify her as an American.

Hassan, husband of Ali's eldest sister Masuma, had planned to leave the day of the invasion to join his wife and children on their holiday in England. Now stuck in Kuwait without them, he braved the checkpoints on an almost daily basis to go to his in-laws' compound so that he didn't have to spend all of his time alone. He took Dina's papers back with him to his home in Bayan one day and buried them in his backyard. Meanwhile, a friend informed Ali about a forger he knew in Bayan. Remembering the story about the English woman, he risked a trip to the nearby town one night to buy Dina some Kuwaiti identification.

With that done, the family felt better about facing a house search, and since the trip to Bayan had gone without incident, Ali decided he would return another time and obtain documents for all of his family in case they were forced to leave Kuwait on short notice.

The Iraqis did not come to the door that day, but the family felt it was just a matter of time before they would.

■ ■ ■

The invaders not only started raiding homes in search of foreigners, they also began a campaign to find members of the Kuwait military reserves. Because the country had such a small population, all Kuwaiti males between the ages of eighteen and thirty were required to serve in the reserves. Since the

Iraqis had taken over all of the military installations and government buildings, it was easy for them to obtain the files of both reservists and career military personnel, which contained names, addresses, and photographs.

Ahmad and Mahmoud were the only ones in the house who were in the reserves. Ali had entered the military academy in 1977, where he served a short time. As a result, he was excused from reserve service. Reda had been out of the program for over four years.

When Bedreah heard this news about the Iraqi searches, she immediately called for another raid through her sons' apartments. Mahmoud's and Ahmad's uniforms, papers, and the military medals and citations they had earned were gathered up and burned.

But the women were in a panic, and the raid didn't stop there. Even though Ali was not in possession of any military items, he excelled in the art of karate, earning many medals in addition to a black belt. Jassim also had received several karate awards, and along with his sister, had earned medals for academic work. Fearing the sports and school medals might be interpreted as military awards and the karate uniforms as a sign that Ali was teaching karate to resistance fighters, Dina and Bedreah confiscated all of these and they, too, were burned—except Ali's hard-earned black belt. Eidan managed to rescue it from the pile and hide it in his apartment.

■ ■ ■

Even though Iraqi bandits were cleaning everything movable out of Kuwait, a few weeks into the occupation Saddam ordered all Kuwaitis back to their jobs. Few went.

He'd also ordered them to stop going to the mosques, even though he was appealing to the Arab countries to join him in a holy war. The order fell on deaf ears. Later in the occupation the Iraqis started staking out the mosques on Fridays, the Muslim holy day and arresting men who defied the order. Kuwaitis still attended the prayer services. Saddam had ordered the Kuwaitis to provide a volunteer to head a puppet government he had established at the onset of the invasion. They had laughed at him.

He had ordered them to apply for Iraqi "citizenship" and change their driver's licenses and vehicle registrations to reflect the new "citizenship." They laughed again. Kuwaitis could be as good at ignoring orders as Saddam was. The few Kuwaitis who did go back to work were people like Abdul-Samad's thirty-six-year-old brother, Rasul, who also lived in Al-Ferdous. He worked in the water plant. Rasul, a small, gentle person with sparkling green eyes, decided to obey the Iraqi order because he wanted to be sure the country did not go without water. Being on the job would help assure the continued flow of water, in addition to ensuring that it would be drinkable. Rumors were floating around Kuwait that the Iraqis either already had, or intended to poison the water.

When Rasul arrived at the plant for his first day back on the job, he found two surprises. First, most all of his fellow employees apparently felt as he did about protecting their country's water supply because they, too, returned to work, and secondly, Iraqi engineers were busily directing the construction of a huge pipeline from Kuwait City to their country. The invaders intended to steal Kuwait's water along with everything else.

■ ■ ■

On August 29, Ali and his family heard on an early morning news broadcast that an "important" announcement would come out of Baghdad that night. Everyone was elated. They felt sure Saddam was going to announce his withdrawal from Kuwait.

Two specific reasons gave them this hope. First, they believed the military buildup in the Middle East had the dictator "on the ropes." Saddam couldn't possibly believe his army was any match for the better-trained and more technologically advanced forces of the Western world. Second, reports they had been receiving from a friend who traveled regularly to Iraq to visit relatives led them to believe the Iraqis would soon revolt against their leader. The friend, a thirty-one-year-old cool, adventuresome man named Adel, had been a police sergeant before the Iraqis took over the police stations. He told Ali the pressure of the economic sanctions was already evident in Iraq, a country where many went hungry even before the embargo.

"All supplies are growing extremely scarce," Adel said. "There are shortages of cooking oil, flour, bread, and eggs. Motorists are even resorting to the black market to get the oil changed in their cars!"

Adel added there was panic buying so national rationing had been ordered. "Believe it or not," he said, "they are shooting their own people. They've begun house searches to ferret out hoarders and then they shoot them when they find them!"

Ali's family was sure that if the military might assembled at the Iraqi dictator's doorstep didn't force him into withdrawing from Kuwait, his own people would.

That evening they all gathered around the television to wait for the announcement. When it came, they were devastated. Saddam had begun changing the names of places inside his "nineteenth province." From now on, the announcer said, Kuwait City would be known as Kadhima, and the Bubiyan and Warba Islands had been renamed Saddamiyat Al-Mitlaa, in honor of Kuwait's new dictator.

"Damn him!" Ali said as he leaped from his seat and shut off the television. "Does Saddam have a slow leak in his brain? How can he keep defying the United Nations?"

Eidan slowly rose from his chair and left the room. The old man's faith in his country's friends was nearly shattered by that announcement. Saddam was being allowed to do anything he wanted. That evening, Eidan buried his belief that the crisis would be a short one.

CHAPTER 7

September 2, the first-month anniversary of the invasion, provided an opportunity for Kuwaitis to show their displeasure with the occupation, and at the same time, put the fear of God into the Iraqi soldiers surrounding them.

By word of mouth, a mass protest was planned that wouldn't require anyone to leave their home. Arrangements were made to broadcast it to the world via satellite television.

Middle East homes are topped with easily accessible flat roofs ringed by low walls, and that night, thousands of Kuwaiti men, women, and children went to their rooftops to join the demonstration. At exactly midnight they shouted *Allahu Akbar!* (God is Great!) over and over, until the Iraqis stilled the roar with gunfire.

The Kuwaitis had learned the intimidation trick from the Iranians. Iranian soldiers would shout the religious epithet before charging into battle against the Iraqis. It scared the hell out of Saddam's forces. A little psychological warfare was about the only thing the majority of Kuwaitis could offer against the invaders.

On the night of the protest, Ali, his brothers, and cousin went to Abass's yard at nightfall, as usual, but when curfew time came, instead of going to Ahmad's balcony to take up their nightly vigil, they went to the roof to join in the shouting.

Dina, Bedreah, and Huda were not told about the demonstration because the men knew the women would argue with them about being a part of it. When thousands of voices cried Allahu Akbar, the roar rumbled through Rumaithiya like thunder. The women thought the town was under a massive attack. Their fears grew, when within minutes, they heard shooting. Thinking her sons and nephew were at their posts on the balcony, Bedreah rushed from the basement to the courtyard, screaming for them to get in the house. No one answered her. Then, fearing they had been shot and were lying dead somewhere in the dark yard, she fainted.

Eidan, hearing his wife's screams, rushed outside where he found his daughters-in-law huddled over the prostrate Bedreah. They thought she had suffered a heart attack. Eidan told Dina and Huda where Ali and the others were.

Dina ran to the roof, burst through the door, and shouted, "You idiots! You've killed your mother!"

They all rushed downstairs where Eidan and Huda had managed to carry Bedreah to a couch. They were reluctant to take her to a hospital, since Kuwaitis were sometimes denied treatment. They figured they would be risking being out after curfew for nothing if medical treatment was denied. All they could do was try to revive her themselves. Bedreah finally opened her eyes. When she saw her sons and Hameed were safe, she began crying. After they told her where they had been and what the noise was about, she made them promise they would never join in a demonstration again.

■ ■ ■

The second week in September, Ali heard on BBC Radio that evacuation flights were being organized for Westerners. Several Middle East countries and some in Asia had ordered their citizens out of Kuwait early in the occupation. The two drivers and an Indian maid the family employed left shortly after the incident with Ali's car, but this was the first word he'd heard about Westerners.

The promise Ali had made to Dina's father about sending her and the children out of the country if a dangerous situation arose had been bothering him. Now that a plane was available for them, he could carry out that promise. Immediately he insisted that she call her embassy and make arrangements for her and the children to leave.

She resisted, repeating that she wouldn't leave without the whole family.

Then Ali heard that his friend Essa's wife, a small outgoing woman named Thoraya, had been told by the American Embassy that she could book passage on the plane for herself and her two children. Female Kuwaitis with Kuwaiti passports were being allowed to leave, but not males. In addition, Thoraya's two children had American birth certificates.

Ali contacted Thoraya and asked her help in putting pressure on Dina to leave.

"You won't be alone," the excited Thoraya encouraged Dina. "We will go out together. There will be nothing to fear once we're in the hands of the embassy."

Sure, Dina thought. *They can't even get themselves out!* Most of the embassies were still operating despite Saddam's August 24 deadline to cease functions, but only with skeleton staffs. Dina knew that some foreign diplomats and their families who had been ordered back to their own countries were being detained in Baghdad, despite promises by Saddam that they would be given safe passage out of Kuwait.

Ali continued his pressure, telling Dina it would be better for him if she left. "I would be able to leave the country on a moment's notice if I didn't have the worry of you and the children," he told her.

After days and nights of arguing, Dina finally gave in and called the embassy, putting her and the children's names on the list of evacuees. The embassy cabled the passenger list to the State Department. That agency then notified Dina's family that she and the children would be in the States on September 12.

The flight left without her. She changed her mind the day before it departed and called the embassy to remove her name from the list. After hearing Dina had canceled, Thoraya also canceled.

Ali was angry when he found out what Dina had done, but in a way, he was relieved, despite his promise to Richard. He knew he would only be half a person if she left.

■ ■ ■

Richard was singing in the shower at the top of his lungs the morning of September 12. He'd planned to go to work at Our Lady of Sorrows Convent, where he was a chef, for a few hours before it was time to pick Dina and the children up at the airport.

The night before he'd slept the best he had since the invasion. There had been many totally sleepless nights, wondering if Dina and her family even had a house to sleep in. *Were they alive?* One thought snowballed into another, and before he knew it, the sun would be coming up again.

The mind always sinks into a pit of despair to think the worst when it doesn't know the truth. Richard's mind had been in such a pit for six weeks. It had been like when he was a little boy, afraid to go into a dark room until someone turned on a light. He'd prayed every night that, somehow, a light would come on to illuminate a path to safety for Dina and her family.

After atrocity stories began leaking out of Kuwait, it had been even more difficult to hold his imagination in check. He knew his son-in-law would be a prime target for the invaders. Ali and his family would never accept Iraqi rule, and Richard feared Ali and those like him would be sought out and elimi-nated, probably along with their families.

But the dark thoughts were behind him now. The light had been turned on. He knew Dina was alive and on her way home. Now he felt terrific!

Stepping out of the shower, he started to dry off. The phone began ringing. Wrapping the towel around his waist, he walked into the bedroom to answer it.

"This is the State Department calling," a woman's voice said. "We're trying to reach a Richard Menard."

Richard sank down on the bed as a shudder of uneasi-ness and fear coursed through his body. *Something was wrong.*

"Yes," he said, "I'm Richard Menard."

"Mr. Menard," the woman continued, "I've been in-structed to tell you that your daughter, Dina, is not on the plane that is scheduled to arrive from Kuwait."

His heart skipped a beat as he asked, "Why?"

"I'm sorry," she said, "I have no other information than that."

Richard thanked the woman and hung up the phone.

I'm back in that dark room again, he thought as he lowered his head into his shaking hands. *What the hell does this mean?* A dozen horrible scenarios popped into his mind. Had the Iraqis broken into the house and killed everyone? Was she being held in Iraq? He had been told the passengers would be bused from Kuwait to Iraq to catch the plane. Had the bus been hi-jacked and the Westerners taken hostage? Would his daugh-ter become one of Saddam's human shields against warplanes from her own country? *Oh, God,* he groaned. *It's so hard when you love somebody and they're a part of your mind and your soul...when you don't know if they're safe, it can drive you crazy!*

He wiped the sweat from his forehead and slowly reached for the phone. He would have to call Pat, who was al-ready at work, and Gina, to break the news to them.

That evening, Richard and Pat went to Lincoln to give Gina moral support. The mental stress was taking its toll on her. She was beginning to "bounce off the walls," as Pat put it. Gina had a stomach ulcer, and Pat, a nurse, worried about her physical condition as much as she worried about the mental stress. The girl was eating ulcer pills like they were candy.

But Gina had accepted the State Department's news much better than they had expected. She wound up giving them the moral support they had come to give her.

"I really think the reason she wasn't on that plane is that she won't leave without Ali," Gina told Richard and Pat. Gina couldn't have said anything more truthful, or that would have helped ease the couple's minds more. Her reasoning made them think a little less morbidly about the situation.

The State Department also had notified Dina's mother that she was on the evacuation flight manifest. On the day Dina was to arrive in the States, Camille called to confirm the flight and learned her daughter hadn't shown up for boarding. She was sure the worst had happened.

■ ■ ■

Word was spreading of increased looting throughout Kuwait and in mid-September the first incident occurred in Ali's neighborhood.

The house next door to his family's was owned and occupied by the ex-wife of a royal family member. The owner had fled the country early in the invasion, but her maids had stayed in the house. One night, robbers with their faces covered by their *qutras*, broke into the house, beat up the maids, and stole everything movable, including a Mercedes parked inside the compound gate.

It made everyone in the neighborhood feel very uncomfortable and vulnerable. Despite the number of watchers that were out on their balconies every night, no one heard or saw a thing until after the robbers left, when the maids went screaming to a neighbor's house. It was obvious that the robbers were not Iraqi soldiers. The invaders would never have bothered to cover their faces. The thieves had to be someone known in the neighborhood, someone afraid that they would be recognized.

■ ■ ■

The Iraqi dictator vacillated between wanting to get as many Kuwaitis out of their country as he could to cut down resistance to the occupation and wanting to keep them as future bargaining chips.

When he was in one mood, the only official border station in southern Kuwait, Al-Nuwaisib, would be open, and when he was in the other mood, it would be closed.

It opened for two days on September 16, after having been closed for a month. Thousands of Kuwaitis fled for freedom. Many crossed over without incident, but many were detained. One minute the Iraqis were seizing young men and putting them onto trucks bound for Iraq, and the next, young men were let past. There was never any explanation to what was done, and it seemed the rules changed constantly.

Those who reached freedom had many stories to tell. Some reported they had seen Iraqis mining oil installations while they were en route to the border. Others let the world know that Kuwaiti schools had been turned into interrogation centers, a building at the university was being used for mass hangings, and the ice-skating rink had been turned into a morgue.

One man told of seeing the general manager of the main supermarket in the town of Al-Ardiya shot because he had refused to display Saddam's picture. Another said the dictator had issued an order that, in addition to Kuwaitis, diplomats who tried to hide Westerners avoiding the roundup would be shot.

One of the saddest tales to emerge concerned the Kuwait City Zoo, where animal cages had been turned into jail cells for human beings. A former zoo employee told of seeing Kuwaiti women thrown into the cages naked after they had been raped and their heads shaved. To make room for the prisoners, the most expensive animals had been shipped to Iraq, while the most dangerous ones were killed. The Iraqis butchered deer, sheep, and other edible animals for food. The others were simply turned loose to roam free until they starved to death.

Kuwaiti officials pleaded with their people not to leave. Besides the risk Kuwaiti citizens took at the border, government officials believed Iraq was trying to depopulate the country. Saddam did have intentions of repopulating Kuwait. Baghdad had promised its people that they could take the jobs and houses left behind by the fleeing Kuwaitis. This had drawn thousands into the country who intended to stay on a permanent basis. Thousands more came for only a temporary stay—while they looted.

■ ■ ■

Amad, a thirty-four-year-old Rumaithiyian, had first-hand knowledge of the looting trips Iraqi civilians were making into his country. He told the men gathered at Abass's one evening that he'd met two such looters.

Ahmad was driving his pickup truck one day on Sixth Ring Motorway, a major highway just south of Al-Jahra, on his way home from visiting relatives when two women in their mid-30s waved him down. Assuming they were Kuwaitis who had experienced car trouble, he stopped. The women did have a problem with their car, but they weren't Kuwaiti. They were Iraqis who had come to Kuwait to steal toys for their children. Crawling into Ahmad's pickup, they asked him to take them to the nearest toy store.

Ahmad began driving, but had only gone about another mile when an Iraqi soldier appeared in the middle of the road. He stomped on the brake, stopping just in time to avoid hitting the man. The Iraqi aimed his rifle at Ahmad's head, got into the back of the pickup, and ordered him to drive off the Motorway and onto a less-traveled road. When Ahmad stopped the truck, the soldier jumped down and told Ahmad and the women to get out. The Iraqi was very belligerent and asked Ahmad why he had the women with him. Ahmad explained that he had been on his way home from Al-Jahra when they waved him down and asked him to take them to a toy store.

The solider sneered and told the three to line up beside the truck. "I sentence you to die!" he shouted.

At that moment, a young Palestinian man drove up and asked the soldier what he was doing. The soldier said that he was going to shoot Ahmad and the women. The Palestinian became very excited. "Good! OK! Go ahead, do it!" he urged.

The soldier turned his gun in the Palestinian's direction and pulled the trigger. The bullet hit the man's car. Frightened, the Palestinian jumped out of the vehicle and began running down the road. The soldier fired again, hitting him in the back and killing him.

Ahmad, a cool, controlled person, hadn't been particularly fearful for his safety up to that point, but now he could see the solider was really dangerous. He began to talk to him.

"Please have mercy on me," he begged the Iraqi. "I have a wife and seven children. They will starve if you kill me."

Suddenly, the soldier's personality changed completely. "I, too, am married," he said. "My wife and I have six children."

"Then you know how I feel," Ahmad continued. "Our families need us."

The soldier talked to Ahmad a few more minutes and then ordered him to leave immediately, "before I change my mind."

Ahmad quickly complied with the order. As he ran up the road, he could almost feel a bullet thump into his back as it had the Palestinian's, but it never came. During his dash to safety, he didn't turn to look at what was happening behind him.

Now he wonders what happened to his pickup and the women. He told his neighbors that he suspected that the women and the solider might have been partners in a racket of stealing vehicles all up and down Sixth Ring Motorway.

■ ■ ■

The day after Dina canceled her trip to America, she went out into the backyard for a breath of fresh air and found Ali slumped on a bench with tears in his eyes.

He'd told her earlier that he was going to the yard to visit with Jafer, a Palestinian friend.

"What's the matter, Ali?"

"This country is no longer ours," he answered, his voice choked with emotion.

Dina didn't think it had been since the day of the invasion, but she asked, "Why do you say that?"

Ali told her that Jafer, who was an ambulance driver for a hospital in Kuwait City, had come to ask him to warn anyone who had any connection with the resistance to stay off the streets. The Iraqis were out in full force picking up suspected resistance members. Those arrested were being tortured and then, if they lived through that, shot to death. When they were done with their prisoners, the Iraqis dumped their bodies in the streets.

Jafer had been ordered to make regular patrols of the streets to pick up the bodies the Iraqis had left the night before.

"He said he was finding many bodies...mostly dead ones, but once in a while someone would be alive and he'd take them to the hospital. The Iraqis toss them by the trash cans, like they were just garbage."

"Did he know any of them?"

"No, but he said they were all young men and boys. What's next? We're sitting here drowning in our own blood, and the rest of the world doesn't care! Nobody's going to come help us...we will be prisoners in our own country for the rest of our lives!"

It was Dina's turn to hold Ali in her arms while he cried out his fear and frustration.

■　■　■

A few days after the September 12 flight left, two more evacuation flights for Westerners were announced on Voice of America and BBC Radio. Once again, Ali tried to talk Dina into signing up.

"Ali!" she screamed. "I said *no*! That's such a little word—why can't you understand it?"

Ali threw up his hands in surrender. "OK, OK...but if you're going to stay here, we're going to move back upstairs!" Everyone else in the house, which now also included Bedreah's eighty-six-year-old mother Bebe, who had come to live with her daughter, had gradually moved back into their own quarters.

Dina put up a tearful argument, but finally consented to go to the apartment for a few hours in the afternoons on a trial basis. The trial went well, so she agreed to move the mattresses back upstairs. However, she wouldn't allow them to be put on the beds. All of them, including the children's, had to be put on her and Ali's bedroom floor. She wouldn't let the children be more than ten feet from her. "We'll be safer on the floor, away from the windows," she explained.

The night was unusually quiet, except for a few short bursts of gunfire, but at 6:30 A.M. they were awakened by a loud explosion and nearby gunfire. They rushed to the window and peered out from behind the drawn curtains. Across the street they saw several men ducking behind walls and vehicles. Their initial thought was that help was finally on the way, but even if that was it, there was gunfire, and Dina wasn't staying upstairs while there were explosions "whumping" and machine guns chattering.

"We're going down!" she shouted as she began gathering up the children.

"Don't be afraid, Mamma," Jassim said as they left the apartment. "It's only a little gunfire." The youngster was very much aware of his mother's nervousness and had tried several times to soothe her fears. His attempts at being brave only agitated Dina even more.

"Just get downstairs, Jassim!" she shrieked.

The gunfire and explosions continued for another fifteen minutes. When all was quiet, Ali went out to the yard to find out what had happened. A neighbor told him the resistance had hit a checkpoint about three blocks from the neighborhood.

The mattresses went back downstairs that day.

■ ■ ■

In mid-September, Ahmad began disappearing from the house every day after lunch. After a few days, Bedreah noticed his absence and became extremely agitated about it. Her son would tell her nothing.

Ahmad and Afaf had been married shortly after the invasion and Afaf was now living in the compound. Bedreah began to question her new daughter-in-law and eventually wore her down. Afaf told her Ahmad was spending his afternoons digging graves.

Most of the grave diggers were foreigners who had left the country at the time of the invasion. Now, six weeks into the occupation, the body count was becoming so high, those who had not fled couldn't dig graves fast enough. The *imam* (an official priest) at the mosque in Rumaithiya had asked for volunteers from each neighborhood to help with the job. Ahmad and Hesham had been their neighborhood's volunteers.

Bedreah's youngest son also had volunteered for another job, one that he hadn't even told his wife about, let alone his mother. When he wasn't digging graves on his afternoons away from the compound, he was passing out flyers encouraging Kuwaitis to resist the occupation in any way they could, an activity that would have earned him the death penalty had he been caught.

The Iraqis had taken over the newspaper offices and print shops when they came into the country and had tried to force the Kuwaitis to buy the newspaper they published. The Kuwaitis left the Iraqi papers on their newsstands, so the invaders then took to passing them out at checkpoints. The Kuwaitis accepted the newspapers in good humor, took them home, and used them to wrap their garbage. When the Iraqis discovered their papers were being used for that purpose, they became furious and issued a new order: wrapping garbage in an Iraqi newspaper would carry an automatic death penalty. Ahmad knew that distributing material printed underground by the resistance would carry the same penalty.

■ ■ ■

After Ali's talk with Jafer, he was determined to obtain a gun. Not so he could join the fighting resistance, just simply for protection.

He approached Farouk one night in the yard and the resistance member agreed to find him a weapon. Several nights later, Farouk came to Ali with a .38 caliber pistol. Ali took it and hid it in a vent in Bedreah's main-floor kitchen.

Then he made a mistake. He told Mahmoud about the gun. Mahmoud urged him to get rid of it.

"We have enough to worry about with an American in the house," Mahmoud reasoned. "We'd all be dead for sure if the Iraqis find a gun *and* an American in the same house!"

Ali told his brother to keep his mouth shut about the pistol, but Mahmoud was so terrified, he told his mother. Bedreah told the others and another war had begun. Ahmad and Eidan thought Ali had made a wise decision in getting the gun, on one side. Mahmoud, Bedreah, Huda, Afaf, and Dina all thought it was a dangerous idea, on the other.

Ali's side held out less than a week before the other four broke them down. He returned the gun to Farouk six nights after his friend had given it to him.

■ ■ ■

Kuwaitis married to Westerners weren't the only ones who had to worry about having a foreigner in their home. Many Kuwaiti families had opened their homes to strangers from other countries who were forced into hiding after Saddam issued his roundup orders. Hundreds of these fugitives owe their lives to the compassionate people who shielded them from becoming one of Saddam's hostages.

Since the Iraqi leader's dragnet hadn't come up with many Westerners, he soon came to the conclusion that they were being hidden by the Kuwaitis. So the dictator issued a new order: any Kuwaiti found harboring a Westerner would be shot.

Shortly after that order was issued, Voice of America and BBC Radio announced the fourth evacuation flight to America. This flight was called "the last one."

Ali and Bedreah used the new order from Baghdad to increase their pressure on Dina. "We can't run the risk of you staying here," they told her. "The Iraqis will shoot us if they discover you're an American."

Dina's resolve was starting to crumble. She barely had enough energy to crawl out of bed in the morning, let alone sustain an intensified argument. She wanted desperately to take a vacation from reality. It would be so nice to see her family *and* feel safe once again.

After only a couple of days of listening to Ali's and Bedreah's haranguing, she gave up and called the American

Embassy, but her mind was working a mile a minute, trying to think of how she was going to get out of leaving.

Even though the thought that she might be a threat to those she loved had shaken her resistance to leaving, it hadn't destroyed it completely.

Dina had become a Muslim in 1984, and she felt that her faith had been the shining beacon that had led to her survival thus far. That night, while at prayer, she remembered something offered through the Muslim religion that she had not yet thought of. It was called *estacara*, the act of consulting the Koran for advice on what to do in a difficult situation.

The next day, being a novice at reading the Koran, she telephoned Thoraya's father, who was recognized as an expert in the interpretation of the Islamic "good book," and asked him to find out what the Koran advised about her leaving on the evacuation flight.

He consulted the book for hours and then called Dina back with his answer: it would not be wise to leave.

"See?" she said when she told Ali and Bedreah what she had done. "That's it...God says 'stay,' so I'm staying!"

Dina called the embassy for the second time and took her name off the list.

■ ■ ■

This time, word of Dina's cancellation failed to reach her family before they went to the airport to meet her. When the flight she was scheduled to be on landed without her and the children aboard, they were devastated. Since she had made the arrangements for the flight, they knew she was still alive, but now they anguished, once again, over what could have prevented her from being on this plane.

Richard called the U.S. State Department. The man he spoke with could tell him only that his daughter had taken her and the children's names off the evacuation list. Gina decided to try to cable her sister again through the Kuwaiti Embassy, even though she had received no response from the one she sent after Dina's first cancellation.

This one said, "Please reconsider. My house is ready for all of you. Love you and miss you!"

The message went through, and after the cable was read to her, Dina thought she could understand how it would feel to have her arms hitched to two teams of horses that were headed in different directions.

■ ■ ■

Four more resolutions came before the United Nations Security Council in September.

On September 13, one was approved that provided guidelines for food aid to Iraq and Kuwait. Adel had been right, the economic sanctions resolution was affecting Iraq deeply.

September 16 saw the passage of a resolution condemning violence against diplomats and demanding protection for them. The situation had grown steadily worse at the foreign embassies in Kuwait. Iraq continued to detain some staff and their families in Baghdad and elsewhere, indiscriminately keeping some while letting others go. Saddam had ordered his soldiers to surround the embassies and cut off water, power, and the food supply line to them. Some embassies and ambassadors' residences were broken into and looted. On the twenty-fourth, the U.N. agreed to consider some humanitarian aid to Iraq, and on the twenty-fifth, it tightened the embargo on air traffic around Iraq (there was some contraband sifting into the country, despite the economic sanctions resolution).

Then on September 27, the emir traveled to the United States to tell the United Nations members, in person, what was happening in his country and to ask for their continued support in Kuwait's liberation. The Iraqi representative stormed out of the session during the emir's speech, but representatives from the rest of the nations gave the Kuwaiti leader a standing ovation when his impassioned plea ended.

The Iraqi government also was busy in September. First it announced it had confiscated all foreign assets from the countries who supported the economic sanctions resolutions, and then it threatened to destroy all Kuwaiti oil fields. Finally it vowed to attack Israel if other nations tried to force the Iraqi troops out of Kuwait.

A bright spot for Saddam came in September. He gained an ally, or at least he thought he had. His former enemy, Iran, came to his side. Ayatollah Ali Khamenei joined Saddam in calling for a holy war against the Western forces. Saddam had bought Iran's support in the middle of August by withdrawing the remainder of the troops he had left in Iran at the end of the Iran-Iraq War in 1988 and releasing some 1,000 Iranian prisoners of that war.

And in Kuwait, the Kuwaitis continued to grow more and more depressed. It had been nearly two months since the United Nations had ordered Iraq out of Kuwait and nothing had happened. They were beginning to believe that everyone, except Saddam, was only going to fight a war on paper.

CHAPTER 8

By the first of October organized resistance was well underway throughout Kuwait. The government-in-exile, which had been closeted in the resort town of Taif in southwest Saudi Arabia since the invasion, was directing the operations. Hundreds of couriers risked their lives to carry messages, money and supplies back and forth between Saudi Arabia and Kuwait.

Resistance came in many forms. Not only were there men and women like Farouk who actively hunted and killed Iraqis, there were men, women, and children who played less militant roles. There were those who simply helped keep their neighborhoods and the Westerners in hiding supplied with money, food and medicine, or devised plans to control garbage build-ups, or those who refused to change their license plates, go back to work, or abandon organized prayer. There were those like Ali who began obtaining papers from the forger in Bayan for people who wanted to make an escape attempt, and Ahmad and Hesham who dug graves and distributed leaflets. Teenagers who confused Iraqi troops and intelligence agents by changing street signs and taking the numbers off houses were considered resistance. People who volunteered to help in hospitals, nursing homes, orphanages, and other vital institutions after the foreign staffs fled (in addition to laborers, many professionals in Kuwait were also foreigners) were part of the resistance.

Even old men like Abraham could help in the effort. What he did was such a simple thing, and yet it created havoc for the Iraqis. After the resolution authorizing use of force to eject Iraq from Kuwait was passed, Abraham spent his days driving from one checkpoint to another, asking the guards one simple question: "Who is in charge here?" The guards, of course, would say, "We are." And Abraham would look puzzled, shake his head, and say, "That's funny. At the last checkpoint the Americans (or the British, or the Saudis, etc.) were in charge." The Iraqis usually panicked and fled their posts, thinking that America and its allies had arrived to throw them out of the country. Then Abraham would laugh and drive on to the next checkpoint.

All of these people were resisting Iraqi occupation, and Baghdad considered them to be as dangerous as those who carried weapons. Saddam knew you didn't have to bear arms to resist effectively, so these "passive" resistance members suffered the same consequences if caught by the Iraqis as the fighting resistance did.

After the secret pathway from Saudi Arabia had been established, arms, money, and food supplies began flowing into Kuwait. The militant resistance members were in charge of these shipments. The weapons were doled out for use by those who would join the fighters, and the money (Iraqi currency, since Kuwaiti currency had been outlawed) and food were smuggled into neighborhoods to be distributed to those who needed it by those who lived there.

The additional arms and manpower bolstered the freedom fighters' confidence. They began raiding Iraqi checkpoints and strongholds during daylight hours as well as at night. Favorite targets were police stations. The Kuwaitis would scout a station for days, learning how many of the enemy were posted there, what time of the day the most men were on duty, and what types of arms the Iraqis were carrying. Then someone would telephone the station and announce that a bomb had been planted in the building. The Iraqis would panic and pour out of the station, right into withering blasts from resistance guns.

Resistance fighters, however, weren't the only ones who claimed raids on police stations. Sometimes the Iraqis forced individuals unattached to the fighting units to vent their anger through single-handed raids. Rajab, a man from Rumaithiya, was one of those individuals. Rajab's son had been arrested as a suspected resistance fighter, even though he was not part of the organization. After the young man was interrogated, he was returned to his home, where he was shot and killed in front of his father by an Iraqi intelligence officer. Rajab, in a blind rage, went that evening to the Rumaithiya station, stalked into the office of the officer who had killed his son, and beat him to death with a lead pipe. The other Iraqis on duty were so frightened by the intensity of Rajab's fury that they ran out of the station like rabbits. After Rajab's mission was completed, he walked out of the station and returned home, unmolested.

As these types of raids increased, so did Saddam's wrath. Death became the automatic penalty for anyone harming an Iraqi, but it wasn't an easy death. Torture always came first.

■ ■ ■

October 2 arrived and Kuwait was no closer to being rescued on the second-month anniversary of the invasion than it had been on the day of takeover. Another mass protest was planned and Kuwaitis, once again, took to their rooftops to shout *Allahu Akbar* for the world to hear.

Despite their promise to Bedreah, Ali, Mahmoud, Ahmad, and Hameed joined in the demonstration. This time when the Iraqi gunfire came, the protesters weren't so quick to leave their roofs. When shots failed to quiet the crowd, soldiers climbed to the roofs of some homes and beat the demonstrators into silence.

Again Ali, his brothers and cousin survived the demonstration unscathed. However, a brother-in-law of another cousin did not. The family learned the next day that the man, whose name was Jafer, was hit in the chest by a stray Iraqi bullet while he was on his roof. Jafer's father and brother wanted to take him to a hospital, but knowing he was mortally wounded, Jafer did not want to go. He told them he was in no pain and wanted to die in his own home, which he did, two hours after the demonstration ended.

■ ■ ■

At Mubarak Hospital in Al-Jabriya, Abo-Ahmad and his wife had seen what the Iraqis could do to a human body. One or two tortured resistance members had begun arriving at the hospital on a daily basis shortly after the invasion. As the days passed, hospital employees began to notice that the severity of the torture the Kuwaitis were being subjected to was increasing.

As had become the habit in Kuwait City, when the Iraqis were done with their victims in Al-Jabriya, they usually threw the battered bodies into or beside trash cans, thinking they were dead. Sometimes they weren't and Kuwaitis would find the bodies and either bring the victim to the hospital or call the hospital to come get the unfortunate person. Most were beyond medical help.

Abo-Ahmad and Um-Ahmad saw people whose fingernails and toenails had been pulled out, eyeballs gouged out, tongues cut out, ears and other body parts chopped off, and skin burned to the bone by electrical shocks or acid baths. In some cases, common wood drills had been used to drill holes in the victims' heads, and always, the females had been savagely raped. The two soon decided the Iraqis had been schooled well in the art of torture and were ingenious in inventing methods of their own.

One of the survivors Um-Ahmad treated, told her that he and several other prisoners had been told by their Iraqi guards that they would be released if they would agree to donate blood for Iraqi wounded, but after their blood had been taken, the torture continued.

■ ■ ■

The day after the October 2 demonstration, Ali went to Abass's yard to tell his neighbors of Jafer's death.

Khalid, a short, chunky, middle-aged neighbor who lived directly across the street from Ali, joined the group about halfway through Ali's story. Khalid, who was always a happy, upbeat person, looked very depressed, so after Ali finished his story, he turned to Khalid and asked him what was troubling him. Khalid said he had been threatened at a checkpoint that morning.

In mid-September the Iraqis had issued regulations that included detention of any man with a beard. Many former Kuwaiti soldiers had taken to growing beards so it would be harder for the Iraqis to identify them from their military pictures.

Khalid, who was very religious, had a long beard and at the checkpoint a soldier had asked him why. Khalid had explained that he wore it for religious reasons. "Then," Khalid told his neighbors, "he grabbed my beard, pulled my head out the car window, and reached for a knife. I thought he was going to cut my throat!" But the Iraqi only threatened to cut Khalid's beard. "He told me if I wouldn't cut my own beard, he'd cut it for me. But I pleaded with him," he said, "and he released his grip. He told me he would let me go this time, but that I better not show up at the checkpoint again unless I was clean shaven."

When Khalid finished his story, he had tears in his eyes. "I am not young enough to be a soldier," he said. "Why can't they leave me in peace?"

The men would find out a few days later how lucky Khalid had been at the checkpoint.

A young *mullah* (one who is learned in sacred law) by the name of Khalifa had come to the Rumaithiya mosque from Al-Salmiya to speak after prayers about the invasion and occupation. Iraqi soldiers, tipped off by an informer, came to the mosque and dragged Khalifa away to the police station. There he was tortured before he was executed in the usual manner—two shots to the head. His body was found the next day on a Rumaithiyan street. His beard had been pulled out by the roots and his eyeballs gouged out.

■ ■ ■

Early on the morning of October 8, another announcement about an evacuation flight for persons with Western passports came over Voice of America. Ali was elated—the previous flight had not been the last one! He still had a chance to send his family to safety and to make good on his promise to Richard.

This time, the whole family banded together against Dina's arguments.

"The house searches for Americans are becoming more frequent," Ali told his wife. "I no longer want my family taking the risk of being shot."

"But *everyone* says I could pass as a Kuwaiti!" Dina shouted.

"But maybe you *wouldn't* really fool the Iraqis," Huda said.

"I have Kuwaiti identification," she argued.

"You know it's forged...it's not totally safe," Ali reminded her. "If you won't think of yourself, think of the children," he continued. "They've seen too much horror already and have been confined for too long. They can't even be children! I don't want them living like this!"

"I don't want to see them die in an airplane crash!" Dina said. She was deathly afraid of flying. The thought of getting on the plane frightened her almost as much as the Iraqis.

Afaf joined in. "Do you want to see them shot by Iraqis because their mother is American?"

Bedreah, Eidan, Mahmoud, and Ahmad took up the attack.

"You're being selfish," Ahmad told Dina. "You are not thinking of us or the children!"

"No!" Dina screamed. "I would be selfish if I left when none of you have a safe way to leave! My conscience will not allow me to do that!"

"You are wasting away here," Bedreah told her. "If you die, the children will have no mother. You have to leave to stay alive!"

"There is no alternative," Eidan chimed in. "You are jeopardizing yourself, your children, and us...you have to leave."

Even Nassima, the sister-in-law Dina had grown closest to, came to the compound from Ahmad to help convince her to leave. "Every day you are here increases our risk," Nassima told Dina.

"So this is how it ends! After coming to Kuwait and learning to love this country, all of you, you just turn around and throw me out," Dina sobbed.

Mahmoud said, "If you love us, you will leave us...you are endangering everyone by being in this house!"

Dina jumped up from her chair. Suddenly the room began to spin around her. Her arms tingled and she couldn't breathe. Everything was growing dark. Nassima caught her as she started to fall to the floor and pushed her back onto the chair. Ali rushed for a wet cloth and wiped his wife's face.

"I'm sorry, sweetheart," Ali said, "but you have to listen to us."

"I have listened," Dina said, shakily getting to her feet. "Now I have to think."

Slowly, sniffling, holding back her tears, she walked towards the stairs and the back door. Nassima followed her, but the rest of the family remained seated.

When they reached the yard, Dina searched her sister-in-law's strong, attractive face, and asked, "Why? Why is everyone ganging up on me?"

"Because we all love you and want you to be safe," Nassima answered, wiping tears from her own eyes as well as Dina's. "Believe me, if we could all be on that plane, we would be."

They sat in the yard for nearly an hour, crying their hearts out. Nassima didn't want Dina to leave. None of the family did. It hurt them deeply to have to force her out of Kuwait.

When her tears ran dry, Dina went into the house, to the derwania where the discussion had taken place. Everyone was still seated in the same place.

"You win," was all she said, then picked up the phone and called the American Embassy. She was told the plane would leave the next day. Passengers were to meet in the Safeway supermarket parking lot in the town of Al-Farwaniya, a half-hour west of Rumaithiya, at 8:00 in the morning. They would be bused to Basra, then flown to Baghdad to catch a plane for England where they would change planes for the trip to the United States. Neither Ali nor any other Kuwaiti should drive her to the parking lot, she was warned. The embassy did not want to be responsible for a Kuwaiti who might be caught accompanying an American to the rendezvous. Dina put her and the children's names on the passenger list, then told Ali she was going upstairs to pack.

As Dina walked into her apartment, tears once again overwhelmed her. She dropped to the sofa, crying as if her heart would break. "I can't leave," she sobbed over and over.

Finally exhaustion overcame her and she dozed off, dreaming of another time she'd had to leave loved ones.

■ ■ ■

"Oh, Poppy," Dina moaned as Richard hugged her close at the Omaha airport. "I can't leave."

It was September 1983, and the plane that would take her away from her family and her country had been called for boarding.

"Dina," Richard said. "This was your decision. You said you had to try to live in Ali's country, and you were right. He is your husband, and you must at least try."

"But, Poppy...."

"Just remember what I've always told you—if you listen, you can hear music in everything. I think you are going to be surprised at how quickly you'll hear it in Ali's country."

It had torn her heart in two to leave for Kuwait, but as her father had said, it had been her decision to do so. It hurt to leave her family, but it would have hurt more if Ali had left her behind.

In the beginning, it had been difficult for Dina to adjust to her new life. She had not learned to speak Arabic before she went to Kuwait, and communication had been a monumental problem. Once she had acquired some fundamentals of the language it was easier to make a niche for herself in her new surroundings.

To her delight, Dina had found many similarities between America and Kuwait—the modern hospitals, supermarkets and shopping malls, the leisure activities of movies, cook-outs, beach parties, and sporting events. Their apartment in Kuwait wasn't much different from their two-bedroom Papillion apartment, except it contained nine rooms instead of five. The kitchen was furnished with all of the appliances she'd had in America and there was Western-style furniture and carpeting in every room.

She had thrown herself into her new life completely, and it hadn't been long before she started to hear the music her father had spoken of. She had heard it in the voices of Ali's family and friends, who had accepted her with love and open arms; in the heartbeat of the country whos people made her feel at home; in the waves of the blue gulf waters; in the comfort of her newfound religion.

She had been surrounded by beautiful music for many years. But now it had been replaced by the harsh, discordant sound of war, and once again, she had to leave a land she loved.

■ ■ ■

When Dina didn't return to the basement after a couple of hours, Ali went to see what was keeping her.

She had just woke up and was pulling a small suitcase from the closet.

"You will need more than that," Ali told her. "It will be getting cold in Nebraska. Take some winter clothes."

"The embassy said to take only as much baggage as I could carry myself," Dina said in a lifeless voice. "I'm not going first class, you know."

It didn't take her long to gather up what few things she intended to take—a change of clothes for herself and each of the children, diapers for Husain, a few personal supplies. When the suitcase was full, Ali found a duffel bag for the overflow.

"Jassim can handle the duffel bag," he told her.

She shrugged and left the bedroom to phone Thoraya.

"The children and I are leaving on the plane tomorrow," she told her friend. "Will you call and make reservations too?"

Thoraya told Dina she had already called the embassy. This time they told her that Kuwaiti nationals would not be allowed to board the plane.

Dina was crushed. *If I had left on that other flight, Thoraya would have been safe with me.* Now her friend would have to stay in Kuwait and face increasing danger.

"Don't worry," Thoraya told her. "I'll be fine...and so will you. You're tough, you'll make it without me."

Dina wandered around the basement the rest of the day in a fog. She couldn't look at anyone without tears clouding her vision.

That night Ali didn't go to the balcony to keep a lookout on the street. He stayed with Dina and the children. He had talked her into taking the mattresses back upstairs to spend their final night, alone, in their own apartment.

Dina didn't argue. She didn't care anymore if the Iraqis blew up the whole house with all of them in it. At least they would all go together. Beginning tomorrow it would be a different story.

Ali sat in his chair the whole evening, holding one of the children, and then another. He held them tightly and breathed in the smell of them.

How am I going to survive without them and their mother?

Too soon it was bedtime and one by one, he tucked each of them into their beds. He wondered if that was the last time he would perform that fatherly rite.

Crawling into bed beside Dina, a sudden thought occurred to him. *I could hold all of them in my arms for a hundred years and still it would not be long enough.*

■ ■ ■

Morning came swiftly. Ali woke Dina and the children at 6:00. Mike, a Palestinian friend whose wife, May, and their daughter, were also taking the flight to America, was scheduled to pick up Dina and the children at 7:30.

While his family dressed, Ali went into the kitchen and set out bowls of cereal. Dina would eat nothing, and the children ate little.

At 7:00 they went downstairs to wait for Mike. Bedreah had packed a bottle of water and some snacks for them to take. Her eyes were red from crying. She had grown to love her daughter-in-law as much as her own daughters. Dina had become the sunshine in her life and her days would be dark without her.

"Please don't make me leave!" Dina pleaded when she saw her mother-in-law's face.

Bedreah took a deep breath. "Don't make it any more difficult for us than it already is," she mumbled.

Dina turned to Ali. "I can't...."

He cut off her words. "I promise I will follow you," he said. "You'll see. One day you'll just find me on your doorstep."

They heard Mike's car pull up. Ali grabbed the suitcase and duffel bag and headed for the front door. Dina and the children followed him outside. As he kissed each of the children good-bye, he noticed that Jassim had tears in his eyes.

"Please come with us, Dad!" his firstborn pleaded. "You always go to America with us."

"I'm coming later, Jassim," Ali replied. "Until I get there, you will be the man of the family. Promise me that you will take care of your mother and help with your sister and brothers."

Wiping his eyes, Jassim said somberly, "I promise."

Ali watched his family climb into Mike's car. He felt like he was on the edge of a cliff...slipping, sliding, toward the rocks below.

Dina stuck her hand through the open window and Ali clasped it.

"Ali, please," she sobbed.

"I love you...I will follow."

Her hand was torn from his as Mike pulled away from the house.

CHAPTER 9

Ali watched Mike's car until it disappeared before going back into the house. The stillness of his apartment made him shiver. It was as hollow as his heart.

He walked into the kitchen and saw the cereal bowls still sitting on the table. "Goddamn it!" he shouted to an empty room. "You didn't finish your cereal!" He picked up the bowls and hurled them at the sink, breaking them into a hundred pieces. Then he sat down and cried like a baby. *I should have made them all finish their breakfast. Maybe there won't be any food for them to eat on the trip…maybe they will never eat again.* A jumble of thoughts crowded his mind. *Why in the hell did I make them leave? I should have found a safe hiding place for them in Rumaithiya, instead of sending them into the enemy's arms! Why was I so stupid? How will I live without them?* Hot tears bathed his cheeks as he pounded his fists on the table in frustration.

"Ali…Ali, where are you?" his father called. Eidan was standing in the apartment doorway. He had heard the sound of the bowls hitting the sink and his son's sobs two floors below.

"You promised to take me to try to find an elbow joint for the sink in your mother's washroom," Eidan continued when he saw Ali at the table.

"I know," Ali mumbled, quickly wiping his eyes. He put his sunglasses on and followed his father to the car, but he had driven only a few blocks before tears once again filled his eyes, obscuring his vision. Pulling over to the side of the road, he put his head down on the steering wheel.

"I am a body with no heart without them," he told his father. Eidan tried to comfort him, but Ali continued to cry for several minutes before he could regain control over his emotions and restart the car.

It took them a couple of hours to find the part, but it helped take Ali's mind off Dina and the children. When you were out on the streets of Kuwait it took all of your concentration to avoid the Iraqis, and when you couldn't avoid them, you had to be as inconspicuous as possible at checkpoints.

When they returned home, he helped Eidan fix the sink, and then it was dinnertime.

Ali had been avoiding his mother since morning, knowing she was suffering nearly as much as he, but he couldn't avoid her now. He walked into the dining room, and the minute they saw each other, they both started to cry.

"If anything happens to them on this trip, it will be my fault," Ali told his mother.

"Hush," Bedreah said, putting her arms around Ali. "The guilt will be on all of us. We all pushed her to leave."

"You're both being overdramatic," Eidan shrugged. "They should be boarding the plane for England now and will soon be safe in America. Don't look for trouble that isn't there."

After he was done eating, Ali knew he had to get out of the house. There was too much there to remind him of Dina and the children. Before he left, he called Nassima and asked if she would come over with her children. He couldn't stand the quiet. The ghosts of his children's voices haunted him. She promised to come later that day.

Then he left for the house of his best friend, Jassim, Hesham's brother, after whom he had named his firstborn. Jassim's family compound was across the street and four doors down from Ali's and he was the only non-family member Ali had told that Dina was leaving. He would understand Ali's depression. Jassim could always make Ali laugh, no matter what.

Jassim wasn't home. Ali slumped down on his friend's front stoop in the sun and let the heat burn into his brain. He was beyond caring what happened to him. He had no life without Dina and the children. As he sat in his misery, it occurred to him that now they were gone, he was free to do something for his country. Something to punish the Iraqis who had turned his happy life into shambles. Ali decided to talk to Farouk about helping the resistance movement.

■ ■ ■

While Ali was sitting at Jassim's house, Dina was sitting in a bus just seven streets away, fighting the temptation to get out of it and walk home.

She didn't know why the buses were parked at a major Iraqi headquarters, formerly the Hyatt Regency Hotel. Nobody did. People on the bus had been asking the driver, but he told them he didn't know. They had been sitting there for nearly three hours. Everyone was expecting to be pulled off the vehicle at any minute to undergo interrogation.

Mike had delivered his passengers to the Safeway parking lot right at 8:00 that morning. They'd had no problem passing the checkpoints. Iraqis liked Palestinians. A guard at one of the checkpoints had even told Mike, "We're going to liberate your country next!"

"Sure, you bastard, you won't even live to get out of Kuwait," Mike muttered under his breath as he smiled at the guard.

Many Palestinians *were* collaborating with the Iraqis, but Mike was not one of them. He knew on which side his bread was buttered. Kuwait had given him a good home and he wasn't going to screw up his life now by embracing the filthy Iraqis!

After he helped his wife and Dina unload the car, he kissed May goodbye and left. She had asked him not to stay until the buses left.

Several hundred people were milling around the parking lot. They were told to form a check-in line at a table that had been set up. Dina looked around her at the soldiers standing watch over the crowd. They didn't seem to know what to do any more than she did. Most were dressed in shabby uniforms and looked like they were bored and lost. Obviously, they did not belong to Saddam's elite corps of warriors.

When she and May were finally given their bus number, they began looking for the vehicle. When they found it, they looked at each other in dismay. It was one of the oldest, dirtiest ones in the parking lot. The Iraqi driver was standing at the door, motioning them to get on. He looked as old and dirty as the bus.

After Dina had the suitcase and duffel bag stored under her seat and the children settled into their seats, she looked around at the other passengers. There were not many Westerners. In fact, she realized, she had seen few Westerners in line in the parking lot. Most had apparently fled on other flights. The vast majority of the people involved in this evacuation must be foreigners with American passports, she guessed. It made her uncomfortable to know hers was probably one of the few passports that was stamped "Born in the USA."

They sat for nearly two hours before the convoy began to move. The children were already getting hot, thirsty and hungry. Dina decided if there was air-conditioning on the bus, it didn't work.

"May," she nudged her friend as their bus followed the others out of the lot, "we're heading in the wrong direction!" The buses were being driven away from Iraq, towards Rumaithiya.

"Be quiet," May said. "Don't panic. You don't want to draw attention to yourself."

Dina didn't have much time to panic over the direction they were headed because once they got out on the main road, their driver began driving like a maniac. The bus had no seat belts so the passengers were nearly jostled out of their seats as the driver wove in and out of traffic at breakneck speed. Dina decided she didn't have to worry about the Iraqis taking her off the bus and holding her hostage, or of being killed in an airplane crash. The way this nut was driving, they would all be dead by the time they reached the border!

Now, as they waited to see what was going to happen at the hotel, a bored and ragged-looking Iraqi soldier climbed onto the bus and began asking passengers their names, addresses and nationality. Dina was terrified. She was sure she would be interrogated when the soldier discovered she was an American. She also was worried that if she gave out her Rumaithiya address the Iraqis would be able to find the family and arrest them for having harbored a Westerner.

Now the soldier was at the row of seats in front of her, questioning May. Husain, who was sitting on his mother's lap, was screaming at the top of his lungs for a bottle. Zade and Yacoub were shouting for a drink of water and Jassim was scrambling under the seat looking for the duffel bag with the supplies in it, when the soldier came to Dina's seat.

"Name?" he shouted over the noise of the children.

Dina pretended she couldn't hear him.

"Give me your name!" the soldier demanded.

"Dina!" she shouted back.

"Full name!" the soldier screamed.

Husain increased the intensity of his howl when he heard his mother and the soldier yelling and began struggling to get out of her arms.

"Dina!" she yelled again.

Now Nadia became frightened at the shouting and started to cry. Zade got tired of waiting for Jassim to come up with the water and climbed out of his seat to join the search, elbowing the soldier's legs in an effort to get past him. Yacoub followed his brother.

The soldier shook his head, scowled at Dina and the children, and moved up the aisle. He apparently didn't think it was worth his effort to try to get more information from her.

She scowled back. "May your camel lose its hump!" she muttered at his back.

It was another hour before the buses began to leave the hotel lot. Now they were heading in the right direction, but they weren't getting anywhere. The highway leading towards Iraq was jammed with vehicles—pickup trucks, buses, and cars—all with Iraqi license plates and all crammed full of loot. Dina looked over at a pickup that was crawling along beside her bus. A dining room table and chairs, two television sets and a sofa were piled high in the bed of the truck. Sitting on top of the pile was an Iraqi woman and several children looking excited and happy. They grinned and waved at the passengers on the bus. Dina wondered if she knew the family from whom the items had been stolen.

After about an hour of creeping along, bumper to bumper, the escort car filled with Iraqi soldiers that was leading the convoy drove over the median into the incoming traffic lane and proceeded to lead the buses to the border on the wrong side of the highway.

All the way through Kuwait, Dina saw the ravages of war—burned-out buildings and vehicles, streets ruined by tanks, trash piled everywhere. This was no longer the beautiful country she had learned to call home. Ali was right. Kuwait was no longer theirs.

Living the Nightmare

When the cities had been left behind, Dina began to see Iraqi soldiers, one or two at a time, scattered throughout the desert. All of them on foot, most of them unarmed, they were headed towards the Iraqi border. She began to wonder if they were deserters trying to get back to their homes. *Poor souls,* Dina thought. *I hope they make it home.* Ali had told her many Iraqis were deserting, even in the early stages of the occupation. Farouk told his neighbors one night that some soldiers even offered to sell their guns and ammunition to the resistance before deserting their units. Those items went for five to ten dinars (a dinar is equivalent to just over three U.S. dollars), while tanks sold for fifty dinars, plus distashas and a small supply of food.

When the buses finally arrived at the first Iraqi town, Safwan, they pulled over and stopped. Once again panic gripped the passengers. They sat for an hour with no explanation. Then the driver, who had gotten off the bus, climbed back on and told them not to worry. There was just some mix-up about some unsigned papers.

The children were so hungry, they could have eaten their socks. They'd had nothing but the cookies their grandmother had packed for them since breakfast, and they had to go to the bathroom. Dina decided she had to take them off the bus so they could at least relieve themselves.

As they returned to their seats, the driver started the motor and began pulling out of his place in the convoy. A rumble of uneasiness rippled through the bus. The driver turned around and reassured the passengers that he was only getting out of line to find a gas station. Once the tank was filled they would rejoin the other buses.

There was a long line of vehicles at the gas station. Dina looked out her window to see if she could see a store open where she could buy food. A nearby restaurant and a supermarket were closed. She was furious. It was now dark. A two-hour trip to the Iraqi border had turned into a nine-hour one and they'd been sitting just inside Iraq for another two hours!

Don't these idiots realize people need to eat? My babies are crying from hunger! All she could do was give them another cookie. There was no more water.

While at the station, the driver wound up getting into a fist fight with another driver over their position in line, delaying them even further. *Damn,* Dina sighed. *What's next?* Finally, the bus was gassed up and they rejoined the convoy to continue the trip to Basra.

When they reached the airport they were herded into the building like sheep and made to stand in line to have their papers processed and their luggage checked. All around them were Iraqi soldiers with guns. Husain had no passport and Dina expected trouble to develop when she was asked for it, but the Iraqi who checked her papers accepted the baby's Kuwaiti birth certificate as a substitute without comment. When Dina was asked for her "Iraqi" address, she was totally confused until it finally dawned on her the soldier was referring to Kuwait as Iraq's nineteenth province—he wanted her Rumaithiya address. She gave him a false one.

After she was done in the processing line, she had just enough time to take the children to the bathroom and wash their sweaty hands and faces before they were called to board the plane to Baghdad.

When they had arrived at the Basra airport, Jassim had called his mother's attention to two Kuwait Airlines 747s that were sitting on the runway. Iraq had stolen all of the Kuwaiti planes after they took over the airport. "I hope those are the planes we'll be taking," he told her.

They weren't. The plane they were led to was as decrepit as the bus they had just left. The seats were barely bolted to the floor and there were no seat belts. In the back of her mind, Dina thought, *They're using old planes because they're going to put bombs on them and blow all of us up!*

She settled the children in their seats and waited for the 40-minute trip to Baghdad. As hungry as they were, she was surprised to see all of them fall asleep immediately.

Living the Nightmare

■ ■ ■

As Ali had told Dina, Iraqi soldiers had been deserting from the day they entered Kuwait and learned they had not been "invited" into the country. One thing the Kuwaitis gave the invaders their wholehearted support in was desertion. They encouraged it—and they helped the soldiers leave Kuwait.

One way Kuwaitis made the Iraqis think about desertion was to turn their radios on full blast to Voice of America or BBC while they were driving in their cars. This kept the Iraqis aware of what the world was planning to do to eliminate their presence in the country.

Another way was to play on the soldiers' religious conscience. Another one of Ali's cousins, twenty-four-year-old Husain (a brother of Abdul-Samad, Rasul, and Hameed), used the religious ploy to cause two Iraqi soldiers to desert.

Driving down the expressway between his home in Salewa and Rumaithiya one day, he saw the two hitchhiking. They were very young, shabbily dressed, and looked harmless, so Husain thought he would spice up his life and take a chance. He stopped and offered them a ride. They turned out to be what they seemed, homesick and sorry they were in Kuwait. Husain, who made his living as a science teacher, began a lecture to "convert" them. Popping a religious tape into his cassette player, he turned the stereo on.

As the two Iraqis listened to the tape, Husain said, "You know, your prayers will not be answered as long as you occupy Kuwait."

Tears came to the soldiers' eyes. "We know we are doing wrong," one of them said. "But what can we do? The officers shoot those who don't follow orders."

"You only have your officers to worry about now," Husain told him. "It will be much worse when the United Nations forces come to liberate Kuwait."

The other soldier looked startled and asked, "What are you talking about?"

"You didn't know that many countries plan to send soldiers here to throw you Iraqis out of Kuwait?"

"I don't believe you," the soldier said.

"Meet me at 10:00 tonight in the parking lot of Hadi Hospital in Al-Jabriya and I will bring you a radio. You will hear my words echoed."

The two soldiers agreed and were at the hospital waiting for Husain when he got there. After the soldiers heard a BBC broadcast referring to the alliance that had formed against Iraq, they broke down and cried, then begged Husain to bring them *distashas* so they could disguise themselves while they tried to get back to their homes in Iraq.

Husain took them the clothes and some food the next night and grinned with satisfaction as he watched them begin their northward trek under the cover of darkness.

Many brave imams also helped "up" the desertion rate by risking their lives pleading with Iraqi soldiers who attended prayer services at their mosques to give up their weapons and go home.

■ ■ ■

In mid-afternoon, Ali gave up on Jassim returning and went to Essa's house. He wasn't home either, so he returned to his own house. He had intended to stay in his apartment after Dina left, but when he opened the door and stepped inside he decided he wouldn't be able to. There were too many more memories there than downstairs.

Ali went next door and asked Huda if she would clean up the kitchen for him and then took his mattress back downstairs. After he deposited it on the floor of one of the smaller rooms, he decided to go to Abass's yard. There he found Essa.

"I was just at your house," Ali said to his friend, "and you weren't home. I didn't think to look for you here."

"I've been here most of the day," Essa said.

"Tell Ali about Yihya moving away," Abass urged Essa. Yihya lived near Essa on the west side of the neighborhood.

Ali was all ears. "What about Yihya, did he run into trouble with the Iraqis?"

"Well, yes and no," Essa said. "They hadn't really threatened him with harm yet, but they probably soon would have. The real problem was, Yihya just got sick and tired of painting his street sign."

Ali frowned. "What are you talking about?" The thirty-four-year-old Essa, a tall, broad-shouldered, easygoing weatherman, had a good sense of humor, and Ali thought maybe he was making another one of his jokes.

"I'm serious," Essa grinned. "He'd painted that sign four times and probably would have another dozen times if he hadn't moved." Essa explained that a group of teenagers had been spray painting over the real name on a street sign in the neighborhood, renaming the street, "Baba (Father) Bush Street," in tribute to American President George Bush. When the Iraqis discovered the name change, they went to Yihya's house, since it was the closest one, and demanded that he paint over the graffiti. Yihya did. The next night, the teenagers painted the same thing on the sign. Once again, the Iraqis instructed Yihya to paint over it. This continued for several days until finally, Yihya had packed up and moved out of his house. After he left, the Iraqis apparently quit checking the sign, Essa said, because the new name was still on it.

Shortly after Essa completed his story, Ali left the men and returned home. Nassima and the children were just arriving. He immediately began a romp with his two nieces and two nephews. It was good to hear the childish shriek of laughter again. He felt like his children had already been gone for weeks.

Early that evening, after Nassima left, Ali listened to the news, but heard nothing about the evacuation flight. It made him uneasy. He knew his family should have cleared England by now and be on a plane to America. He expected to hear some news about the flight. Other evacuation flights had been tracked closely by the media and he was sure this one also would be. Bedreah told him there could be a hundred reasons why there was nothing on the news yet, but Ali couldn't shake the feeling that something was wrong.

■ ■ ■

My God, it's beautiful, Dina thought as she walked into the Baghdad airport about midnight. She'd had to wake the children to take them off the plane. They were grouchy and irritable, especially Yacoub. He was a "bear cat" when he was awakened under the best of circumstances. Now he insisted on being carried, too. Dina was struggling to hold onto him and the baby. Jassim, Zade, and Nadia were left to haul the heavy suitcase and duffel bag.

The Iraqis put on a good show for their television camera crews, who filmed the evacuees' arrival. Several tables of bottled water, unwrapped fruit, and cookies, and packaged snacks had been set up in the airport. Dina put Yacoub down and grabbed a handful of packaged items before she sank down on the floor with the children gathered around her. The evacuees had been warned not to eat any food the Iraqis might offer them because passengers on the first evacuation flight had suffered from food poisoning. But she felt the packaged snacks were probably safe and the children were so very hungry.

After they ate, she took them into the bathroom where they could wash and get a drink from the faucet. She was sure the water from the faucet was safe, but wasn't so sure about the bottled water. When they came out of the bathroom, they were met by an American Embassy official.

"I'm so sorry for the delays," the man told her, "but we could do nothing about them. Are all of you well?"

"As well as we can be after being confined on a hot bus for over thirteen hours without any food or water and then on an airplane that should have been junked when Orville and Wilbur died," Dina snapped.

"I know it has been difficult," the man said, his eyes filled with sympathy, "but it will soon be over. They should be calling your plane for England in about an hour."

Tears came to Dina's eyes. "I'm sorry," she apologized. "I don't mean to be rude...it's just that we're all so tired."

"I understand," the man smiled gently. He wished her a good trip and left.

Dina plunked back down on the floor again to wait for the boarding call. She really didn't care what anyone thought about her sitting on the floor. She was too exhausted to think about it.

The embassy man was right. In exactly an hour, they were called for boarding. Dina had hoped they would have a better plane from Baghdad to London, but it was the same rickety monster they had taken from Basra.

■ ■ ■

The plane had barely cleared Baghdad air space before the children were once again sound asleep, but their mother was far too nervous to close her eyes. She wondered what was happening at the family compound. If the Iraqis, somehow, had found out her last name and true address, they would have had time by now to have everyone in the compound under arrest.

Please be safe, Ali, she prayed silently. *Please follow me quickly...I won't be able to live without you!* A sob caught in her throat as she remembered the first time she had ever seen him.

It had been on an unusually warm evening in late March 1979. She had gone to the campus library to study for a humanities test, and there, sitting at a table near the front door, was Ali. He'd looked so sad and forlorn. He had fought homesickness from the first day he arrived in America. *Poor guy,* she thought. *He looks like he's lost his best friend.*

Just then, he glanced up from his book and saw her. Dina smiled at him and he smiled back. The next thing she knew, he was walking towards her.

"Hello, my name is Ali."

"Oh, hi," she said. "I'm Dina."

His face broke out into a big grin as he said, "It is very nice to meet you, Dina."

"That's quite an accent," she said. "Or is it just a come-on?"

"I do not know the word 'come-on'," Ali said. "I am from Kuwait and I apologize that my English is not good."

"*Kuwait?*" Dina slowly repeated the strange word. "Where in the world is *Kuwait?*"

Ali was more than happy to explain where his country was and to talk about its people, especially his family. It helped the homesick feeling.

Dina was more than happy to listen as Ali told about Kuwait and everyone in it. She was fascinated with this dark, good-looking person.

They had agreed to be "just friends" in the beginning, but within a matter of weeks they both knew their relationship was headed far beyond friendship. Ali proposed to her in December of that year, and they were married the next February in both a Muslim and Catholic ceremony.

Oh, Ali! she thought now. *We've had a good, happy life together. This can't be all God is going to allow us!*

■ ■ ■

When their plane arrived in London at 6:30 A.M., nearly a day behind schedule, the welcome the evacuees received was unexpected. *We're finally back in civilization,* Dina sighed.

Living the Nightmare

Embassy staff came onto the airliner to greet them, carry the luggage, help with the children, and escort the passengers to the terminal shuttle buses.

"We know this has been a long and difficult trip," the spokesman for the group told the passengers before they left the plane. "If there is anything we can help you with, don't hesitate to ask." The man then explained that when they reached the terminal there would be food available and that they would be deluged with media personnel.

"You do not have to speak with them," the man said, "but if you do answer any questions, just be careful what you say. We have no way of knowing how far their reports will go."

Then he told them there also would be more papers to fill out before they were taken to a hotel. The passengers groaned and the man smiled and said, "but this time it will only take a few minutes to complete them. We just need a record showing that you have arrived in England safely."

The evacuees cheered and the deplaning began.

The first thing they saw inside the terminal was the food. Table after table was filled with sandwiches, juice, pop, and cold water. It couldn't have tasted better to them if it had been cooked by the finest French chef. Now feeling safe, Dina let the children eat as much as they wanted, which was surprisingly little. Their stomachs had already shrunk from lack of food.

Several reporters approached her while she was eating, but she politely refused to talk to them. She was too exhausted and was afraid she would slip and say something that might endanger Ali and his family.

Soon the evacuees were rounded up and given the promised papers to fill out. The embassy staff member who picked up Dina's papers asked if she would consent to a military debriefing when she arrived in Nebraska. She told him she had little to tell since she had not gone beyond the confines of the neighborhood during the occupation, but consented to the interview. The passengers also were checked for any physical wounds, and medical personnel expressed concern about a bandage Yacoub had on his head. The youngster had fallen and cut his forehead the day before they left Kuwait, and Dina was questioned closely to assure the wound hadn't been inflicted by an Iraqi.

After the paperwork and cursory medical exams were completed, the evacuees were allowed to make one three-minute international phone call. Dina called her sister, then they were loaded onto buses and transported to a London hotel.

As soon as she shut the door to her room, she stripped the children, bathed them, and put them to bed. Then, just as she was ready for the luxury of a bath herself, the phone rang. It was Gina. She had called the State Department to find out in what hotel Dina was being housed.

The sisters spent a tearful 15 minutes on the phone, but each was crying for a different reason. Gina was simply happy her sister was safe. Dina cried for the safety of Ali and his family.

"I'm not the same," Dina said. "You won't recognize me when I get off the plane." She explained her loss of weight and her adoption of the Muslim dress.

"I don't care if you're skinnier than me and have a gunnysack on," Gina laughed. "Nobody does." Then she told her sister she realized this wasn't a happy homecoming for her. "We'll help you as much as we can to get information about Ali," Gina promised.

That call was followed by one from her best friend, Donna Ellenberger, then one from Richard, and then one from Camille.

Finally Dina got her bath. She'd never felt more dirty in her life. She also had never felt so happy, and so depressed, all at the same time.

As she was getting out of the tub, the children began waking up, so she called room service for a real meal for them, the first they'd had since 7:00 A.M. the previous morning. They were disappointed with the English cuisine, but ate all of the ice cream their mother ordered as a treat. Not long after they ate, everyone was back in bed.

Before he nodded off, Jassim asked, "Mamma, do you think Dad will be at Aunt Gina's when we get there?"

Oh, how I wish,! Dina thought. "No, Jassim, he won't be, but I'm sure he'll be there soon."

"He promised to buy me a catcher's mitt when he gets there," Jassim mumbled sleepily.

God willing, Dina thought as she fell asleep.

The next morning they were up early, ready for their trip back to the airport. They boarded a plane for Raleigh, North Carolina, arriving there in the afternoon. They were escorted off this plane by military staff and taken to a holding room. Dina waited three hours before she was called for immigration processing.

To her surprise, this was where she was hassled because Husain didn't have a passport. *How ironic,* she thought. *I get through the Iraqi paperwork without a problem, and now, I'm back in my own country, getting the third degree over not having a passport for the baby!*

Here, also, were tables full of food and medical aid stations where they were checked over again. In addition, there were several tables where the evacuees could sign up for financial support during their stay in America and where they could get loans processed for their plane fare to other parts of the country. The State Department only provided transportation to the United States. The evacuees were responsible for getting to their ultimate destination from wherever the plane from England landed. By the time Dina was processed through the airport, it was too late for her to get a plane to Nebraska, so she and the children were driven to a Raleigh hotel for the night.

The next morning they were on a plane for Lincoln.

CHAPTER 10

Ali continued to worry. Throughout the early evening hours of the day Dina left, he stayed glued to the BBC news broadcasts, willing the announcers to say something about Dina's flight. Then suddenly, as he paced past the radio for the hundredth time, he heard an announcer say, "...passengers were harassed...." His heart caught in his throat as he turned the radio up.

"According to our reports," the announcer continued, "they were taken to the Hyatt Regency Hotel for questioning."

Now his mind twisted in agony. Was the announcer talking about the evacuation buses? He soon found out that was the subject.

Sick with fear, he wondered what to do. Had they interrogated Dina? She had been scared to death that she would be questioned. Had the children been separated from her? Husain had no passport. Had they been released, or were they still at Iraqi headquarters? He was hesitant to call the embassy to see if anyone there had any additional information. Rumor had it that the Iraqis had recently hired foreign collaborators to tap phone lines in an effort to follow resistance movements. If his family's phones were tapped, he might jeopardize their lives by asking about one of the American evacuees.

He felt like his brain would explode with all of the questions churning inside it. He knew he had to get out of the house or go mad, so he made a quick decision to go to Nassima's. Rushing into the kitchen, he told his mother where he was going. She pressed him to tell her why, but he couldn't tell her about the news broadcast. She would go to pieces and he didn't have the patience to take care of her.

Grabbing a few clothes and a carton of cigarettes, he left for Ahmadi about 7:30 that evening. He wasn't stopped at the first checkpoint, but at the second, on the outskirts of Bayan, a belligerent soldier pulled him over and asked for his driver's license and civil card. The soldier acted as if he were going to give Ali some trouble, but then he spied the cigarettes Ali had tossed on the front seat. Ali quickly offered him a couple of packs, the soldier muttered a "thank-you," returned his driver's license and civil card, and motioned him through the barricade.

He wasn't stopped again until he approached the outskirts of Ahmadi. There another soldier asked for his driver's license and civil card. This one also looked like he was spoiling for a fight, but, he too, spied the cigarettes. Again Ali handed over a couple of packs and got the same results he had with the first two packs.

As he was driving away from that checkpoint, another soldier stepped from the side of the road and motioned with his gun for Ali to pull over.

Damn it, Ali thought. *I will be out of cigarettes before I ever get to Nassima's!* As he pulled to the side of the road, he reached over and shoved the rest of the carton onto the floorboard.

"I'm looking for a pickup truck," the soldier, who at least seemed friendly, said when he reached the car. "Would you know of anyone who has one for sale?"

Sale, sure, Ali thought. *He means do I know where he could steal one.*

"No," Ali answered. "I used to have one," he lied, "but I sold it about a year ago."

"Well, if you do hear of someone, will you let me know?"

Jesus Christ! Ali wanted to scream. *Are you guys all nuts or what?* But he just smiled and said, "Of course I'll let you know."

"Thanks," the soldier said, waving Ali on. "I'll be seeing you, then."

"All you'll ever see is my ass," Ali muttered under his breath as he drove away.

Driving into Ahmadi he suddenly realized he was completely disoriented. *God, I'm so tired,* he thought. Every nerve ending in his body was bruised. He drove around the dark streets for a few minutes, but couldn't get his bearings. Stopping at a convenience store, he found a telephone and called Nassima's house. Mohammed answered the phone.

"I'm lost!" Ali said, almost hysterically.

"Tell me where you are and I'll give you directions," Mohammed said.

"No," Ali shouted. "Come get me! There are too many checkpoints!"

His brother-in-law asked what was wrong, but Ali told him he would explain after he arrived at the house.

While he was waiting for Mohammed, Ali watched with hatred in his eyes as several Iraqi soldiers wandered in and out of the store, stealing pop, candy, and other snacks off the shelves. He thought *it would feel so good to put my hands around an Iraqi throat and squeeze until there was no life left.*

Mohammed, a tall, big-boned man with a serious demeanor, arrived after some fifteen minutes and escorted Ali to his house where they were met by an anxious Nassima.

As he slumped into a chair, she asked, "What's wrong, Ali?'

He told his sister what he had heard about the evacuation buses on the news earlier. "I'm so afraid for them," he said, "and I don't know what to do!"

"There is nothing you can do," Nassima said. "If you go to the hotel to look for them you will only endanger yourself. You would be of no help to them, even if they're still there, which they probably aren't."

As they sat talking, drinking tea, and eating sweets, a news flash came on the Gulf States television channel. It was the report about the buses being detained at the hotel.

Just then the phone rang. It was Bedreah, concerned about whether Ali had made it to Ahmadi, and about what was troubling him when he left the house. He told her once again that he just needed to get away for a while. She put Mahmoud on the phone and told him to try to find out what was troubling his brother. Ali broke down and told Mahmoud, but warned him against telling Bedreah. He had barely gotten the words out of his mouth when he heard his brother tell his mother. As Ali knew she would, Bedreah panicked and grabbed the phone from Mahmoud.

"You should have told me!" she screamed at Ali. "What are we going to do?"

"Mom," he sighed. "There is nothing we can do but wait." Then he hung up. *Let Mahmoud tend to her hysteria,* he thought. *It was his big mouth that had caused it!*

It was nearly 1:00 A.M. by now, and Ali could no longer stay awake. The tension of the day had completely drained him. He said good-night to his sister and brother-in-law and went upstairs to bed.

There was less night noise in Ahmadi than in Rumaithiya, which had become a virtual hotbed of resistance activities. Because of all of the oil refineries surrounding Ahmadi, the Kuwaiti fighters pretty much left the Iraqis in that area alone. The absence of the sound of gunfire and explosions allowed Ali to fall asleep the minute his head hit the pillow, but it was a restless sleep.

He dreamed that he and his son Jassim were being chased by Iraqi soldiers. He had found Jassim at the hotel and had spirited him away from his captors. The Iraqis were shooting at them and Jassim was hit by a bullet.

Ali woke up in a cold sweat, screaming Jassim's name.

■ ■ ■

The next morning, still restless and worried, Ali decided to leave his sister's house and go talk to his Aunt Miriam. Not only was he worried about Dina and the children, he was anxious to find out if his aunt had heard anything about Abdul-Samad or any of the other air force base personnel.

On his way to Miriam's Ali stopped by his house to tell his mother where he was going. She had calmed down considerably from the night before. Mahmoud had succeeded in convincing her there was nothing that could be done, even if Dina and the children were still at the Hyatt Regency. She had decided that she would have to trust that God would get them safely to America.

As Ali returned to his car, his brother-in-law Hassan drove up. He asked Ali where he was going.

"To Aunt Miriam's," Ali answered.

"Do you have any Kuwaiti money on you?"

"Yes, why?"

Hassan told Ali the Iraqis were searching people at the checkpoints he had come through on his way from Bayan for Kuwaiti or foreign money. The Iraqis had started arresting Kuwaitis found with either the outlawed Kuwaiti dinars or foreign currency. Ali took his Kuwaiti money back into the house and then got into his car and headed for Al-Sulaibkhat.

He was challenged at the first checkpoint. He shivered involuntarily when he saw the challenger. He was an officer dressed in a plain, olive-colored uniform—the uniform of Saddam's secret police.

"Give me your driver's license and civil card, you rich son-of-a-bitch," the officer ordered.

This is going to be a rough one, Ali sighed as he handed the cards over. Then the Iraqi asked him for his wallet. Ali gave that to him. The officer opened the wallet and a sneer crossed his face.

Stepping closer to the car, he demanded, "What is this?"

Ali turned pale. *Oh, shit!* he thought.

The Iraqi was holding a single French 100 franc note in his hand. "Explain this," the officer shouted.

Ali had taken his mother to France shortly before the invasion for treatment of her eyes. He'd forgotten he still had the French money in his billfold. He told the officer the truth, but the officer scowled and called Ali a liar. "You deal in illegal foreign currency," the Iraqi accused.

Ali denied the accusation, but the officer just snorted and ordered him out of the car. An evil grin crossed the Iraqi's face as he drew his revolver from its holster. "I can shoot you now," he said, "or maybe you would like to meet some of my friends at headquarters...they would be very happy to visit with you for a while."

"Please, sir," Ali pleaded. "I am a good person...I'm not a forger. Just release me and you can have the money."

The officer slapped Ali in the face. "You are trying to bribe me," he roared.

Ali held his tongue while his face grew red with anger.

The Iraqi slapped him again. "Answer me!"

"I am not trying to bribe you," Ali said, gritting his teeth. "I am simply trying to tell you I got that money when I took my mother to France two months ago."

This time the officer laughed and threw the driver's license in Ali's face. It fell to the ground.

"Pick it up!" the officer said.

Ali bent down and retrieved the license, sure that he was going to get a bullet in the back of his head while he was bent over.

"Now get back in the car and get out of here!"

Ali clenched his fists. "May I have my civil card and bill-fold?"

"We will contact you about them later. Just go before I decide to use this." The pistol was pointed at Ali's head.

Ali got into the car and drove on through the checkpoint. After he was out of the officer's view, he stopped the car and pounded the steering wheel in a rage. He wondered how much more he could take from an Iraqi before he would wind up being shot for using his fists. *The bastards have even more fun humiliating us and making us beg for our lives than they do shooting us*, he thought.

■ ■ ■

Ali wasn't the only Kuwaiti who was wondering how much longer the world was going to expect them to tolerate the Iraqi brutality and humiliation before help would be sent. They all knew that other countries were aware of what was going on inside Kuwait because they heard the reports themselves over the "free" radio stations. Abo-Ahmad and Um-Ahmad, both compassionate and caring people, were among those who wondered how much longer they were going to be able to continue their jobs without losing their minds.

The two Rumaithiyans (formerly from Egypt, they were now living in an extra building in Abass's family compound) had been loyal to their jobs at Mubarak Hospital from the first day of the invasion. What they had seen in the beginning of the occupation had been bad enough. The wounded soldiers had been one thing to deal with, and even though some wounds were horrendous, they were wounds expected from battle.

Since the tortured resistance people began coming in, it had become a nightmare. The wounds inflicted on these civilians were deliberate and despicable. Abo-Ahmad and Um-Ahmad went back to Rumaithiya nearly every night depressed and discouraged over some incident that had occurred that day at the hospital.

But they always went back the next day. They were needed by the few Kuwaiti patients who were left in the hospital, and as long as they kept their ties with the hospital, the couple could keep their friends and neighbors supplied with medicine they needed but could no longer obtain.

When the Iraqis came into the country, they began throwing Kuwaitis out of the hospitals—even those on life-support—to make room for their wounded. Newborn babies were taken out of their incubators and left on the cold floor to die so the machines could be shipped to Iraq. It is estimated that the Iraqis stole 90 percent of the medical supplies and equipment from Kuwaiti hospitals and medical centers, and they didn't only steal blood from the bodies of their prisoners, they emptied the blood bank too.

When the Iraqi theft intentions became apparent, some hospital employees tried to hide equipment by taking it home with them. Two men in Rumaithiya, a father and son, were executed after medical equipment they were trying to hide was found in their home during a routine house search.

Medical centers in several areas had been shut down due to a lack of equipment, supplies, and doctors. Many of the doctors in Kuwait were foreigners who left at the beginning of the occupation. Those who stayed ran the risk of being shot if the Iraqis thought their wounded were not getting proper treatment. If an Iraqi officer or soldier died because of his wounds, no matter how severe the injury might be, someone at the hospital was likely to lose his or her life.

Terror and death were constant companions of Abo-Ahmad and his wife.

Um-Ahmad, a small, timid woman, suffered a miscarriage after being threatened by an Iraqi soldier. Her crime? The hospital gate was closed when she arrived for work that morning, so she honked the car horn to get the soldier's attention to open the gate. It made the soldier angry and he stomped to Um-Ahmad's car, stuck his pistol in her face, and warned her never to honk her horn at him again.

Shortly after his wife lost their baby, Abo-Ahmad heard a commotion at the hospital entrance and went to investigate. A man was arguing with two Iraqi soldiers who were bent on stealing his car. Suddenly, to Abo-Ahmad's horror, one of the soldiers whipped his pistol out of its holster and shot the man dead. Then they pulled his body out of the car, threw it on the ground, got into the car, and drove away.

The man's wife, whom he had brought to the hospital for treatment, had been standing beside the car, pleading for her husband to get out of it. When he was shot, she went into hysterics and threw herself on top of his body. Abo-Ahmad picked her up and carried her into the hospital to a treatment room. Then he went back outside to get the corpse and take it to the hospital morgue.

Sometimes, however, there were bright spots for the couple. One day Um-Ahmad was called upon to help treat several Iraqi soldiers who had been brought to the hospital with their tongues so swollen they could barely swallow. The doctor determined they had eaten a women's depilatory. The Iraqis told the doctor a clerk in a convenience store had told them the hair remover was a sandwich spread. The resistance worked in subtle ways.

■ ■ ■

Too upset to continue to Miriam's, Ali turned around and went back home after his encounter with the secret police officer.

That afternoon, about 2:30, he was in the bathroom when an explosion nearly knocked him off the stool. Pulling his pants up and yanking the door open, he scrambled toward the stairs, sure that a bomb had hit the house. He was joined on the stairway by Ahmad, who came running up the hallway from the kitchen.

Living the Nightmare

Another explosion, then a third and a fourth pounded in their ears. Dashing through the main floor of the house, they determined there was no damage there, so they sprinted up the stairs to the other floors. Finding no damage there, either, they continued to the roof, bent on finding out what was happening. More explosions ripped through the air as they climbed the last flight. Once they reached the roof, they heard a *whoosh* and felt the hot breath of a projectile streak past their heads. As they fell to the rooftop, another huge explosion tore through the neighborhood.

Picking themselves up, they ran back down the stairs and into the front yard. When they reached the flower bed, the explosions quit. Cautiously, they went to the gate, opened it, and peered into the street. About a block away was a heap of burning metal that had once been a flatbed truck. The resistance had hit an Iraqi military truck transporting short-range missiles on Naser Al-Mubarak Street in broad daylight!

Suddenly, several truckloads of Iraqi soldiers hurtled onto the street from Al-Fahaheel Expressway. The soldiers were in a panic and were shooting at anything that moved.

Ali and Ahmad ran into the house, bolted the door, and stayed there until the gunfire faded. They expected the soldiers to start a house-to-house search for the freedom fighters involved in the incident, but none developed.

After everything was quiet, Ali, his brothers, and several other neighbors spent the rest of the afternoon roaming through the neighborhood to see if everyone was safe. Several houses had been hit by the exploding missiles, but there were no casualties. One neighbor had been especially lucky. A missile had gone through a wall in his son's third floor bedroom, lodged in the opposite wall above his desk, but didn't explode. His son had been at the desk only moments before, but had gone downstairs when the explosions began.

■ ■ ■

The second night Dina and the children were gone, there was a knock at Ali's door. It was Essa.

"Ali," he said, "we need your help."

Ali stepped outside the door and shut it. He didn't want the others to hear what Essa was saying. Whatever it was, he knew Bedreah would object to it.

"What's the matter, Essa?"

"One of the guys found out there is a basement full of supplies in one of the supermarkets. We have a truck to haul them away, but we need more help to get the job done quickly before the Iraqis get wise to us."

"How could the Iraqis have missed that?" The markets had long since been looted and closed.

"I don't know," Essa grinned, "but it's their loss and our gain. Come on Ali, let's go!"

Since Ali would no longer have to explain his absences to Dina, and because it would take his mind off worrying about her, he went with Essa and several other men and helped fill the truck with food, cigarettes, diapers, and bottled water.

They brought the truck back to the neighborhood and began delivering the cache door to door. Not wanting anyone to know who was making the deliveries, they simply dropped the items on doorsteps. You never knew who might be an Iraqi spy, or who might fall into the hands of the Iraqis and, under interrogation, reveal the activities of others in the neighborhood.

They finished their own neighborhood that night, and then the next night they took supplies to the next neighborhood, and so on, until all of the supplies had been doled out. Ali wound up wrenching his back while lugging the 100-pound sacks of flour and sugar, which was hard to conceal from Bedreah. She hounded him to tell her what had happened to his back, but he stubbornly ignored her.

■ ■ ■

Dina was to have arrived in Lincoln on October 10, the day after she left Kuwait. However, due to the delays in Kuwait, Iraq, and then again in North Carolina, her plane landed on the afternoon of October 13.

Because of the circumstance of her return, her family had discouraged friends from meeting the plane. They wanted her to have a few days to recuperate from the journey before being swamped with well-wishers.

Only Gina, her ex-husband Jeff Baker, and their daughter Marcel, Richard, Pat, Dina's friend Donna, her husband Paul, and their three sons were at the Lincoln airport to greet her. They were all shocked at her appearance. She walked towards them as if she were in a trance. The sparkle in her beautiful eyes was gone. Pale and far too thin, she looked like a shadow of the Dina they once knew. Dina smiled when she saw them, but it was a wan, hopeless smile. There were tears of joy, and sorrow, in her eyes. Even though none of them had ever seen her in Muslim garb, they barely even noticed she was dressed differently. The pain in her face distracted from all else.

"Hold me tight, Poppy!" she said to Richard as he clasped her in his arms. "I'm not sure I won't turn around and get back on that plane."

"It will be all right, honey," Richard said. "You'll see. It will all turn out all right now that you're safe."

"Only half of me is safe," she sobbed.

Inevitably, the media was well represented at the homecoming. Dina forced herself to speak briefly with the reporters before Richard hustled her into his car for the trip to Gina's house.

As they pulled into the driveway, more tears came to Dina's eyes. Flying on a pole in front of the house, along with the American flag, was a homemade Kuwaiti flag. *Leave it to Gina*, Dina thought, *to know what would make me feel at home.*

There were more surprises inside the house. Gina had turned her finished basement into quarters for her sister, niece, and nephews. Each had a bed, including the baby. She had set up Marcel's outgrown crib for Husain. Gina ran a daycare center in her home and the mothers of her daycare children and other friends had donated beds, bedding, extra towels, food, toys, even clothes for Dina and the children when they found out they had left Kuwait with few of their own. There also were piles of gifts for everyone. It was like Christmas and birthdays all rolled into one.

Everyone knew Dina was tired, so they left shortly after they arrived, but Dina was too on edge to sleep. After the others were gone, the sisters talked for a long time. In bits and pieces, Dina began to tell Gina of the evil that had overtaken her adopted country and of her fear for Ali and his family's safety.

"I feel so guilty," she kept telling Gina. "I'm safe but they're still in so much danger."

"I know you feel guilty," Gina told her, "but think of the relief they're all feeling knowing that you and the children are safe. That has to take a big weight off their minds."

■ ■ ■

No one in the family compound was feeling any relief over Dina and the children being safe, because no one knew that they were. Ali agonized through the third, fourth, and fifth days after they left without any news about them. The tension finally built to the point that, on the sixth day, he knew that no matter what the cost, he had to find out about the flight.

After breakfast that morning, he went to Essa and Thoraya's house to discuss what he could do.

"The only way I can think of to find out about them is to call the embassy," Ali told his friends. "But I'm so afraid the call might be traced by the Iraqis."

Thoraya suggested that she make the call, but Ali argued with her, as reluctant to endanger her family as he was to endanger his own. But Thoraya ignored him, picked up the phone, and dialed the embassy number. A man answered and she asked if the evacuation flight had made it to England.

"Oh, yes," the man said.

"Can you tell me if a woman by the name of Dina was on the flight," Thoraya continued.

"Tell me the last name," the man said.

"Please try to find this person without my using her last name," Thoraya said. "I don't want to put her family in any danger."

"I understand," the man said. "Please hold." Within minutes he was back on the line.

"Yes," he answered. "She and her five children were on the flight, and they continued to the United States where they landed in Nebraska yesterday."

Thoraya put the phone down and grinned at Ali. "They are safe in Nebraska!"

Now Ali felt he could breathe again, but he was still uneasy. *Why had it taken them so long to get to Gina's?* He knew that question would be on his mind until he saw them again and learned the answer. *If I ever see them again,* he sighed.

■ ■ ■

The morning after Dina's arrival, Gina woke her houseguests with breakfast in bed. Dina protested the extra effort. But Gina told her, "I'm giving you a week to get over your depression and get with the program, but until then, it's my house, and if I want to, I'll treat you like a queen!"

They both laughed. *If anyone can keep my mind off my problems,* Dina thought, *it will be my silly sister.*

Within days, Dina began to relax. Although the pressure of not knowing what was happening to Ali and his family still weighed heavily upon her, there was a great deal of peace of mind knowing the children were out of danger. She threw herself into assisting Gina with the daycare, which helped keep her mind off Kuwait, and there was always one friend or another dropping by to see her, or calling her on the phone.

From the moment she got up in the morning until the moment she could no longer stay awake at night, the television was on. There wasn't a word of news that came out of the Middle East that she didn't hear. She videotaped many of the reports, running and rerunning them in hopes she had missed some tiny hint of good news, but there never seemed to be any.

Her family and friends joined her in writing letters to congressmen, senators, embassies, anyone they thought might be able to obtain information on Ali and his family. There was simply no way anyone could find out if they were dead or alive.

The two sisters grew even closer. Gina did not follow through on her threat to give Dina a week to get over her depression. She continued to wait on her hand and foot, gaining the nickname "Cindy" (for Cinderella) from Dina. Most importantly, Gina took over the father's role with the children, passing out the discipline Dina didn't have the heart to give them.

After a week had gone by, Dina began to think about enrolling Jassim, Nadia, and Zade in school. Being totally surrounded by Western culture and language was difficult for them, and they clung closely to their mother and Aunt Gina. Dina knew it wasn't going to be easy on them, or her to make them go to school, but she knew she had to enroll them. She still was paranoid about letting them out of her sight.

One night as she was putting them to bed, she told them she was going to start looking for a school the next day. All three threw a royal fit.

"I am not going to any English school!" Jassim shouted at his mother.

Zade, out of respect for his older brother's decision, screamed, "Me either!"

Nadia simply started to cry.

But, true to her word, the next day Dina called the Lincoln School District office to ask about getting three Arabic-speaking students enrolled. She and Ali had taught the children some English, but Dina knew it wasn't enough for them to survive in an American classroom. A school official told her she should contact Park School, which offered English as a second language to elementary students. The next day she went to the school and registered the children for classes. Jassim would enter the fifth grade, Nadia the second, and Zade kindergarten. They started school two weeks after they came to the States. Nadia nearly broke her mother's heart the first day. She cried all the way to the building and was still crying when Dina picked them up after school, but soon all three settled into the routine as well as she could expect.

Eventually they learned to be at home at Park, which Dina attributed to the patience and understanding of their teachers, principal and other staff. It warmed her heart to see all of those strangers go the "extra mile" to become friends with her children.

■ ■ ■

Ali, Mahmoud, Ahmad, and Hameed had continued their every night vigil on Ahmad's balcony, despite Bedreah's objections.

In addition to watching what the Iraqis were hauling out of the country, they also watched what was being brought into it. Information gathered on weapons and troop transportation was passed on to Farouk or other friends who were part of the fighting resistance. The group also kept their eyes peeled for Iraqi soldiers who might be out on looting or raping sprees and for foreign collaborators who also roamed the streets at night wreaking havoc on the country that had opened its arms to them. To defend themselves and their family in case they were attacked by one of the marauding bands, they carried kitchen knives. After Dina was gone, Ali had approached Farouk about getting him another gun, but Farouk told him all weapons were now being given to resistance fighters. Ali was helping the movement, but not as a fighter. Farouk told him he was not eligible for a gun.

Every man in Kuwait was most especially worried about their women being raped. It was a despicable crime in the Muslim world, but rape didn't seem to bother the religious conscience of many Iraqi soldiers.

On this night, while Ali was on the balcony, the threat of rape was very much on his mind. He had visited another cousin, Abo-Ali, that afternoon and given him Kuwaiti money for him to exchange into Iraqi currency so he could take his family to Saudi Arabia. Abo-Ali had become obsessed with the thought that his wife or daughters—ages nineteen, eighteen, seventeen, and sixteen—would be raped.

His fears had mounted a few days earlier, when Iraqi soldiers broke into the house of a neighbor and raped the women. He was afraid the criminals would come back to the neighborhood, and this time, his house would be the target.

"I'm so torn," Abo-Ali told Ali. "I know it's dangerous to try to escape, but it's dangerous here, too."

Ali talked to his cousin for several hours, trying to help him come to a decision. Finally, Abo-Ali had decided to leave Kuwait. Tonight, Ali was hoping that would turn out to be the right decision.

■ ■ ■

A few days later when the neighborhood group was gathered in Abass's yard, Essa appeared with tears in his eyes. He had just learned of the death of an eighteen-year-old cousin.

The youngster, whose name was Maithem, had been arrested at a checkpoint in Ahmadi in early September, along with two friends. The Iraqis searched the car the three were in and found a resistance pamphlet similar to the ones Ahmad was passing out. The three youths had no idea where the pamphlet came from, but the Iraqis wouldn't believe them. The two friends had been released after three weeks of confinement, but Maithem continued to be held. He was especially suspect since the pamphlet had been found in his vehicle.

When the friends returned home, they called Maithem's parents and told them where he was, revealing that he had been tortured pretty badly. His mother and father went to the police station the friends identified, but were told their son was not there.

"He has been transferred to another facility," an Iraqi officer told them, "but we expect to release him in about another week." He would not say to which station Maithem had been taken.

After the week passed and their son didn't show up, Maithem's parents went back to see the Iraqis and were told that Maithem had been transferred to still another facility. "But you will see him in a few days," the officer promised.

That promise had been kept yesterday, Essa said. Maithem was brought back to his house in the town of Sha'ab about six in the morning. While his family still slept, the Iraqi officer put two bullets in the back of the young man's head, killing him instantly. He was then left on his front steps where his father saw him, as the officer had promised, about an hour later when he came out the door to water his garden.

A description of the officer provided by a neighbor who had witnessed the execution assured Maithem's father that the killer had been the same officer he had been dealing with at the police station.

■ ■ ■

Dina underwent the debriefing she had agreed to in England a couple of weeks after she arrived in the States. It was one of the most interesting experiences she'd ever had.

She went to the FBI office in Lincoln for a session with agents from the Office of Special Investigation (OSI), a U.S. Air Force agency, on a Thursday morning. They took a break for lunch, then the session resumed at Gina's house at 1:00 and lasted until about 5:00.

She couldn't believe the OSI had a map of Kuwait that was so clear she could pick out her house in Rumaithiya. She was asked to circle her house, was questioned about the construction of it and other buildings in the area and to provide physical descriptions of Ali and all of his relatives. She became excited when asked to do this.

"You are going to evacuate as many Kuwaitis as you can before the war begins," she surmised, but the agents wouldn't confirm her guess.

Dina couldn't answer the OSI's questions about the deployment of Iraqi soldiers around the city, explaining that she had been too afraid to leave the neighborhood.

During the interview, she discovered that the intelligence people were interviewing everyone who came out of Kuwait, then matching up the stories to confirm they had the truth.

The biggest thing Dina felt good about telling the agents was that it was the "gut" feeling of every Kuwaiti she knew that the Iraqis would not put up a fight, once they were pushed into a corner.

■ ■ ■

As October ended, the world continued to wage its paper war against Saddam. On August 14, it was learned that Iraq had transferred $3 billion to $4 billion in confiscated gold bullion, currency and goods from Kuwait Central Bank to Baghdad. Then on September 20, Iraq confiscated assets of all countries imposing economic sanctions against it. Therefore, on October 29, the U.N. Security Council passed another resolution, this one holding Iraq responsible for financial losses suffered by Kuwait and other nations because of the invasion.

This was small comfort for the Kuwaitis who were still clinging to the desperate hope that the world would rescue them before Saddam could annihilate them.

CHAPTER 11

By November 11, Major Abdul-Samad and several hundred other prisoners from the air force base had spent time at two prison camps and had just taken up residency in a third.

Conditions at the first camp, Al-Rasheed, had been more than primitive. Over 650 prisoners had been confined there, including the air force men who had been taken away from their colleagues at the fire station. There had been much rejoicing when Abdul-Samad's group arrived at Al-Rasheed and found those men alive.

Iraqi political prisoners were also housed in that camp. Abdul-Samad met one of Saddam's bodyguards, in addition to a relative of the dictator's wife. The bodyguard had made the mistake of telling his boss that a group of foreigners had offered him a bribe of $1 million to kill Saddam. The Iraqi leader thanked his guard for his honesty by throwing him in prison. Abdul-Samad never did find out why a member of Saddam's wife's family had been banished.

Al-Rasheed was a very secure prison, surrounded by electrified trenches that had been filled with water and a high, barbed-wire fence. The prisoners' beds were the ground and the sky their blanket. There were only four toilets for the entire camp, and they were constantly clogged and overflowing. They drank dirty water and ate two tiny servings a day of yellow lentils, cooked cucumbers, and bread made from barley, which was dry as stone. On rare occasions they received a few pieces of meat that they were told was lamb, but it was so foul tasting, they believed it was really dog or cat.

Occasionally a water-spraying truck would be brought to the compound and the prisoners could crawl under it, into the field of spray, and have a shower of sorts.

The only clothes the Kuwaitis had there were what they had been wearing when they were captured. They were never given extra clothing, and in some cases, lost some of what they came to the camp with. Abdul-Samad and many other men had their boots taken at gunpoint by guards shortly after they arrived at Al-Rasheed.

However, conditions improved considerably at the second camp, Al-Mawsel. That water was pure and sweet, and it reminded Abdul-Samad of the water in Scotland, where he had attended college. Sanitary conditions were much better. There were ample, fairly clean toilets. Best of all, Iranian prisoners before them had planted a garden. Those Iranians had been part of the group Saddam released as a bribe for Iran's support, and when they left, the garden was inherited by the Kuwaitis. This boosted the spirits of Abdul-Samad and his friends tremendously. They worried constantly of becoming ill due to the lack of fresh fruits and vegetables.

The prisoners slept indoors on concrete floors at Al-Mawsel, but the Iranians had left some pillows and blankets behind so the Kuwaitis could sleep a bit more comfortably than they had at Al-Rasheed. Each man was issued a *distasha* when they entered the camp, which allowed everyone the luxury of always having one set of clean clothes.

There were also Iraqi prisoners at Al-Mawsel—kind, unselfish Iraqis. When their families brought food on visits to the camp, these Iraqis shared it with their fellow prisoners.

Sometimes the families would even bring extra food and distribute it directly to the Kuwaiti prisoners.

But, after only a short time in Al-Mawsel, the prisoners had been bused to a third camp, Al-Bakoba, which was located very near Baghdad. As soon as they arrived there they decided they might as well be back at Al-Rasheed. Al-Bakoba showed no outward signs that it would be anything like the relatively civilized Al-Mawsel.

In the three months since their capture, however, the Kuwaitis had learned a little bit about surviving as prisoners. They took their blankets and pillows to Al-Mawsel with them, and Abdul-Samad had managed to transport some seeds from the Iranian garden to the new camp. He planted them immediately and was soon growing a vegetable crop that included onions, peppergrass, and white radishes, welcome additions to the meager diet the Iraqis provided.

The pillows, blankets and small garden might be shrugged off as infinitesimal comforts to those living in a sane world, but for the prisoners in a world gone mad, they were monumental.

■ ■ ■

One lonely, miserable day followed another for Ali until October gave way to November. Without Dina and the children, he became increasingly depressed and irritable, angry and alone in a timeless void.

November brought reminders of three birthdays he would miss helping to celebrate—Yacoub's on the ninth, and Jassim's and Husain's on the thirtieth. He would not be present at his youngest son's first birthday party.

He knew his family was safe, but he had no idea how they were managing. They were to go to Gina's house, but were they still there? What did they do to occupy their time? Were they all well? Ali knew Dina's family would make sure they didn't want for anything, but not knowing what was happening in the States made him anxious.

Hassan had given up on making the dangerous trips from his home in Bayan and had moved in with his in-laws shortly after Dina left. He was as eager to join his family in England as Ali was to join his family in America, but they had never talked seriously about trying to flee. Even though Ali had promised Dina he would join her in America, he only half believed he would be able to do so. Kuwait's leaders had pleaded for Kuwaitis not to leave the country, and in Ali's family, patriotism ran a strong second to religion. This left the fulfillment of his yearning to be with Dina and the children in third place.

But early one November morning, Ali decided he couldn't stand being without them any longer. There had been a full moon that night while he and his brothers were at their post on the balcony and a weird feeling had come over him as he gazed at its brightness. He saw Dina's lovely, once-happy face in the bright face of the moon. *I am losing my mind,* he told himself. *If I don't see her soon I will go insane.*

As dawn crept in, Ali left the balcony and went to the basement to wake Hassan. He had heard the border had re-opened and he'd made up his mind that he was going to try to get out of Kuwait.

"Let's go!" he said to his brother-in-law. "I can't stand it here another minute!"

Hassan, a tall, very good-looking man, rubbed his sleep-filled eyes while he tried to figure out what Ali was talking about.

"Go…go where?"

"Saudi Arabia."

Now Hassan was awake.

"OK," he said, leaping from his mattress and grabbing his clothes. "I'm all packed, you know." He had been packed since the day of the invasion when he'd expected to be leaving for England.

"Wait," Ali grinned as he watched the Kuwait Oil Company chemist yank his pants on. "Not right now. We have plans to make first."

The two spent the day getting ready for the trip and at 3:00 the next morning, they climbed into Hassan's car and left. The family had mixed emotions about them making the trip. They wanted them to go to their wives and children, but hated to see them leave. Once they were out the door, the family would have no way of knowing if they had made it out of the country or not.

Rain beat down lightly on the cold, moonless night, but the weather served to help the two easily clear the checkpoints they encountered on the way to the border station at Al-Nuwaiseeb. All of the guards were wet and miserable, which lessened their desire to challenge the Kuwaitis.

But their luck ended about forty kilometers from the border. There they found a line of 60 to 70 cars filled with Kuwaitis heading for Saudi Arabia—and three checkpoints, all in a row.

Hassan parked the car and the two went to find someone who knew what was happening.

A man in the car in front of them told them the guards at the first checkpoint were telling everyone to have certain documents ready, the papers were checked at the second checkpoint, and then at the third the decision was made on whether you would be allowed to continue to Saudi Arabia or not. He told Ali and Hassan that the first checkpoint was to open at 8:30. It was now only 5:00.

The two returned to the car and Ali told his brother-in-law that he was going to get out and go back to Rumaithiya.

"You are joking," the quick-tempered Hassan shrieked. "You can't go back—I can't go on without you!"

"I have no civil card," Ali said, "and no passport. I will never get through three checkpoints...I would be lucky to talk my way through one!"

Hassan knew Ali's civil card had been taken from him, but he didn't know about the passport. Irritably, he asked, "Where's your passport?"

"I sent it in for renewal just before the invasion," Ali explained. "Of course, I've never gotten it back."

"Well, we're at least going to *try* to get you through," Hassan growled. "You know, I'm too scared to go on alone, and I won't turn back!"

The two sat in silence, chewing on some bread and cheese Bedreah had packed for them while they waited for the checkpoints to open.

About seven o'clock, more soldiers arrived, led by a very large man in the uniform of an intelligence officer. He ordered the soldiers to fire their rifles in the air, and once he had the Kuwaitis' attention, told them they had to move their cars to form one line. Ali and Hassan looked around them, and to their surprise, there were another 200 to 250 cars that had gathered in the area after they had arrived.

The Kuwaitis began moving their vehicles to comply with the order and as Hassan got his car into line, the big man passed by, heading for the rear of the line. Ali and Hassan heard him scream insults and orders to someone in a car somewhere behind them. Ali shuddered as he recalled his confrontation with the secret police officer.

At 9:00, the cars started moving forward slowly. By noon there were only four cars ahead of Ali and Hassan. Then there were only two. Ali took turns being excited and frightened. One minute he felt he could talk his way through the checkpoints, and the next he knew he would be yanked out of the car and sent to Baghdad.

As Hassan inched towards the first checkpoint, they noticed a civilian car heading toward them. In it was a man dressed in civilian clothing and Hassan thought he might be some Kuwaiti official coming from Saudi Arabia to help get his people through the checkpoints. As the vehicle approached them, the man looked straight at Hassan and began waving and shouting, "Go back! Go back!"

Hassan immediately began turning the car around, but Ali grabbed the steering wheel.

"No, go on. We'll pretend we didn't see him."

Hassan began to shake like a leaf. "Ali, there's something wrong—that guy was trying to warn us!"

Ali looked out the back window in time to see the man who had shouted at them point their car out to the intelligence officer, who then started walking toward them.

"Turn around and go back," the officer said when he reached their vehicle.

"No, no," Ali protested. Putting his hand on Hassan's shoulder, he added, "Look at this poor guy, he's worried to death. His wife and children went through in one of the cars ahead of us. We have to follow them!"

The officer sneered and said, "I said to get out of here!" Then he turned and headed back toward the end of the line.

Hassan looked like he was going to faint. Ali got out of the car and walked around to the driver's side. "Move over," he told his brother-in-law. Hassan hesitantly slid across the seat.

A few minutes later, the officer was back at the car window again.

"I thought I told you two to leave," he said, as he motioned two of the soldiers to the car. They had their guns at the ready. "Maybe we need to show you how to obey orders."

"But, you let his wife and children through," Ali tried again.

"Get your asses back to wherever you came from!" the officer roared.

Ali pulled out of line and headed back to Rumaithiya. All the way home he and Hassan tried to figure out the mystery of the man who had shouted at them. Was he giving them a warning, and if so, about what? Or was he somehow tied in with the Iraqi officer? They finally decided he must also have been an intelligence agent and that they were damned lucky they hadn't been arrested.

■ ■ ■

The first snowfall came to Lincoln in early November.

Jassim, Nadia, Zade, and Yacoub were so excited Dina could scarcely hold them down. They had never seen snow and ran in and out of the house constantly, reporting their impressions of the cold, wet stuff to their mother and Aunt Gina. A neighbor instigated a snowball fight and the Kuwaiti children shrieked with laughter, thoroughly enjoying an activity in which they had never participated. Watching the snowball fight was a bittersweet experience for Dina. She laughed at the children's excitement, but tears came to her eyes when she thought about Ali not being there to see it.

Dina had still heard nothing from or about him. All of the time spent on letters and phone calls trying to get information had been for naught.

She kept herself busy with the daycare (and watching news reports) and had begun to get out of the house more on shopping excursions. She was amazed at the outpouring of warmth and concern from employees in the stores where she shopped. When they found out she had been evacuated from Kuwait they never failed to ask if she'd heard anything from Ali the next time she was back in the store. A look of sympathy would come over their faces when Dina would tell them there had been no word.

■ ■ ■

One evening after Ali and Hassan returned from their aborted trip out of the country, Ali went to Abass's where he found Arafat, another neighbor he hadn't see for some time.

Arafat was an army captain, who, like Faud, had avoided being captured the day of the invasion. He was normally a cool, calm individual, but that night he was highly agitated.

Ali and the rest of the neighbors prodded him to tell them why he seemed so anxious, and after a few minutes, the story poured out of the man. Arafat had learned that morning that one of his friends, whose name was Mohammed, had been killed at an Iraqi checkpoint. "He had come to my house last night to talk and play cards with some other friends," Arafat said. "We were having a good time, laughing, joking, trying to get our minds off the occupation. We hadn't even thought about the stupid curfew, so when we broke up about 2:00 A.M., I told everyone they should stay overnight and go home in the morning. Everyone did, except Mohammed. He insisted on driving to his home in Shamiya. He said his parents would worry if he didn't come home."

Essa asked how he had been killed.

"He was shot in the head near an Iraqi checkpoint. His father thinks the Iraqis couldn't resist stealing his new car and Mohammed put up a fight. He was really proud of that car— it was his first new one."

Arafat told the men a passerby spotted the body early that morning, found Mohammed's wallet still in his pocket and contacted his parents. They, in turn, called Arafat.

"He was just lying there in the street, like a sack of garbage, not even a block from a checkpoint," Arafat said. "How can they do such a thing? How can they shoot someone over a car?"

No one could answer Arafat's questions.

■ ■ ■

On November 28, the U.N. Security Council passed its eleventh resolution. This one condemned Iraq for seeking to alter the demographic composition of Kuwait. The following day the final resolution was approved. This was the dictum authorizing the use of force to throw Iraq out of Kuwait, but it gave a "pause of goodwill" until January 15, 1991, for Iraq to leave the country on its own.

Passage of the twelfth resolution renewed the Kuwaiti people's faith that the world would rescue them, even if it meant that many nations would have to go to war to do so. However, they were extremely concerned about what Saddam would do to them and their country during the "pause of goodwill." The passage of each resolution had thus far brought increased terror, and they knew Iraq would not break the pattern.

Iraqi civilians and military personnel continued to strip Kuwait. In addition to cleaning out retail stores and homes, they emptied libraries of their books (Ali's facility, however, was not looted), museums of their artifacts, and private and government offices of their computers and other equipment.

The Iraqi government had even had designs on stealing all traces of Kuwaiti citizenship. That plan was foiled by a suspicious Kuwaiti who, seeing what was happening in the country at the beginning of the occupation, took the computer disks containing records of all Kuwaiti citizens and transported them to Saudi Arabia.

■ ■ ■

On December 2, the first organized protest against Saddam's terror took place in London. It was called the "National Stop the Atrocities March" and was sponsored by an organization that was urging the world to free Kuwait.

Hundreds of people marched from the Kuwaiti Embassy to Trafalgar Square. The demonstration was prompted by an International Television News interview with Saddam on November 11. The dictator was questioned about reported atrocities in Kuwait and his response was, "Have you seen these atrocities yourself? I have not heard of such acts being done."

Another of Saddam's lies. He knew what was happening in Kuwait. Many of his own men had given interviews to the media telling of the horrors they had seen before they deserted.

An Iraqi army captain called Kuwait "a butcher shop" after he deserted to Turkey in November. An Iraqi private who also walked out on the carnage and went to Turkey told an American news reporter that he had seen officers in his company rape several women and then order them shot. One of the officers was hung after he refused to carry out the execution order.

"Saddam is not only terrorizing the people of Kuwait," another Iraqi soldier said, "he is terrorizing his own soldiers."

■ ■ ■

While the protesters in England were marching and Saddam was denying, in Kuwait people were dying horrible deaths.

One was an attractive, high-spirited, thirty-two-year-old Kuwaiti woman named Asrar, who had a master's degree in computer science from Denver University. When Asrar first went back to Kuwait from the United States, she started a daycare center where she also taught English. Later she became interested in the plight of handicapped youngsters and began working with them.

After the invasion, Asrar began her association with the resistance by supplying movement leaders with information on Iraqi actions and strength, but she soon took on the additional task of smuggling money and medicine into Kuwait from Saudi Arabia. Then she figured out a way to use a satellite uplink unit and television camera to broadcast stories from inside Kuwait to the outside world, right under the noses of the enemy. She also used the same equipment to assist Kuwaitis and foreigners trapped in the country to contact friends and relatives in other countries by telephone to let them know they were safe.

The sixth of ten children, Asrar still lived with her father, Mohammed, who tried to get her to quit the dangerous business she was in, but she told him she couldn't just sit by and do nothing. "I have started a job," she said, "and I want to finish it. I want to be one of those who makes freedom possible again." Asrar's work to help her countrymen ended at a checkpoint in the Abdulla Al-Salim area in early November. The Iraqis had been running around in circles since August trying to find out who it was that was making the satellite broadcasts and they finally homed in on Asrar. But it had taken them nearly two months to capture the shrewd and cautious woman.

After her arrest, the Iraqis went to her home and arrested her father, brother, and a nephew and took them to the same interrogation center where they had taken her. They brought Asrar into the room with her family and an officer put a pistol to her father's head and told her he would kill the old man if she didn't tell him what he wanted to know. Asrar stood in silence, ignoring the officer, until he, in a rage, ordered two of his men to beat her in front of her family. She was pummeled by the guards until she fell, unconscious, into a bloody heap and was dragged away. That was the last time her family saw her alive.

The men were held in that jail for several weeks, and while they were there they knew she was still alive, even though they never saw her. A Kuwaiti prisoner who had been pressed into service as a cook kept them informed about her and told them she had become the jail's "cheerleader," encouraging other prisoners to resist the Iraqi questioning. "She has told them nothing," the cook said. "She just spits in their faces. Asrar is tougher than two men."

After they were transferred to another jail, news of her became spotty. Her father, brother, and nephew were held a total of fifty-eight days before they were released on January 14.

Immediately upon his release, Mohammed went to the first jail and learned that his daughter was still alive. He went home and gathered up all the jewelry, money, and other valuables he could find and took them to the jail, where he readily found an officer willing to accept the bribe. The Iraqi promised that Asrar would be "brought home shortly."

When the old man returned home, he found blood outside his house. Somehow he knew that it was his daughter's. A neighbor was waiting to tell him that, as soon as he had left, the Iraqis had indeed brought Asrar home—dead. "I believe they were watching for you to leave," the neighbor told Mohammed.

Asrar's brothers had taken her body away to a morgue in hopes of easing their father's pain, but he insisted on being taken to see her. When he arrived at the morgue he knew why his sons had not wanted him to see their sister's body. It was riddled with bullet holes and her head had been split in two with an ax.

As Mohammed sat in pained silence beside the body, he noticed the pockets of Asrar's dress were bulging. He reached into one and pulled out a packet of prayers, and in the other he found a pair of broken eyeglasses. This was all he had left of this martyr...this brave and vivacious woman he had called daughter.

■ ■ ■

One night in early December, Ali's Palestinian friend Mike, came by the compound to tell Ali he was strongly considering leaving Kuwait.

"I can't take it anymore," Mike said. "I'm sick of living scared every day, and I miss May."

Ali could understand how Mike felt and would have loved to be able to go with him, but he couldn't bring himself to try another escape attempt. As a Palestinian, Mike wouldn't be stopped—Ali probably would be.

Ali hated to see his friend leave because he knew if Mike left, chances were he would not be allowed back into the country after it was liberated. Ali felt the punishment for collaborating Palestinians would be severe, and Mike and other innocent Palestinians like him, would probably be caught up in the mania for revenge.

"You know, if you leave, you'll probably not be allowed to come back," Ali said.

"I know, Ali, but I'm afraid I'll go insane if I stay."

A week later, Mike was on his way to the States. With him went a letter Ali had written to Dina.

■ ■ ■

Early in December, Ali's family received good news. Abdul-Samad had been found alive in a prison camp near Baghdad.

Miriam had made numerous attempts to find information about her son, but had run into nothing but dead ends in her search. She had then contacted an Iraqi acquaintance and asked him to look for Abdul-Samad in Iraq. The Iraqi had found him.

Miriam was ecstatic with the news and immediately began haranguing Iraqi officials in Kuwait for permission to travel to Al-Bakoba to visit her son. It took several days to obtain the authorization, but it finally came through and she and another son, Kareem, found themselves on a bus headed for Baghdad.

They were not allowed to go to the prison camp. Instead the prisoners were brought to a building several miles from the camp for the visit. The Iraqis did not want the families seeing the abhorrent prison conditions. To make them look more presentable, the prisoners were issued blue coveralls to replace the filthy, worn-out *distashas* they had been given at Al-Mawsel.

When Abdul-Samad walked into the building, he immediately saw his mother and brother. His mother's dear, chubby face looked twenty years older.

Miriam rushed to her son and showered him with kisses. Sobbing, she asked, "Did they hurt you? Have you been tortured? You are so thin. Do they not feed you?"

"I am fine, mother," Abdul-Samad answered. "I have been treated well. The camp is a good place." He hated to lie to her, but he did not want her to know the true conditions. And, in fact, he had not been, and never was, physically tortured. There were many in the camps who were, but Abdul-Samad was spared that suffering.

Glancing around, Abdul-Samad asked, "Where is my father?"

"He is not feeling well enough to travel," Kareem answered.

"It's not serious, is it?"

"No. Just the illness of old age."

Abdul-Samad wanted to question further about his father's health, but Miriam turned his attention toward a large basket she had brought. In it were cooked chickens, fresh fruit, and canned goods. She also had brought blankets and pillows. Abdul-Samad had difficulty trying to keep from cramming all the food into his mouth at once. He forced himself to accept only a small portion of chicken and an apple to eat in front of his mother. He did not want her to know he was nearly starving.

The Iraqis allowed the prisoners an hour with their families. When his mother and brother left, they promised they would be back the next week with more food, Abdul-Samad's wife and children, and two other brothers, Husain and Hameed. Abdul-Samad felt uneasy when his father wasn't mentioned, but he knew that if there was something wrong, no one would tell him the truth anyway. They wouldn't want him to worry.

The week passed slowly for Abdul-Samad, and then, on visitation day he discovered that his name was not on the list of those who would be permitted to see their families. He was devastated and immediately began to look for someone who could help him go to the visitor center.

At the center that morning, Abdul-Samad's wife was in hysterics. She was sure something terrible had happened to her husband. A friend of Abdul-Samad's assured her that her husband was fine and was working on a way to get to the center, but she continued sobbing until one o'clock in the afternoon, when Abdul-Samad finally walked through the door.

The visits continued weekly until the air war began. By then the prisoners whose families visited them were well-stocked with food, blankets, money, and cigarettes. They were able to share their "wealth" with the other prisoners at Al-Bakoba.

■ ■ ■

Essa's family received another blow in December when another young member died, another eighteen-year-old cousin whose name was Jafer.

Jafer had had the bad luck in late October to come home from a friend's house just as Iraqi intelligence agents were leaving his house after they had conducted a routine search for guns. They hadn't found so much as a slingshot, but when they saw the tall, husky youth, they arrested him because "he looked suspicious."

Jafer was taken to the police station where he was interrogated for several days and then he was taken back home where he was shot twice in the head—once under the chin and again near the temple. He was still alive, but in a coma when his family found him, so they took him to a hospital where his aunt, who was a doctor, nursed him for six weeks. At the end of the six weeks he had gained consciousness and strength and his family took him home.

However, the youth took an unexpected turn for the worse and died that day, about a week after he returned home.

The following photo section is a collection of pictures taken in Kuwait by Ali and others during the Iraqi occupation. There are no captions because identification has been difficult to acquire. The centerfold photos were retrieved from a videotape of a news interview conducted on an Omaha, Nebraska television station.

The following pages are oil fields that were targets of Iraq.

Dina and family upon her return to the States.

Dina and family as they are interviewed in the States about the plight of Kuwait and her family still there.

Concern for her family in Kuwait is apparent on Dina's face.

The family after being reunited in the States.

Photos of Ali have been excluded for security reasons.

Death and destruction was evident in cities, on highways, and in almost every facet of Kuwaiti life.

Our Achievements in Numbers

After the successful conclusion to the Gulf War, attention quickly focused on the task of rebuilding war torn Kuwait, and the vicious destruction wrought on the oil fields by the Iraqi aggressors.

As early as November 1990 an international team from KOC, the fire fighters and Bechtel began planning and preparations to reverse the incredible damage. In March 1991 the first four fire fighting companies were mobilised to Kuwait. The first oil well was controlled on 20 March 1991, less than three weeks after liberation. Over the next seven months, with the support of a multitude of contractors and service companies, the following accomplishments were achieved:

- A total of 727 burning and gushing oil wells were extinguished and controlled.

- An average of nearly three wells per day was achieved, with a peak rate of 13 wells per day. The record number of wells controlled in one week was 52.

- Fire fighting teams were mobilised from Kuwait, USA, Canada, Iran, China, Hungary, France, Romania, Britain and Russia; building to a peak of 27 teams by October 1991.

- A total of 361 water lagoons (the size of small lakes) were prepared to support fire fighting operations.

- Water supply rose to 25 million gallons of water per day, with a total of 1.5 billion gallons of water being used. This represents enough water to fill a lake two metres deep, one kilometre wide and three-and-a-half kilometres long (or enough water to cover the entire surface area of Kuwait by some 12mm).

- To supply this water, over 400 kilometres of flowlines were laid, and a total of 280 kilometres of special access roads to oil wells were constructed.

- Gatch supplied for roads and hardstands totalled 1.8 million cubic metres, enough to build a pyramid 100 metres wide, or 100 metres deep towering 540 metres high.

Rebuilding efforts in Kuwait following the war. Flyer above shown in English; at right in Kuwaiti native language.

منجزاتنا بالأرقام

بعد إنتهاء حرب الخليج وتحرير الكويت تركز الإهتمام على عملية إعادة التعمير وإزالة آثار الدمار والخراب الذي ألحقه المعتدون العراقيون بآبار النفط.

وكانت عملية مكافحة الحرائق قد بدأت في وقت مبكر فمنذ نوفمبر ٩٠ بدأ فريق دولي تابع لشركة "نفط الكويت" و "بكتل" وهو فريق متخصص في إطفاء حرائق النفط، في التخطيط والإعداد لمعالجة هذا الدمار المروع، وتم بالفعل في مارس ١٩٩١ تجنيد أربع شركات إطفاء للعمل في الكويت وأمكن السيطرة على أول بئر في ٢٠ مارس ١٩٩١، قبل مرور ثلاثة أسابيع على تحرير الكويت. وخلال الشهر السبعة التالية، وبمساعدة عدد كبير من شركات المقاولات والخدمات المختلفة، تم إنجاز الآتي:

- تم السيطرة على ٧٢٧ بئراً مشتعلة ونازفة.
- أمكن السيطرة على ثلاثة آبار في المتوسط يومياً، وكان أكبر عدد من الآبار التي تم السيطرة عليها في يوم واحد هو١٣بئر ومن محاسن الصدف إنها كانت أثناء زيارة سمو ولي العهد للفريق الكويتي وبلغ أكبر عدد قياسي للآبار التي أمكن السيطرة عليها في أسبوع واحد ٥٢ بئراً.
- تم إستخدام فرق إطفاء من كل من الكويت والولايات المتحدة وكندا وإيران والصين وهنغاريا وفرنسا ورومانيا وبريطانيا وروسيا، وبلغ عدد هذه الفرق ٢٧ فرقة إطفاء في اكتوبر ١٩٩١.
- تم أنشاء ٣٦١ بحيرة صناعية صغيرة لإستخدامها في أعمال إطفاء حرائق آبار النفط الكويتية.
- زاد الإمداد بالمياه على ٢٥ مليون غالون من الماء يومياً، وبلغ إجمالي كمية المياه المستخدمة ١/٢ ١ مليار غالون ، وهذه الكمية الهائلة تكفي لملء بحيرة كبيرة عمقها متران وعرضها كيلومتر واحد وطولها ثلاثة كيلومترات ونصف الكيلومتر. (وهي كمية كافية لتغطية مساحة دولة الكويت كلها بإرتفاع ١٢ مم).
- لتوفير هذه المياه تم مد شبكة أنابيب للمياه المتدفقة بلغ طولها ٤٠٠ كيلومترا، وقد جرى إنشاء شبكة طرق الوصول إلى الآبار النفطية يبلغ طولها ٢٨٠ كيلو متر.
- بلغت كمية الغاتش المستخدمة في شق الطرق وإقامة المنصات حوالي ١.٨ مليون متر مكعب، هذه المواد تكفي لإقامة هرم عرض قاعدته ١٠٠ متر وإرتفاعه ٥٤٠ مترا.

CHAPTER 12

To this day, Ali's oldest brother, Saleh, doesn't know why he is still alive. He gives equal credit to both God and his wife, Zarah.

The Iraqis came to his apartment in the town of Abdulla Al-Salim one sunny, but chilly day in December. Within a few short minutes, he believed he had seen his last sunrise.

Saleh had received a phone call from a neighbor that morning, warning that the Iraqis were conducting house-to-house searches in the neighborhood. He immediately instructed Zarah and their two daughters—Ahoud, sixteen and Altaf, fourteen—to put on their black capes and full face and head coverings, hoping to discourage any thoughts of rape the soldiers might have. Saleh then raced around the apartment, stripping the walls and table tops of flags, photographs, magazines—anything he was afraid the Iraqis might take offense over.

Soon came the dreaded knock. Saleh went to the door, opened it, and there stood two regular army officers and six soldiers. *Thank God*, Saleh thought, *they're not secret service or intelligence agents.* "Come in," Saleh invited, in the most gracious tone of voice he could muster in his fright, "you are welcome."

One of the officers scowled at him, pointed at the two cars parked in front of the apartment, and asked, "Are those your vehicles?"

"Yes," Saleh answered. "One is mine and the other is my wife's. You are welcome to both of them."

The officer ignored Saleh's offer and said, "Go look in the back seat of that car," he said, pointing at Zarah's vehicle.

Saleh obediently walked to the car. As he approached the back door he noticed it was unlocked. The electric lock had quit functioning several weeks ago and had to be operated manually. Saleh guessed that Zarah had forgotten to lock the door the last time she had used the car. "The door is unlocked," Saleh said to the officer.

"Just open it!" the officer commanded.

Saleh opened the door and peered into the back seat. There on the floor was a handful of spent shell casings. *Oh, my God*, he thought. *I'm a dead man.*

One of the soldiers grabbed Saleh, a tall, strong man, by the back of his distasha and yanked him away from the car as if he were a small child.

Breaking out in a cold sweat, Saleh said, "I swear to God I don't know where those came from...someone must have—"

The officer cut Saleh's words off. "Don't swear!" he commanded.

"But sir," Saleh continued. "Honest to God—"

"I told you not to swear!" the officer shrieked. "Tell me about your involvement with the resistance."

Saleh was now sweating profusely, despite the cool air.

"I swear to—" Saleh caught himself this time and started again. "I do not belong to the resistance, sir. That is my wife's car, and I do not know how those shell casings got in there."

"Go back inside and tell your women to cover up," the officer instructed. "We will give you five minutes, and then we're searching the apartment."

Saleh shakily walked to the front door, opened it, and found Zarah standing in the foyer. She had not heard the words spoken outside, but she knew when she saw her husband's face that a serious situation had developed.

Saleh stepped into the foyer, shut the door, walked over to the sofa, and sank down on it in a heap. He was shaking like a leaf and there were tears in his eyes. "They found shell casings in your car."

"Oh, my God," Zarah cried. "Where did they come from?"

"I don't know. You forgot to lock the car yesterday, and somebody must have thrown them in there, perhaps even the soldiers who are out there now." He stood up and walked over to his wife.

"Zarah," he said, putting his arms around her, "They are coming in for a search. They won't find anything, but they'll be taking me away with them when they leave."

"No!" Zarah screamed. "No! I won't let them!"

"There's nothing anyone can do about it. When I leave, I want you to remember one thing...I'll be in God's hands. Don't come looking for me.... If God wants me to survive this, He'll find a way."

Zarah was so angry and frightened, she could have chewed a tank in two. "I will not let them take you!" she shouted. She turned towards the door, and as Saleh reached to grab her, the Iraqis started pounding on it. Zarah yanked it open and faced the two officers.

"What do you want?" she demanded. "You can search my house if you want, but you will find nothing. We are not resistance!"

Saleh groaned. *What the hell's the matter with this woman? She's going to make them even more angry!*

The officer facing Zarah took a step backwards, a look of surprise on his face. A plump, stubborn woman, the irate Zarah looked as if she were well capable of inflicting some heavy-duty damage on anyone who crossed her.

"Uhh…uhh…." he stuttered as he backed down the steps. "We've decided not to search your house…we've decided the shell casings are not yours."

"You're damned right, they're not ours!" Zarah screeched. "I told you we are not resistance!"

"We will be going now," the other officer stammered as he turned around and hurried from the doorstep.

After the Iraqis left, Saleh went back out to Zarah's car. The shell casings were gone.

■ ■ ■

As was expected, the situation became even more desperate in Kuwait after the November 29 U.N. resolution was passed.

Saddam had steadily increased the number of troops in Kuwait and after the final resolution, he sent in more, moving the total to nearly 400,000 in December.

Multistory buildings were confiscated for use by anti-aircraft gun crews. Ali and his family worried that their house, because it was a corner, multilevel building located near a main thoroughfare, would be confiscated. Two houses in the neighborhood were taken over. In addition to putting the big guns on their roofs, all of the windows on the upper floors were bricked up, leaving only holes large enough for use by snipers.

More checkpoints were erected. Now there was one less than fifty yards from the compound. Soldiers moved into the school Jassim had attended, which was located across the street in a different direction from Abass's house. Ali watched as every desk, book, blackboard, and eraser was hauled out and loaded onto trucks bound for Iraq. He would discover later that nearly all of the schools in Rumaithiya had been cleaned out in a similar manner.

Food became even harder to find. Flea markets began closing as hoarded supplies dwindled and inflation hit at a rate of nearly 200 percent. When people found food, they couldn't afford to buy it.

But, as bad as the food situation was in Kuwait, it was even worse in Iraq. Adel, one of Ali's ex-police friends, was still making regular trips to that country. He said people in outlying areas were resorting to picking the grain out of sheep and cattle droppings to grind for flour. In the cities, Iraqis stood in line for hours for a few pieces of bread. "Saddam is making his people suffer even more than we are suffering," Adel assured his friends.

■ ■ ■

One cold December night, as the men gathered around a fire they had built in Abass's yard, Khalid joined them. He excitedly began telling them about an incident that had occurred the day before in a town south of Rumaithiya, Sabah Al-Salim.

An Iraqi soldier had been executed and hung on a street post by his superior officer after the soldier had broken into a house in that town and raped a woman. Rape had been one of the crimes that had increased greatly since the final resolution had been passed by the United Nations.

Khalid told the men that the soldier was still hanging from the post, with a sign tacked to his body warning other Iraqi soldiers of the fate that was in store for them if they were caught raping or looting.

The soldier had been caught when a neighbor of the woman went to Iraqi headquarters to report that the woman's house had been broken into. The officer went to the house with a contingent of men and found eight soldiers taking turns with the woman. The other seven escaped.

This was the first time Ali had heard of any action being taken against an Iraqi rapist, so he wasn't too willing to believe Khalid's story. He grinned at his neighbor, tapped his forehead, and said, "The bats in your belfry are really busy to-night! What makes you think that's a true story?"

"I saw the body," Khalid shrugged.

Ali was still reluctant to believe, but Adel backed up the story and insisted on taking Ali to the spot where, he said, the soldier still hung. Ali reluctantly got into Adel's car and rode to Sabah Al-Salim with him. Sure enough, there hung the Iraqi. The rapist had been shot in the head and his brain was hanging out one side. Two days of hanging in the sun had not helped preserve the corpse. Ali thought he was going to lose his supper when he saw the body. Several soldiers were guarding it, warning people not to take pictures. Adel parked the car and got out, motioning Ali to follow him.

"Look at the son of a dog," Adel said in a loud voice. "He got what he deserved."

Ali could have tied his friend's tongue in a knot. "Shut your mouth," he hissed. "The soldiers will hear you!" He started pushing Adel back toward the car. "Let's get the hell out of here!"

On the way back to Rumaithiya, the ghoulish sight would not leave Ali's mind. He couldn't believe the Iraqis had doled out such harsh punishment to one of their own over the rape of a Kuwaiti woman.

A few days later, he learned from Arafat that the other seven Iraqi soldiers involved in the incident had been arrested. Arafat said that he had watched as they were executed by a firing squad.

"After the execution," Arafat said, "I heard on an Iraqi radio station that those men were criminals wanted in Iraq even before the invasion."

So that was the explanation, Ali thought. The Iraqi officer had executed the men because they were wanted for crimes in Iraq, then tried to make the Kuwaitis believe it was for the rape of a Kuwaiti woman.

■ ■ ■

As the Kuwaitis anxiously waited to see if Saddam would pull his troops out of Kuwait during the "pause of goodwill," it was easy to imagine there were hopeful signs. Everyone wanted so badly for the occupation to end.

One day in the middle of December, Ali received an excited phone call from a friend in Ardiya, a town just south of Kuwait City.

"Ali," the friend shouted, "they're pulling out!"

"Who's pulling out?" Ali knew what his friend was talking about, but the news was so sweet he wanted to hear the announcement one more time.

"The Iraqis are pulling out!" the friend repeated. "They're moving their equipment out of Ardiya!"

His friend's happiness took a hold on Ali. He laughed and said, "This is the best news ever...but are you sure?"

"It really looks like they're leaving...there are trucks all over the streets."

Ali hung up the phone and went to tell his family the good news. It was nice to see the smiles on their faces after he finished telling them his friend's story, but within hours they found out the report was not true.

It was true that the Iraqis were moving men and equipment in several suburbs surrounding Kuwait City, including Ardiya, but only to reposition them in other areas. News reports on both Voice of America and BBC Radio indicated no withdrawal was underway.

■ ■ ■

Throughout the occupation Saddam tried hard to convince his own people, and the whole world, that the Kuwaitis were happy with their new dictator.

One night Ali was watching an Iraqi television station and saw a group of about a hundred people gathered in an area near the ministries complex in Kuwait City. A huge picture of Saddam had been erected on one of the buildings. The people were laughing and cheering, shouting, "Saddam, Saddam, long live our leader" and other slogans.

Ali could scarcely believe his eyes. It galled him to think any Kuwaiti would cheer Saddam. The next day, to his relief, he found out the demonstrators were not Kuwaitis. Iraqis, made up to look like Kuwaitis, had been bused into the country from Basra to put on the show in front of Iraqi cameras.

Ali scolded himself for not having recognized that the demonstrators looked too dirty and disheveled to have been Kuwaitis. Even though people in both countries wore the same type of clothes, you could always tell a Kuwaiti from an Iraqi. A Kuwaiti was always neat, and above all, clean.

■ ■ ■

Even though Ali knew there was even more danger in leaving the compound after the November 28 U.N. resolution was passed, he couldn't help himself. Sitting around, doing the same thing every day, drove him crazy.

One afternoon he talked Essa and Abass into driving to Kuwait City with him to see the damage they had been hearing about.

They soon saw the Iraqis had done a good job of devastating the city. Many buildings had been bombed and burned out. Those that hadn't been destroyed had been looted. The Al-Muthana Shopping Center was only a shell, the exquisite boutiques empty of their expensive wares. The gold shops had been stripped, as had the car dealerships the men saw along the way.

When they passed the shopping center, they were reminded of a story another friend, Abdulla, had told one night.

Abdulla had been driving by the shopping center one morning shortly after the invasion and had noticed a large group of Iraqi men, women, and children gathered there. Standing at the center's entry door was a soldier with a gun and a whistle. At precisely 10:00 A.M., the time the stores usually opened for business, the soldier stepped away from the doorway, blew his whistle, and the group roared into the center on a looting spree.

Abdulla had parked his car and gone in, too, just to see what was happening inside. The Iraqis were dragging items out of every store in the center, except one. In front of it, which was stocked with expensive watches, was another soldier with a gun. He wouldn't let anyone inside, saying, "This shop is reserved for my commanding officer."

After a couple of hours of madness, the soldier blew his whistle again and people started leaving the stores. Those who didn't head for the main door were chased out by soldiers with nightsticks. "It was a mess," Abdulla had told the men. "The looters fought among themselves like animals over every piece of merchandise in the center."

Ali, Essa, and Abass were glad they hadn't seen the looters stripping and vandalizing the stores. It was depressing enough just to see the barren and battered stores. They decided to cut their tour short and go back to Rumaithiya. Seeing their beautiful capital city in ruins made them sick to their stomachs.

As they drove towards home along the beach road, Arabian Gulf Street, they began to notice the buildings facing the gulf had been turned into fortresses. There were anti-aircraft guns on the roofs and soldiers with machine guns could be seen in the windows of the upper stories. The Iraqis were obviously preparing for an allied sea invasion.

Slow, happy grins lit their faces. They hoped this was a sign that a rescue effort was getting nearer.

The next day, while Ali was out in the yard, Yusuf, another neighbor, told Ali that he had gone to his chalet in southern Kuwait the day before and found two Iraqi soldiers in it. Yusuf said he asked the soldiers why they were there and the soldiers said they were "hiding out" until the allied invasion was over. They said they had seen American ships in the gulf through their binoculars, and believed an invasion was imminent.

"They told me I could have anything of mine in the chalet, except the radio and white clothing," Yusuf told Ali. "They said they wanted the clothes to make surrender flags. They called Saddam a 'crazy bastard' and said they weren't going to die for him!"

Ali grinned again.

However, a few days later, a Voice of America news report wiped away his smile. In the report, the deputy commander of U.S. forces in the gulf area was quoted as saying that his troops would not be ready to mount an offensive against Iraq by the January 15 deadline.

■ ■ ■

The week of December 10 found only a few foreign embassies operating in Kuwait. Little by little, the staffs had filtered out of the country. U.S. Ambassador Nathaniel Howell and four other U.S. diplomats were among the last to leave, departing Kuwait on December 13.

A few foreigners trapped when Iraq closed its borders had been allowed to leave, but no Americans were released until December 10. The number of human shields was declining, but Saddam still had eighty-eight people tucked away to deter an allied bombing raid on Iraq.

Latif Jassim, Iraq's information minister, announced to the world that it would only be "wishful thinking" by any nation to imagine that Iraq would ever withdraw from Kuwait. "We will not compromise," Jassim said, "nor will we give an inch in Kuwait."

■ ■ ■

Shortly before Christmas, Dina learned Ali and his family were still alive. Mike had made it to the United States with Ali's letter to her intact.

She was ecstatic. All of them were still alive and well, and Ali was still promising to join her in America.

That letter was the best Christmas present she had ever received. As she read and reread it, she thought of another valued present she had been blessed with. It had come the first Christmas she spent in Kuwait.

Ali had known the holiday would be a difficult time for her, so he had planned several surprises in hopes of easing her through it.

Unbeknownst to Dina, he had packed the small artificial tree and decorations they had used in their Papillion apartment to bring with them. It went up in their living room the day before Christmas. Dina was so grateful she cried with joy while she decorated it.

Then, on Christmas morning, he'd made arrangements for her to telephone her parents and Donna. Hearing the familiar voices, Dina cried again.

At dinner time everyone in the house gathered in Bedreah's dining room. There was the biggest surprise of all. Her mother-in-law served a stuffed turkey that Ali had secretly bought. Dina cried again.

Later in the day, Ali's sisters came with gifts for her and the children. More tears.

That Christmas had brought Dina the gift of acceptance from Ali's family. It had been her most precious gift until Ali's letter arrived.

■ ■ ■

One night while Ali was on the balcony he thought he heard a car start, but then he decided it was his imagination. The next morning he found out it had not been his imagination. Someone had stolen Mohammed's car.

Nassima, Mohammed, and their children had moved into the family compound that week. Mohammed usually parked his car at the curb outside the compound fence, but when Ali went out that morning to visit with Abass, he noticed the car wasn't where it usually was.

"Mohammed's car is gone," Ali said to his friend. "I wonder where he went so early this morning."

"It was parked where it usually is at midnight," Abass said.

Ali decided he better go back into the house and see if Mohammed was there. He was. He woke up his brother-in-law and told him his car was missing.

"I should have known better than to park it outside the fence," Mohammed groused after he had checked out Ali's report. "I should have known the Iraqis would steal it."

"You have to report that it was stolen," Ali told him.

Mohammed laughed. "Why? What the hell good would that do?"

"Think," Ali said. "What if it was a foreign collaborator who took it, and then he goes out and commits a crime with it. The Iraqis would trace it back to you and arrest you."

Mohammed decided his brother-in-law had a point. He hadn't thought about the theft from that angle. He asked Ali to drive him to the Rumaithiya Police Station.

The officer who took down the information was very cool and brusque, but Mohammed tried to be polite. When the Iraqi asked him who he suspected of the theft, Mohammed wanted very badly to say, "You bastards!" but he kept his composure.

"I don't know," he answered, "possibly one of the foreigners who has been hiding in the country."

The officer told Mohammed to check back at the station in another three days to see if the car had been found, something Mohammed never bothered to do. He knew the vehicle was gone for good.

■ ■ ■

In addition to providing the fighting resistance with information on the movements of Iraqi troops and equipment, Ali also was assisting the group by maintaining his relationship with the forger in Bayan who had manufactured the false Kuwaiti papers for Dina. He had forged driver's licenses and car registrations for his family and had assisted the resistance in obtaining forged documents for numerous other Kuwaiti families.

One night he returned from Bayan with a pocket in his distasha stuffed full of forged papers to find Abass, Essa, and Adel still sitting on the benches outside Abass's fence. It surprised him because it was nearly 11:30. The men usually broke up their evening visits early enough to be back in their homes by curfew time.

Ali took a seat on one of the benches and then asked, "What's going on?"

"Nothing," Essa answered. "We just didn't feel like going inside tonight…where have you been so late?"

"Oh, nowhere in particular," Ali answered. Farouk was the only one in the neighborhood who knew Ali was making regular trips to the forger. He didn't want to get his close friends involved in a risky business.

The men exchanged small talk for a few minutes, and Ali forgot all about the dangerous papers in his pocket. Suddenly an Iraqi truck with a dozen machine-gun toting soldiers in the back of it pulled up in front of them. Just as suddenly, Ali remembered the papers.

He was sitting sideways, with one foot on the bench and one on the ground. The papers were in the pocket hanging over the front of the bench, not ten feet from where the Iraqis were. He didn't move a muscle. In fact, no one on the benches so much as twitched. They knew if they stood up and ran they would be shot first and questioned later.

"OK," the officer who was driving said. "One by one, each of you walk over here."

None of the men moved. Ali felt like his whole body was dead already, but he smiled and tried to look as nonchalant as he could.

"Now," ordered the Iraqi. "You," he pointed at Abass.

Abass slowly got to his feet and walked to the officer.

The Iraqi surveyed Abass up and down and then asked, "What are you men doing?"

"Just visiting, smoking, drinking tea," Abass answered.

"Tell me what time it is," the officer demanded.

"Just after 11:30," Abass said after consulting his watch.

"Don't you know there's an 11 o'clock curfew?"

"No," said Abass, innocently.

"Don't you watch television?"

"Yes, but I've never heard such an announcement on television." Kuwaitis were only supposed to watch the Iraqi TV stations, and Abass knew for a fact that the curfew had never been announced on an Iraqi station. It was a big joke all around the country.

While Abass was talking to the officer, Ali prayed, *Please, Allah, make it easy—just one shot in the head. Let it all be over with one shot in the head!*

Abass began backing away from the truck. Ali heard him ask the officer if he would like some tea.

The officer declined Abass's offer and then shouted at the four Kuwaitis. "You guys have to knock this off! There is a curfew and the next time I drive by here none of you better be here!"

The truck pulled away from the curb.

Adel and Essa stood up and left immediately.

"Ali," Abass said, "we better do as they say."

Ali remained seated.

"Come on, Ali," Abass said. "Go home."

Ali tried to stand up, but fell to the ground. His legs had no strength. In a fog, he started crawling towards his house. Then he heard laughter behind him.

"What the hell's the matter with you, you chickenshit?" Abass roared with laughter.

Ali paused, willed himself to stand up, and then said, "If you had known that I have a pocket full of forged papers, you would have been dead from fear by now." That said, Ali stalked across the street and disappeared behind his fence.

Abass turned and walked towards his front door, shaking his head in disbelief. He'd had no idea his friend was helping the resistance fighters so extensively.

CHAPTER 13

As the January 15 deadline neared, Saddam seemed even more determined that he would not withdraw his troops from Kuwait. On January 9, U.S. Secretary of State James Baker met with Iraqi Foreign Minister Tariq Aziz in Geneva, Switzerland, in a last-ditch attempt to talk the Iraqis out of Kuwait. The meeting was a failure. It was certain that Iraq would not leave Kuwait without a fight.

January 15 came and went without U.N. action. On January 16, the United Nations issued a final appeal for a peaceful withdrawal. By this time 400,000 U.S. troops and 260,000 allied troops aligned against the estimated 545,000 soldiers Saddam had dispersed to Kuwait and southern Iraq, but once again, he ignored the U.N.

Then, on January 17, at 12:50 A.M. gulf time, hundreds of American, British, French, Saudi Arabian, and Kuwaiti planes left Saudi air bases to demonstrate to the dictator what the penalty was to be for ignoring the world's pleas to withdraw. In all, forces from twenty-eight nations, including Arab League members, stood together as the drive to move Iraqi troops out of Kuwait began.

Living the Nightmare

Leading the allies in the attack on Iraqi forces in both Iraq and Kuwait, the United States launched 150 Navy Tomahawk Cruise Missiles from ships stationed in the Arabian Gulf. On the heels of the missiles came the U.S. Air Force's F-4G Wild Weasles, F-111 strike fighters, F-117A Stealth bombers, B-52 bombers and F-15 Eagle fighter planes, along with the U.S. Navy's F-14 Tomcats, the U.S. Army's Apache attack helicopters, British Tornadoes, French Jaguars, Saudi F-15s, and the Kuwaiti Skyhawks that had sneaked away from the air base. In the all-out attack, Coalition forces went after Iraq's radar, command centers, missiles sites, air bases, and suspected nuclear and chemical warfare production facilities. Specific orders were given to the pilots to avoid civilian casualties as much as possible. Since Saddam had put much of his military machine inside heavily populated areas, this was an extremely difficult task for the pilots.

In addition to bombing military sites in and around Baghdad, in western Iraq, and at various locations in Kuwait, Strategic Air Command (SAC) B-52 bombers carpet bombed Saddam's elite Republican Guard units near the Kuwaiti border in southern Iraq.

By the third week of the campaign, the United States and its allies had declared air superiority, with few losses for the allies. Some 3,000 missions were being flow daily, over 30 Iraqi planes had been shot down, and over 100 enemy planes had fled to Iran where Saddam's former enemy, turned ally, now suddenly turned neutral, interned them.

■ ■ ■

Nassima and her family had moved into Dina and Ali's quarters when they came to the compound to live, and since Ali wouldn't have to be alone with the ghosts in his apartment anymore, he had taken to sleeping in his own room again. Now, in the early morning hours of January 17, he felt himself being yanked out of his warm, comfortable bed.

"What...What?" he mumbled, flailing his arms at the intruder.

"Get up, Ali! We have to go downstairs!" It was Mohammed.

Ali scowled up at him. "What are you talking about?"

"The war...it has begun! Listen to the bombing and gunfire. Hurry! We have to go downstairs where we will be safer."

"Oh, calm down," Ali said gruffly. "You know this happens practically every damned night! It's the resistance. Go back to bed."

"No," Mohammed insisted. "This is different. We have the radio on. This is the war!"

Ali's feet were on the floor in one leap. "You heard it on the radio? Which radio? Free radio or Iraqi radio?"

"BBC," Mohammed grinned. "Now come on, everyone else is downstairs."

Ali followed his brother-in-law to the basement where he looked into the face of the other family members, including Saleh and his family, who had moved into the compound a few days earlier. Fear. Disbelief. Relief. Joy. All these emotions seemed to blend into one expression on all of their faces.

"Smile!" Ali shouted excitedly. "Be happy! This is the liberation! We are being freed! Hassan...you and I will see our wives and children soon!"

The men danced around the room with Ali and Hassan, but the mothers sat tensely with their children huddled around them. The sounds of the bombs and anti-aircraft fire were constant and deafening. The house shook from the violence of the explosions.

God had finally answered their prayers. The world had come to their rescue. Now all Kuwaitis prayed that they would survive the rescue process.

■ ■ ■

Living the Nightmare

At 5:45 P.M. on January 16, Dina and Gina were sending the last of the daycare children out the door when they heard the voices of two CNN television reporters giving a running commentary on explosions they were hearing in Baghdad.

The report hit Dina like a hammer. *Had the long-awaited— and feared—day come? Had the allies begun their push to free Kuwait?*

She walked to the sofa on rubbery legs and sank down on it in a daze. Tears filled her eyes, obscuring her view of the television screen. The reporters seemed unsure at first if the distant explosions they were hearing were the sounds of bombs, but a while later they announced that a large portion of the city was blacked out and the explosions were much louder. As Dina cringed on the sofa, the noise of the explosions pounded out of the television. It felt as if they were hitting her in the stomach. Then one of the reporters said that bombs were now falling in the center of the city and the sound of anti-aircraft fire could be heard.

Dina could only wonder if the scene being described in Baghdad was the same as what was happening in Kuwait. She'd had much time to think about how Kuwait was going to be rescued. She did not want to see an all-out war, fearing that if that happened, everyone in Kuwait would be killed. She'd hoped against hope that someone would say some magical word that would catch Saddam's ear and he would agree to withdraw, peacefully.

That had not happened. Now the allies had begun the arduous task of throwing Saddam out. She was both excited and depressed. After a few bombs were dropped, would the dictator give up? Would a bomb hit his bunker? How many military and civilian lives would this cost? Would Ali and his family be among those who would die?

Gina's voice brought her out of the fog. "It's Masuma," her sister said, handing her the phone.

Since she'd arrived in the States, Dina had spoken several times with Ali's sister at her vacation spot in England. Now

Masuma was calling to see if Dina had heard more news than she was hearing in London. After comparing notes, both agreed neither knew more than the other.

■ ■ ■

The prisoners at the Al-Bakoba prison camp were also having trouble sleeping the night the air war began. Disappointment that the allies hadn't begun their rescue effort on the appointed day dominated their thoughts and made them restless. They had learned during visits from relatives, and through broadcasts on radios they had managed to obtain and hide from the Iraqis, that January 15 had been set as the deadline for Iraq to withdraw. That date had come and gone without a whisper of action. The prisoners feared that the final U.N. resolution would become another in a string of empty threats aimed at Saddam.

Abdul-Samad and his colleagues had been working on an escape plan since the first of the year in preparation for the war. The prisoners felt it was entirely possible that when bombs started dropping, the Iraqi guards would run away and hide, making an escape attempt possible. The prisoners had drawn a map to guide them to the Iranian border, which they considered the nearest point of safety. They had bundled together sweat suits, running shoes, and flashlights their families had brought to them so they could leave the camp on a moment's notice.

Abdul-Samad was examining details of the plan in his mind when, at around one o'clock in the morning on the seventeenth, he thought to himself, those animals sound terribly frightened. The barking increased in intensity until Abdul-Samad rose from his blankets to look out a window. A few yards away he saw several Iraqi soldiers running toward the prison headquarters. Suddenly the lights in all the buildings on the grounds went out. As Abdul-Samad turned from the window, the thunderous sound of anti-aircraft guns assaulted his ears. Then he heard the sound of bombs.

"The war has begun!" Abdul-Samad shouted. "The allies are bombing!"

Everyone jumped up and ran outside. The ground beneath their feet trembled as bomb after bomb exploded and round after round of ammunition left the barrels of anti-aircraft guns.

Those guns are very near the prison, Abdul-Samad shuddered. *They would surely be an allied target.*

The prisoners looked toward Baghdad and watched in awe as brilliant flashes of light appeared over the city. Colorful tracers from the anti-aircraft guns blended with the fires from the bomb explosions to create a dawnlike thanksgiving.

■ ■ ■

Almost twenty-four hours to the minute after allied planes struck Baghdad, Saddam answered the attack by firing a salvo of Scud missiles at Israel and Saudi Arabia. He was making good on his threat to attack Israel, and he would continue the ruthless campaign against civilians throughout the war.

Another act of retaliation came on January 19 when the Iraqis blasted pipelines and storage facilities and emptied loaded tankers to spill an estimated 4 to 6 million barrels of crude oil into the Arabian Gulf. The main spill was at Sea Island Terminal off the coast from Ahmadi. It covered some 600 square miles of sea surface and 300 miles of coastline, killing an uncountable number of fish and wildlife. The gulf's counterclockwise current and prevailing northwesterly winds guided the oil south, blackening the Saudi coast.

A few days later, U.S. fighter jets struck at the Ahmadi oil facility in an attempt to cut off the flow. Smart bombs from F-111 jets dropped on outlet pipes at the oil complex halted the major flow, but the ecological damage had already been done.

■ ■ ■

Few Kuwaitis went outside their doors the first few days of the air war, but by week's end, they were becoming used to the sounds of bombs and anti-aircraft guns and the smell of gunpowder and smoke from burning Iraqi tanks. They became a little more brave and ventured out of their own yards, or to a neighbor's, but it wasn't until the end of the second week that they began going any distance from their homes.

By then they were beginning to believe the war was going to last forever. When the allies first started bombing there had been many guesses about how long it would take for them to pound Iraq into powder. Some said Saddam would give up after only one day, others thought it would take several days, or maybe even a week. Few Kuwaitis had guessed on January 17 that the dictator would hold out for some six weeks.

In the early days of the war, Ali and the other men in the house watched the war from the roof. The sight of the tracers from Iraqi anti-aircraft guns was spellbinding and the sight of allied planes streaking through the sky on their missions was exhilarating. They applauded when they saw smoke on the ground that signaled the planes had hit their targets. They laughed when jet streams from American planes spelled out USA in the sky to taunt the Iraqis. They jeered when Iraqi gunners on the roofs of the neighboring houses and Jassim's school fired at the planes. They never saw the Iraqis hit a single one, even though Ali thought that sometimes it looked like the gunners could reach out and touch the pilots. The Kuwaitis were amazed at the accuracy of the allied pilots as they targeted the Iraqis and their guns, blowing them off the roof of a building without damaging the building itself.

"This isn't going to last very long," they told each other. They really believed Kuwait would be liberated before the end of the month.

■ ■ ■

One day while Ali and Ahmad were on the roof, they saw an Iraqi truck coming down a side street. They crouched down and watched as it slowly moved towards them. There were two Iraqi soldiers in the truck bed, both with machine guns in their hands.

"They are looking for men to pick up," Ali whispered. He had received a phone call that morning from a friend in Kuwait City, telling him that Iraqis were cruising neighborhoods in the city arresting men, regardless of age, for transportation to Iraq. The friend said that Iraqis wanted to get as many men out of Kuwait as possible so that they could not join the Coalition forces in a door-to-door fight for possession of the country.

The truck stopped and the brothers watched as a man who lived two streets away was ordered into the vehicle. Then the Iraqis continued up another street and stopped beside another man. By the time the patrol rolled out of sight, Ali and Ahmad had seen five men from their neighborhood forced into the truck.

■ ■ ■

The January cold finally forced a change in the nightly neighborhood meetings. After the bonfires failed to keep the men warm, Ali, Abass, and Fuad set up a tent in Fuad's backyard. Then they dragged a barrel into the tent and built a fire in it. This kept them fairly comfortable, but it wasn't long before the Iraqis discovered the tent and ordered them to remove it.

Nearly every neighborhood in Kuwait had erected a tent to use as a meeting place when the weather grew cold. Some neighborhoods the Iraqis never bothered. In others, the residents were just warned and told to tear the tents down. But, in a couple of neighborhoods, the Iraqis tore the tent down themselves and arrested the men inside for being resistance members. Ali and his neighbors decided the reason they weren't arrested was that the Iraqis didn't think resistance would be crass enough to operate in a neighborhood where there were military contingents stationed at two houses and a school. The Iraqis were wrong in much of their thinking.

After the tent came down, the men began meeting in the house of a neighbor by the name of Hussain. Dressed in dark clothes, they would slink through the shadows of darkness, one by one, to gather behind Hussain's locked door to swap stories until curfew time when they would begin leaving in the same manner they had come.

The Iraqis, naturally, had taken out their rage over the allied bombing on the Kuwaitis. Now, nearly every night, one of the neighbors had a tale of death to tell.

One night a neighbor reported the death that day of a friend by the name of Sadeq. Sadeq had been arrested as a suspected resistance member at his house in Rumaithiya one day in October while he, his wife, children, brother, and sister were eating lunch. The Iraqis took him to the police station where he was severely tortured for several days before he was taken back to his house where he was left for dead on the doorstep.

Sadeq's sister, a nurse, found her brother and took him to the hospital she worked at, where she registered him under a false name. Sadeq had lost much blood during his ordeal and once his neighbors heard of his plight, they risked their lives to donate blood for him. Sadeq had earned the love and respect of his neighbors by always being the first to volunteer to help anyone who had a problem, and by risking his own life to distribute food and other supplies to them after the occupation began—the reason the Iraqis had arrested him. After he had recuperated sufficiently enough to be moved from the hospital, he was secretly taken to the home of a friend. After a few days there, Sadeq insisted on going home, even though everyone warned him about how dangerous that could be. As one neighbor pointed out, "Someone in the neighborhood must be an Iraqi informer."

"If it is destined that I should die," Sadeq told them, "I will die."

And die he did. Somehow the Iraqis found out Sadeq had survived the torture session and were waiting for him when he got home. Once again they took him to the station and tortured him. Once again, they brought him back home and dumped him on his doorstep. Only this time, for good measure, they put two bullets in his head. Hearing the shots, his sister flew to the door and found him in a pool of blood, but miraculously, still alive. She took him back to the hospital, but the trip was in vain. Sadeq died shortly after he was readmitted.

■ ■ ■

The resistance became an even greater target for the Iraqis after the air war began. They widened the scope of their searches to a ridiculous degree—even into hospital labor rooms.

The neighborhood found this out through the birth of a baby to Hesham and Jassim's younger brother, Ahmad, and his wife. Jassim told the men one night that Iraqi intelligence agents had raided the labor room at an area hospital while his sister-in-law was in labor.

"Can you believe these people?" Jassim said. "Is there nothing sacred to them?"

Obviously not—they had been raiding mosques in search of resistance members since they entered the country.

■ ■ ■

Ali and his brothers always tried to keep the gas tanks of all the family cars full and the vehicles in top running condition in case it was necessary to evacuate Rumaithiya.

Buying gas was never an easy task after the invasion. Once Saddam found out that few Kuwaitis were going to change their vehicle registrations to Iraqi, he issued an order barring those without Iraqi license plates from purchasing gas, and started confiscating cars without Iraqi plates. Some Kuwaitis took to riding bicycles after their cars were taken away. The Iraqis then began confiscating bicycles.

Bedreah suggested to the men that the family have one of the cars changed to Iraqi registration, but received a loud and unanimous "no" from all of them. She argued and cajoled for weeks, but this was one time the men would not back down. They felt changing the registration would be giving in to the Iraqis.

There were many ways to circumvent Saddam's order forcing the Kuwaitis to change their vehicle registrations. Kuwaitis helped each other. The men in the neighborhood decided that three of them would change their registrations. Those three would fill their gas tanks and then other neighbors who needed gas were welcome to siphon a few gallons out of their tanks.

As the occupation wore on, a gas shortage developed. The embargo on Iraq had cut off shipments of raw materials the Iraqis needed to refine oil into gasoline, so they solved their problem by hauling Kuwaiti gasoline back to their country. This forced many Kuwaiti gas stations to close and it became doubly difficult to buy gas.

When Ali was out on the streets, he learned to keep his eyes open for a station that still had gas, and at which the soldiers seemed to be ignoring the vehicle registration order.

One day, while sitting in line at a station, an Iraqi soldier struck up a conversation with him. The soldier was one of the saddest-looking men Ali had yet seen. He was terribly thin and his uniform was filthy and torn. Ali said to him, "You look tired and hungry." The soldier smiled wanely. "I am," he said. "The only food we have to eat is what we can steal from you people. The allied bombing has cut off nearly all of our supply convoys."

This was good news for Ali, but the soldier seemed so nice he felt sorry for him. Obviously he didn't believe in stealing to eat, and he hadn't tossed him out of the gas line because of his Kuwaiti license plates. He offered the soldier a cigarette.

The Iraqi gratefully took it and then hesitantly asked, "Do you think you could bring me some bread the next time you come to the station?"

"Of course," Ali said.

"Be very careful when you hand it to me," the soldier cautioned. "If the wrong person sees you do it, we could both be shot."

Ali nodded his head. He was thinking about a friend who had nearly been shot by an Iraqi officer who saw him trying to give food to a soldier at a checkpoint.

As the conversation progressed, Ali got up enough nerve to ask the Iraqi a question that had been nettling his mind since the invasion. "If Saddam wants Kuwait, why is he destroying it?"

Another sad smile crossed the soldier's face. "He's jealous. He doesn't want Kuwait to look more beautiful or have more wealth than Iraq. We have been ordered to take everything we can from you rich bastards."

"We're not all rich," Ali said.

"If you've ever been to Iraq," the soldier said, "you know that, to us, all of you are rich."

Ali could see the man's point. He was aware of the poor standard of living in most of Iraq.

The soldier haunted Ali's thoughts that night. He hated the Iraqis, but the thin, gentle face of this one would not leave his mind.

The next day he took a loaf of bread and a couple of packages of cigarettes to the man. The Iraqi had tears in his eyes when Ali handed him the bundle.

■ ■ ■

Iraq launched the first major ground assault of the war on January 30, when it probed allied ground forces in five areas of southern Kuwait. Four of the assaults fizzled before they were hardly underway, but during the fifth, which was in the Kuwaiti-Saudi Arabia border town of Khafji, thirty-six hours of heavy fighting was necessary before U.S. Marine units, along with troops from Saudi and Qatar, could dislodge units from Saddam's highly thought of Fifth Division.

During the battle, the dictator's trickery and treachery were once again displayed. Saudi troops were caught off guard by the Iraqis when a line of Iraqi tanks approached with their turrets reversed, a signal of surrender. As the Saudis held their fire, the Iraqis came closer, swung their guns around and opened fire at the last minute.

When the fighting ended, thirty Iraqis were dead. Four hundred more were captured. From those captured, the allies learned the attack had been planned as a major offensive into Saudi territory. The battle at Khafji was underrated by the allies at the time it occurred, but soon they decided it had been a significant event. Because of the Khafji incident the allies learned that the Iraqis were not prone to fight tenaciously, but that Iraq could sustain a drive, despite the lack of aerial support.

Even the Iraqis learned something from the battle. Although they could launch a ground offensive without air cover, it was suicidal to do so. And they learned that the allies would be stubborn fighters, even though they weren't fighting for their own land. Iraqi officers had been telling their men that the allied troops would balk at shedding blood for Kuwait.

Living the Nightmare

■ ■ ■

One day in late January, Ali was standing outside Abass's house talking to Farouk when a car with four Iraqi soldiers cruised by. The two friends looked at each other and decided they better get back to their own homes, but before they had taken two steps, the car was back. This time it stopped and the Iraqi sitting in the passenger seat, one of the ugliest, meanest-looking soldiers Ali had yet encountered, got out, unholstered and cocked his revolver, and walked toward the two. The resistance fighter's knees went weak. He was sure the Iraqis had caught up with him and he was going to be arrested again.

"I'm leaving," Farouk hissed at Ali.

"No, you jackass!" Ali hissed back. "If you move, you'll be shot!"

Farouk knew Ali spoke the truth so he stayed put.

When the soldier was in front of Ali he pointed at Abass's Jeep, which was parked at the curb, and said, "I want that vehicle!"

"This is not my house," Ali answered, "and that is not my Jeep."

The Iraqi sneered and then asked, "Why didn't you change your license plates?"

"It is not my Jeep," Ali repeated. As the officer turned to Farouk, Ali said, "It's not his, either."

"Then get whoever owns it out here, you dumb ass!" the Iraqi shouted, waving his pistol in the air.

Ali turned towards Abass's house and yelled, "Abass! Come out here a minute!"

Abass's father, Ismail, appeared in the doorway. "Abass is not home," he said.

The Iraqi turned around and motioned the other three soldiers out of the car. While they were walking toward the house, Ali briefly explained to Ismail what the problem was.

"I do not have the keys to the Jeep," Ismail told the Iraqis. "It is my son's and he is gone, but you are welcome to it. However, as I said, I do not have the keys."

At that moment, Abass, who had been at the house next door, walked up. He looked at the soldier and asked, "What do you want?"

"That vehicle," the Iraqi again pointed at the Jeep.

"No!" Abass said, his face turning red with anger.

Ali turned to Abass and whispered, "Think man! Don't jeopardize yourself and your family over a car!"

"I won't let them take it like this," Abass insisted.

"To hell with the Jeep," Ali growled. "It is nothing. You're thinking stupid!"

Finally Abass looked the Iraqi straight in the eye and said, "Okay, but I don't have the keys. My brother has them and he is not home now."

The Iraqi shrugged and turned towards the street, summoning his companions to follow him. When they reached the Jeep, one of them produced a wire and unlocked the vehicle, then unscrewed the door lock and put it in his pocket. The Iraqis walked back to their car, got in, and left.

When they disappeared, Ali and Farouk went home and Abass and his father went into their house. Later in the day, Ali looked out his window to see that the Jeep was gone. His curiosity got the better of him and he went back to Abass's house to find out what had happened to the vehicle.

"They took the door lock somewhere and had a key made," Abass said. "Then they came back and drove it away."

"Those bastards are real smart, huh?" Ali chuckled.

"Yah. They've got my Jeep," Abass frowned.

"No," Ali said. "Think about it. A wanted resistance leader, Farouk, is standing here when they walk up and they don't even give him a second look. All they can think about is a lousy damn car!"

Abass started laughing. "You're right, Ali. The Iraqis will be no match for the liberation forces!"

CHAPTER 14

Talal moaned, fighting the consciousness that was creeping into his mind. He knew he was slipping out of the black abyss of nothingness because the cold was back. And the pain. The piercing, pounding pain that was only gone when he was in that place of darkness. All around him he heard weak, tormented voices begging to be rid of their misery, even if it meant death.

Suddenly he heard a scream. His eyes flew open. Had that noise come from his throat? No...not this time. The Iraqis were working on another prisoner. Talal hadn't screamed for a long time. The best he could muster any more when they worked on him was a raspy-sounding "caw." He had screamed his throat raw the first week he was in jail.

Now, in early February, nearly nine weeks after he'd been arrested for collaborating with the resistance, he was in the third Iraqi interrogation center. Talal almost smiled. That figured out to three weeks in each, and he'd still not told the Iraqis anything of value. He wondered if that was only because he didn't know anything to tell. He had never been involved with the resistance. If he had, he wondered if he would have been strong enough to endure the torture without telling the enemy something.

Slowly Talal rolled from his back to his right side, drawing his knees upward to his belly in hopes of staving off the wave of pain and nausea he knew would hit him the moment he moved. He shivered, wishing his wardens would give him just a scrap of blanket to cover himself. His clothes had been taken away, and he'd remained naked since the day he was arrested. They had never given him a blanket, not even when they saw that his skin was blue from cold.

The slam of a door followed by heavy footsteps sent a shudder coursing through his body. *Oh, God,* Talal groaned. *They're coming for me again. It's my turn again. Please, God, this time don't let me surface from the abyss. Please let me stay in that dark, warm, painless place forever!*

"Get up!" a guttural voice barked.

Talal's eyes moved up from the stone floor of the cell to the face of the man who had spoken. It was the same officer who had come for him the day before. Talal could not make himself move. He remained shivering on the hard bunk.

The officer walked over and grabbed him by the arm. "I said get up!"

"I can't," Talal whispered. "I have no strength."

The officer pulled him to a sitting position. Tears came to Talal's eyes as the pain assailed his groin once again.

"Get dressed!" another officer ordered, as he threw a shirt, slacks, shoes, and socks at Talal.

Talal could hardly believe his ears. *Dressed? Did the Iraqi say "get dressed?" Were those really clothes?* Talal decided he was dreaming.

The first officer slapped Talal alongside of the head. No, he wasn't dreaming. He felt the slap.

Talal reached for the shirt, intending to pull it on. He couldn't make his hands work. They felt like something foreign dangling from the ends of his arms. Weren't they supposed to do something other than just stand there and quiver?

"Oh, shit!" the second officer said as he grabbed the shirt. "You rich bastards don't even know how to dress yourselves!"

Talal sat on the bunk like a baby, tears of pain and embarrassment soaking into his beard, now prematurely flecked with gray, while the two Iraqi officers dressed him.

This doesn't make any sense, he told himself. *Why are they putting clothes on me? Is there a new type of torture I haven't experienced yet? One that required the prisoner to be dressed?*

The two officers lifted their prisoner to his feet and dragged him through the cell door, and away from the interrogation rooms.

Surprised, Talal croaked, "Where am I going?"

"Home," one of the officers answered.

Home! The word slammed into Talal's brain. *Home! Safety. Comfort. Warmth. Home! Oh, God,* he asked silently, *why is my mind playing such horrible tricks on me? The Iraqi couldn't have said I was going home....*

"We have no further use for such a worthless piece of crap," the other officer said. "You are not even man enough to admit you would help the resistance defend your country!"

The two officers threw Talal into a car, drove him to his home, and tossed him on the doorstep.

■ ■ ■

Early in the second month of the new year, Ali began to believe all of the Iraqis stationed in Rumaithiya were concentrating on his neighborhood. The streets were full of them, scurrying around like frustrated rats in a maze.

One night there was a knock on the front door and as Mohammed rose from his chair to answer it, Bedreah and Eidan intercepted him.

"No," Bedreah said. "We will go. All of you scatter and hide."

"You're not going to the door, Mom," Ali said, heading for the stairs.

"We *are* going," Eidan said forcefully. "We have decided we have less risk than any of you boys—you know the Iraqis are now going door-to-door picking up young men."

"Not just young men, Dad," Ahmad said.

"Do as I say!" the old man shouted.

Eidan and Bedreah climbed the stairs and opened the door. There stood three ragged Iraqi soldiers.

"We have not had a bite of food for three days," one soldier said. "Could you spare us some bread?"

"Certainly," Eidan said. "We will be back in a few minutes."

He shut the door and Bedreah hurried down the stairs and returned quickly with bread, tea, and rice. Eidan reopened the door.

"God bless you," one soldier said, turning to leave.

Then one of the other soldiers stepped forward. "One more thing, if you please," he said to Bedreah. "Would you have any cigarettes?"

"No," Bedreah lied. Cigarettes were now a particularly valuable bargaining tool and she knew her sons would be furious if she gave any away to an Iraqi.

"Please," the soldier pleaded. "Just one. You must have at least one cigarette in this big house. My nerves are so bad from the bombing. Please!"

He looked so pitiful Bedreah couldn't stand it. She went back down the stairs, found three packages of Marlboros, and took them to the soldier.

"Oh, dear mother," the Iraqi babbled when she handed the cigarettes to him. "May God bless you for eternity."

Bedreah smiled, closed the door, and then began wondering what she was going to tell Ali about what happened to the cigarettes he had just brought home that day from a successful scavenging trip.

■ ■ ■

On February 7, Rumaithiya lost its local telephone service. Even though all of Bedreah and Eidan's immediate family was living in the compound, a total of twenty-four people, they still had sisters, brothers, cousins, and other relatives whose safety they worried about. After the phones went dead, the only way they could find out about them was to send Ali to their homes.

Even though making the trips was dangerous in itself, what bothered Ali most when he was away from the safety of the compound was seeing the increased humiliation that was being heaped on his countrymen. Nearly every time he went into the streets, he would see another poor soul being subjected to Iraqi brutality.

One day as he was on his way to his Aunt Miriam's, he found himself in a traffic jam. Thinking an accident was probably the cause, Ali shut the car motor off and got out to see if he could find out what was happening. It was no accident. Several car lengths ahead of him, Iraqi soldiers had pulled a Kuwaiti man out of his vehicle. Two soldiers were punching and beating him while a third held a machine gun pointed at him. Ali clenched his fists and got back into his car.

After about twenty minutes, traffic began moving again. The beaten Kuwaiit had been thrown up against a street pole, where he was lying in a pool of blood. As the cars passed the scene, the Iraqi with the machine gun yelled at the drivers. "See what can happen to you? You better be good…we can do anything we want to you!" Then he bellowed out an insane-sounding laugh.

■ ■ ■

Sometime in early February, Ali woke in the middle of the night to the sound of moaning and gagging. Someone was heaving his guts out. He rolled off the mattress (everyone except Ahmad and Afaf had begun sleeping in the basement again after the air war started) and went to the nearest bathroom, where he found Ahmad on his knees in front of the stool. Bedreah was holding his head, which was sinking dangerously close to the bowl full of vomit.

Peering through the doorway, he asked, "What's the matter?"

"As you can see," Bedreah snapped, "your brother is terribly sick!" She went on to explain that the same thing had happened several years ago and he had to be taken to a hospital for treatment before the vomiting would stop.

"Get dressed," she ordered Ali. "We have to find a hospital that can help him."

Ali glanced at his watch. It was 2:00 in the morning. "Mom," he sighed, "you know how dangerous it is to be out on the streets at this time of night. We'll have to wait until daylight."

Ahmad raised his head from the stool. "Ali, she's right. I have to get to..." His voice trailed off as another spasm of nausea overtook him.

"Isn't there some medicine here you can give him that will help until the sun comes up?"

"No," Bedreah nearly shouted. "We tried everything when this happened before and nothing helped. We have to go to the hospital!"

When the seizure left Ahmad, Ali helped him stand and half-carried his 200-pound brother into the kitchen. Ahmad was clutching his stomach and groaning with pain. He was dressed warmly in a sweat suit but he began to shiver. "God, I'm so cold," he said.

Ali went for a blanket, but before he could get back to the kitchen, Ahmad was already staggering back to the bathroom.

Bedreah raced to her room and threw her clothes on. Ali shrugged, and went to find his clothes and some shoes and socks for his brother.

They got Ahmad into the car, and Ali pulled out onto the main road, heading in the direction of Hadi Hospital, a private institution in Al-Jabriya. He thought maybe there would be a better chance that a doctor and medicine would be available there. He knew through reports from Abo-Ahmad that things at Mubarak and other government hospitals had grown even worse since the bombings started.

A steady drizzle had been falling since dusk and the guards at the first checkpoint they encountered looked wet and wretched. *They're getting younger and younger,* Ali thought as he looked at the huddled group. He guessed the oldest to be about seventeen, while the youngest looked no older than fourteen or fifteen. He cursed Saddam for the youths' misery.

The older guard came to the car window and asked for identification. Ali handed him some papers and the youth peered into the back seat, where Ahmad moaned in pain as he vomited into the bucket. "That's my brother," Ali explained. "We have to get him to a hospital." The youth's face twisted as if he, too, were in pain. "Yes," he said, as he waved them through the roadblock. "Go quickly."

Ali put the car in gear and roared away. When they arrived at the hospital, a soldier at the door ushered them inside. The man at the reception desk sent them back outside.

"The only doctors here are for emergency maternity cases," the man explained. "Try Mubarak Hospital."

Ali and Bedreah dragged the miserable Ahmad back to the car and headed for the government hospital. A group of soldiers stood outside the hospital gate, and Ali was sure they were in for trouble, but a guard waved them through after barely glancing at them.

Inside, the man at the registration desk sent them to the internal medicine department, where an unfriendly looking foreign doctor met them. Ali looked around and saw three bodies lying on stretchers, covered completely with sheets. He turned pale.

"Mom," he nudged Bedreah, "we have to get out of here. All those people are dead!" For some reason, Ali felt the doctor might be responsible for that.

Ahmad began vomiting again and Bedreah ignored Ali. "Do something!" she shouted at the doctor. "He is going to die!"

The doctor scowled and grunted something unintelligible, but led them to an examining room where he instructed Ahmad to lie down on a table. Then the doctor began pushing around on his stomach, prompting him to scream in pain.

"I have no medicine," the doctor said, "but I will give him some pain pills. You will have to go find another hospital." He gave Ahmad two pills and a glass of water. Ahmad swallowed the pills and immediately threw them up. The doctor gave him a look of disgust and handed him two more pills. This time they stayed down, but didn't seem to relieve the pain. The doctor said he could do no more, and Ali and Bedreah once again hauled Ahmad back to the car. This time they took him home, hoping the pills just needed time to work.

After an hour the situation had grown worse instead of better. Ali began to believe that his brother could die if he didn't get some help soon. Bedreah woke Afaf to tell her that Ahmad was very ill and that Ali and she were going to try, once again, to find a doctor to help him. Afaf insisted on going with the trio.

This time Ali headed for Mowasat Hospital in Al-Salmiya, taking side streets and back roads to avoid as many checkpoints as possible. They were challenged at one of the road-blocks they couldn't avoid, but Bedreah was successful in talking their way through.

When they arrived at the hospital they were told there were no doctors in the building and that the pharmacy was closed until the morning shift arrived at 7:00. That would be a wait of two hours. Ali feared his brother didn't have two hours to wait.

"There has to be someone here to help us," Ali said to the Egyptian man who was on duty at the registration desk. "You can see my brother is in terrible pain."

The Egyptian turned a sympathetic eye toward the sick man and then asked Ali if he knew if Ahmad had ever been treated for an ulcer. "His symptoms are similar to those I had when a doctor discovered I had an ulcer," the man said.

Ali thought for several moments, and then his face brightened. "Yes...yes, I believe he was, several years ago."

The Egyptian told them to wait in the reception area and disappeared. In about fifteen minutes, he returned with a small bottle of pills. He told Ahmad to take two of the pills now and two more in six hours. Ahmad took the pills and after resting for about half an hour, he seemed to be in less pain and quit retching.

Ali asked what the pills were and where the Egyptian had gotten them if the pharmacy was closed.

"They are the pills I take to relieve my ulcer," the man grinned. "I happened to remember I had some in my coat pocket in the locker room." Then the man's expression sobered and he said, "You know, I could be shot for giving them to you. Please don't tell anyone where you got them."

Tears came to Ali's eyes as he thanked the Egyptian. Acts of kindness and concern from a stranger had been rare for many months, and the thought that this one was risking his life to help his brother overwhelmed him.

Ahmad's problem apparently was an ulcer. He had no further pain after he began taking the pills.

■ ■ ■

The next day, while the family was eating dinner, they heard a knock at the back door. Ali left the table to answer it and found Essa standing on the step with a big grin on his face.

"Ali, Talal is alive." Ali and Essa had gone to high school with Talal. They knew he had been arrested at his home in December on suspicion of helping the resistance, but had heard nothing about him since.

"How do you know?"

"I saw him. He's in terrible shape. He looked like an old man...his hair and beard are gray...but he is alive."

After Essa left, Ali went back into the house for a jacket. He didn't care what the danger was, he was going to see Talal. Grabbing the coat, he hurried back up the stairs, but didn't make it out the door before Bedreah saw him and asked where he was going.

"To the yard," Ali answered. He hated to lie to his mother, but he knew she would have one of her tantrums if she knew the truth. Talal lived several streets away and Bedreah would forbid him to go. This trip would not be considered official family business.

Ali left the compound on foot, eyes and ears alert for Iraqi patrols as he worked his way between houses to reach Talal's street.

Wafa, Talal's wife, answered Ali's knock at the door. Her face was pinched and pale and her eyes were hooded with fear.

"Oh, Ali," she said, heaving a sigh of relief, "I was afraid it was the Iraqis again."

"Essa told me Talal is home."

"Yes," she nodded, tears filling her eyes. "His body is here...the Iraqis kept his spirit." She stepped aside so Ali could enter the house, then closed and bolted the door.

Ali followed Wafa to the *derwania* where Talal was seated, cross-legged, on a floor cushion. Essa was right—he looked like an old man. He did not get up, or show any sign that someone had entered the room.

"Talal," Ali said softly as he sank down on a cushion in front of his friend. "I'm so glad you are alive!"

Talal's eyes met Ali's. They were flat and hard. "Alive?" he said in a hoarse whisper. "Am I alive?"

Ali lowered his eyes. He could almost feel the pain radiating from his friend's lifeless stare. "When did they release you?"

"Last week," Talal shrugged, clenching and unclenching his hands, which lay trembling in his lap. There were deep, angry-looking indentations on both of Talal's wrists. Ali reached out to take Talal's hands into his own, but he pulled them away. "No," he said, "don't touch me."

Ali's eyes returned to the once strong, confident, always happy face. This man had been blessed with an even greater sense of humor than Essa had. Ali wondered if Talal would ever joke or laugh again.

"Talal...."

"*Sshh*," Talal cut off Ali's words as he uncrossed his legs and rose from the pillow. "Don't ask me any questions, please," he said, as he left the room.

Ali turned to Wafa. "Has he been this way since he came home?"

"Yes," she nodded. "I've tried to get him to talk, but he won't tell me anything. It would be good for him to talk, but words just seem to stick in his throat. He doesn't eat, won't answer the *azan*, just sits and stares."

Ali rose from his cushion. "It will take time, Wafa," he said. "We must all try to be patient with him. Can I come back tomorrow?"

"Please do. I think he will open up to you or one of his other friends before he does me."

Ali left, but returned to Talal and Wafa's every day for over a week before Talal began to relax, and in bits and pieces, he told Ali of his ordeal.

For the first three days of his imprisonment, Talal told Ali, he had been hung by his feet, naked, to a ceiling fan, which was then turned on to its fastest setting. When he was taken down, he underwent shock treatments with electrical wire hooked to his chest and arms. Then, still naked, he was strung back up on the fan, this time by his wrists. Then the Iraqis tied a heavy rock to his penis and dropped the rock. Talal passed out from the pain. As soon as he came to, the Iraqis repeated the procedure. Talal passed out again. This time he woke up in a cell, still naked. His penis was grotesquely elongated and totally numb.

"They took my manhood, Ali!" Talal sobbed. "I am no longer a man!"

When the Iraqis at that prison decided they were not going to get Talal to talk, they transferred him to another location where the torture continued. His hands were tied behind his back, he was blindfolded, and then forced to kneel for several days on a concrete floor in a busy corridor of the prison. As prison guards passed by they would hit or kick him, "150 to 200 times a day," Talal said.

Then he was taken to still another house of torture. In addition to being tortured himself, here he was forced to watch young Kuwaiti women being tortured. He was left alone one time in a room with one of the women. He asked her why she had been arrested and she said the Iraqis accused her of writing political slogans on walls and street signs. "But I didn't," she cried. "I am innocent!" Also at this prison, Talal told Ali he had seen a naked man forced to sit for days on a broken Pepsi bottle.

"I couldn't even sleep to escape what was going on," Talal said. "The screams of the other torture victims kept me awake day and night!"

Now Ali could understand why Talal's voice was so hoarse. He, too, had done his share of screaming as he underwent the Iraqi cruelty. Talal's vocal cords were probably permanently damaged, just as his manhood was.

CHAPTER 15

Despite the horrendous pounding his country was taking from the allied bombing, Saddam remained obstinate in his refusal to budge from Kuwait until February 21. On that date, he offered to withdraw "fully and unconditionally" one day after the cessation of hostilities. In return he demanded all twelve U.N. resolutions be dropped. The offer came out of a meeting between Soviet President Mikhail Gorbachev and Iraq's foreign minister. In the meeting, Gorbachev, independent of U.N. approval, offered Tarik Aziz an eight-point plan for the withdrawal.

Upon review of Gorbachev's plan, and in view of Iraq's demand that the resolutions be dropped, the United States refused Saddam's offer. The United States and its allies insisted that Iraq comply with all of the resolutions, show legitimate signs of withdrawal before a cease-fire was initiated, and agree to a deadline for completion of the withdrawal. Otherwise, U.S. officials pointed out, what would prevent another bit of Saddam's infamous trickery and treachery?

The United States suspected that without a deadline for withdrawal, the dictator would simply move a few hundred of his troops out of Kuwait and leave the rest entrenched indefinitely.

■ ■ ■

Three more of Ali's cousins wound up in the hands of the Iraqis in February. Abdul-Samad's brothers—Husain (the one who talked the two Iraqis into deserting), Rasul (the water plant employee), and Kareem, an electronics engineer—were arrested at a checkpoint late on the afternoon of February 20 while they were on their way to their parents' home.

They were taken to the Al-Ferdous Police Station and thrown into a small, windowless cell. There they heard the scream of a man for the first time in their lives. As they sat huddled in the cell, the screams continued for what seemed like hours until the victim was brought to their cell and dumped on the floor. That man's screams were soon replaced by those of another torture victim.

The brothers sat in shocked silence after the arrival of their cell mate, wondering when it would be their turn to scream. After a few minutes, they heard a noise at the door and turned to find an Iraqi intelligence officer looking into the cell through the small, barred opening in the door. They thought the officer was probably there to take one of them to the torture chamber. Instead, the Iraqi just stood there for several minutes, staring at the heap of humanity on the floor.

When the Iraqi turned to leave, Rasul stood up and walked to the door. "Wait," he said to the officer. "Can you tell me why my brothers and I have been arrested?"

The officer shrugged and said, "I am from intelligence. I know nothing about this police station."

Rasul began to plead with the officer. "Please release us, or at least release one of us so he can go tell our family what has happened." The officer shrugged again and walked away without answering.

Soon another intelligence officer walked by the cell. This one was very young, and Rasul hoped, sympathetic. He called to the officer and, pointing at Husain and Kareem, repeated that they were brothers and asked that one of them be released. The officer took all three of their names and left, returning a few minutes later with another officer.

"I am looking for one named Rasul," the second officer said.

"That is me," Rasul acknowledged.

The officer opened the cell door and motioned for him to come out. "You may go now," the Iraqi said.

"No," Rasul said. "Please release one of my brothers instead."

"You go," the officer said. "You are the only one with the proper papers."

Shortly after the Iraqis ordered Kuwaitis back to work, they issued a special letter to everyone employed at the water and electric plants, which exempted them from arrest because of the importance of their jobs. When Rasul was arrested, he had tried to call the soldiers' attention to the letter, but they ignored him and took it away from him, along with his other identification. Rasul now reasoned that after he had given the young officer his name, the Iraqi must have gone through the papers taken from him and found the letter.

Rasul hesitantly moved toward the cell door.

"It is all right," Kareem said. "Go and tell the family what has happened. We will be fine until you return."

Rasul felt as if his heart would break as he walked out the front door of the station. Slowly he began walking down the street toward home. But then he stopped, turned around, and retraced his steps. He had to try at least once more to get his brothers released.

Walking up to one of the soldiers lounging outside the station, he said, "I will give you anything you want if you will help me free my brothers."

The soldier nodded in agreement and motioned for Rasul to follow him to the back of the station. As they neared the back door, it suddenly flew open and a Kuwaiti man, hands tied behind his back, was shoved out by an intelligence officer. Then as Rasul watched in horror, the officer unholstered his pistol and shot the prisoner twice in the back of the head. The man fell dead at Rasul's feet.

Shock immobilized Rasul for a moment. Then, as the officer nudged the body with his foot to roll it over on its back, Rasul began to back away from the scene. The officer's eyes left the dead Kuwaiti and fell on Rasul. Rasul turned quickly and began to run. He didn't stop until he reached his house, which was several miles from the station.

When he arrived home, he immediately called his mother to report what had happened. Miriam barely let him finish his story before hanging up and heading for the station. The Iraqis already had Abdul-Samad; she would not allow them to take two more sons from her.

Miriam pleaded with the officer at the information desk to let her see Husain and Kareem, but he told her they were not there.

"Try the juvenile detention section," the officer suggested.

Good, God, Miriam thought. *They jail children too?*

"My sons are not children," Miriam shouted. "Husain is twenty-five years old and Kareem is twenty-nine. They would not be put in a juvenile section!"

The officer just smiled and said, "I'm sorry, mother, but your sons are not here."

Frustrated and sick with worry, Miriam left the station and went home. *If they weren't at the station just a few hours after Rasul left them, where could they be?* A chill went down her spine as an obvious answer popped into her head. *Iraq! They have already been sent to a prison camp in Iraq!*

For two days Miriam returned to the station, but the answer was always the same: "We have no one here by that name." Several times she saw buses loaded with prisoners heading for the Iraqi border. She ran after them, shouting her sons' names. Once she even managed to stop a bus by standing in the road and refusing to move. But she wasn't successful in boarding it to look for the two.

■ ■ ■

After Rasul left, his brothers sat dejectedly in the cell, trying to blot out the screams of the torture victims, which were sometimes punctuated by the sounds of gunshots.

Kareem, a short, dark-haired man, whose religious convictions paralleled Abdul-Samad's, kicked himself for getting arrested. He had been warned. Yesterday he and his wife had gone to visit his Aunt Bedreah and her family. Ali had told Kareem then that the resistance was telling everyone to stay home. The Iraqis were outraged at the possibility of the allies launching a ground offensive and arrests were at an even higher peak.

"You won't see me at your house until this thing is over," Ali had told Kareem. "I am not leaving my neighborhood any more."

But Kareem had not listened to his cousin, and now, here he was, in jail. His thoughts were interrupted about eight-thirty that night with the appearance of a very tall, heavyset guard at the cell door. Unlocking it, he walked in and asked, "Who is Husain?"

Husain, who was only about five-feet-five, stared up at the guard, searching his face for an indication as to why he had called his name. The guard's face was ugly and impassive.

"I am," Husain answered shakily.

"Come with me," the Iraqi ordered, grabbing Husain by the arm and shoving him toward the door.

Kareem was on his feet in an instant. "Where are you taking him? He is my younger brother. Take me instead."

The guard grinned and slammed the door in Kareem's face. "Don't worry," he said, "we are only going to ask him some questions."

"I know how you bastards ask questions," Kareem shouted. "Please don't hurt him! Take me!"

Husain and the guard disappeared through the iron door at the end of the hallway, and the next thing Husain knew he was standing in a line of men in a large room. In the center of the room was an officer holding a pistol. Husain's feet froze to the floor as he saw the officer select one of the men in the line and walk him through another door. He waited to hear the sound of the officer's gun being fired, but he could hear nothing.

Several minutes later the officer returned to the room. "Now I'll take this one," he said as he grabbed Husain by the shoulder and rammed the barrel of the revolver into the side of his neck. The Iraqi began walking him toward the door the other man had been taken through. Husain's eyes glazed over with fright, and his legs began to shake.

"Open the door!" the officer commanded.

Husain felt for the doorknob. He couldn't focus his eyes to see it. When he got the door open, the officer shoved him through it. The door slammed shut and Husain felt the barrel of the revolver dig deeper into his neck. Husain closed his eyes and began to repeat the Muslim prayer: "There is only one God, Allah, and His Prophet...."

Suddenly the officer laughed and pulled the gun away from Husain's neck. "Get on the bus, you chickenshit!" the Iraqi ordered as he holstered the pistol. "All you Kuwaitis are afraid to die!"

Husain opened his eyes to a bus partially filled with men. Slowly he shuffled up the steps and dropped into a seat. He watched with hatred in his eyes as the Iraqi officer went back into the jail to fetch another victim for his special brand of torture. After a few minutes, Husain quit watching the officer bring men out of the prison. It made his head ache to see the fear in his compatriots' eyes when they came through the door. He leaned back in the seat and closed his eyes. A few minutes later he felt someone shake him.

"Husain! Wake up Husain!"

He opened his eyes to see Kareem standing over him.

"Oh, praise God, you are alive," Kareem grinned. "I kept hearing screams and shots after they took you away and I was so afraid they were torturing you or had killed you!"

Husain looked up at his brother in surprise. "How did you get here? Did an officer with a gun bring you?"

"No," Kareem answered. "The Iraqis just opened all of the cell doors and ordered us to go outside and get on a bus. But, oh, thank God, I cannot believe you are alive!" he said again as he hugged his brother. "And I got on your bus! God is watching over us, Husain. I know now that we will both survive this ordeal."

As the bus pulled away from the police station, Husain told Kareem about the scare he had had. Then they sat wondering where they were going.

In a short time they found out. The buses stopped at the juvenile detention center.

Had Miriam taken the guard's suggestion, she might eventually have found her sons.

■ ■ ■

Early on the morning of February 24, over 680,000 U.S. and allied ground troops converged on Kuwait to free it from the bonds of tyranny.

Increased air attacks signaled the beginning of the ground attack as the Coalition forces struck from every direction. Coming from Kuwait's southern border, allied troops punched through mine-sown Iraqi defenses in only two and one-half hours on a drive toward Kuwait City. In northern and western Iraq, the allies drove eastward toward Basra and southward to take on the main concentration of the Iraqi Republican Guard at the Kuwaiti border. Off the coast of Kuwait, U.S. Marine amphibious forces seized the island of Failaka at the entrance of Kuwait City's harbor.

By mid-afternoon, the lightning-quick offensive found liberators positioned less than twenty-five miles from Kuwait's capital city.

■ ■ ■

On the night the ground war began, Ali's family suspected something was about to happen. The impending assault had been like a silent intruder in their house for days: rarely discussed for fear of disappointment, but always present in everyone's mind.

Saddam had been threatening for some time to poison the air as he had the water and he held good on the threat. Two days earlier the family had watched daylight turn into night when the Iraqis dynamited the Sea Island oil facilities, as well as all but two of the oil fields and refineries in the country. Seven hundred thirty-two oil wells were now burning, spewing poisons aloft. Oil from those wells that didn't catch fire poured onto the desert sand, forming huge, black lakes.

Usually Iraqi retaliation came after something had upset Saddam. This time, the family felt, the Iraqi terror was a harbinger of something big to come. *Could it be the ground war?*

All evening the bombing seemed to increase in intensity. They wondered if it was a signal that the ground campaign was near. They tried to hold their emotions in check, for they had been disappointed so many times before. At 6:00 P.M., everyone listened intensely to the news broadcasts, but heard nothing new.

The air was so thick with suspense that no one could settle down for sleep. At one o'clock the next morning, most of the family was still up when a newscaster on a Saudi Arabian radio station shouted, "Operation Desert Storm is underway! Coalition forces have entered Kuwait!"

At first the family sat in stunned silence, afraid to believe they had heard the newscaster correctly. Then the announcement was repeated, and pandemonium reigned in Bedreah's basement. Everyone was screaming, laughing, crying, and hugging, as they finally felt the bonds of enemy occupation begin to snap loose.

■ ■ ■

On the morning before the ground offensive began, a group of Iraqi intelligence officers came to Al-Bakoba prison camp. Abdul-Samad learned shortly after they left that they had brought an execution order from Baghdad. One of the prisoners who worked in the camp kitchen had overheard the officers give the instructions to the camp commander.

"If the allies launch a ground attack, we will be slaughtered," the Kuwaiti told Abdul-Samad later that day.

That night, Abdul-Samad sat on his blanket thinking about what the kitchen worker had said. He decided that he had two choices: either panic and make an escape attempt, which would surely fail, or put his trust in God.

As he sat pondering, his mind drifted back to a couple of months before when he, Ali, and their uncle Khalil had taken one of their many fishing trips out into the gulf. That morning had been particularly beautiful, and the three had left the dock in high spirits, anticipating a good catch. Their hunch had come true. By early afternoon, they had caught all the fish they could handle.

As they began thinking about heading back to shore, the sun suddenly disappeared behind a huge bank of black clouds, and within minutes a terrible storm was underway. Abdul-Samad's small boat was nearly swamped several times as the trio maneuvered it back to shore.

Living the Nightmare

God had spared Abdul-Samad from death in that storm, and now a peaceful calm began to settle over him, seemingly assuring him that God would also protect him from the Iraqi storm. He lay back down on the cold concrete, pulled his blanket up, and slept a deep, untroubled sleep.

Twenty-four hours later, when Operation Desert Storm began, Abdul-Samad received further assurance that an execution order would not be carried out at the prison. Al-Bakoba's staff was far too busy plotting escape plans for themselves if the allies came to the camp. They had little time to think about how they would execute over 650 prisoners.

■ ■ ■

After three days at the juvenile center with no food or water, Husain, Kareem, and the other prisoners were loaded onto several buses bound for Iraq, just hours before the ground war was launched. They traveled northward for several hours before they saw streaks and flashes of light in the sky and on the ground, and heard the sound of explosions. The prisoners knew immediately that the allies were attacking.

As the action grew louder and closer, the buses stopped alongside an Iraqi road. The drivers and guards exited the vehicles and closed the doors behind them, sealing the prisoners inside. Then they hid in ditches until the raid ended. The Kuwaitis huddled together, watching missiles from dozens of allied aircraft streak through the sky, and praying that one wouldn't hit their bus. The window glass shook and the vehicles rocked like paper in the wind from the vibrations of the explosions.

After the air attack subsided, the Iraqis reentered the buses, but they drove for only a few minutes before a second air raid developed. The dark sky lit up as if it were daylight, and the Iraqis again left the buses to hide—all except one. After this raid ended, Husain and Kareem learned that one of the guards had remained on the bus, and had raped a seventeen-year-old male prisoner during the height of the attack.

As the buses continued their journey, they passed scenes of total destruction—bombed out tanks, buildings, roads, and bridges. The allies' aim seemed excellent, the prisoners agreed.

When the buses stopped again, they were in the town of Al-Zubeir. The driver and guards on Husain and Kareem's bus got out, again carefully closing the door behind them. As the Kuwaitis sat waiting, an old Iraqi man appeared at the side of the bus. Husain risked opening a window to plead with him to bring water. "Four days we have been without water," Husain told him. The Iraqi left and came back with a bottle of water. It was greasy and had a strange flavor, but the two brothers drank some anyway before passing the bottle to others on the bus.

Shortly after the man returned with the water another violent air attack began. When Husain looked at the sky, he thought it was on fire. The bus was parked near a large oil reservoir and the allies had made a direct hit on it.

As they waited for the attack to end, a vehicle with several Iraqi officers inside pulled up. One of them had the helmet of an American pilot in his hand. He waved the helmet and shouted at the prisoners, "Do you see this? Do you see this? This belongs to a Zionist! We just hit this pilot down!" The prisoners turned their heads away. The raid ended abruptly, and the buses again began moving.

This time when they stopped, the Kuwaitis found themselves inside a prison camp surrounded by barbed wire and electrified trenches.

■ ■ ■

As soon as the allies began moving into Kuwait, the Iraqis began a hasty, unorganized retreat. The Kuwaitis had guessed correctly—the majority of the invaders had no desire to fight.

On their way north, the Iraqis left as much devastation and misery as possible behind them. One of the most senseless acts of destruction was the demolition of nearly all of Kuwait's power stations. As the first Coalition forces moved into Iraq and Kuwait, the Iraqis began blowing up the electrical plants.

The power station in Bayan, which served Rumaithiya, was one of the first to go. As the news that Operation Desert Storm was underway came over the airwaves, a terrific explosion shook Ali's neighborhood. The few lights that had been in Bedreah's basement flickered off. Ali jumped up and ran upstairs to his apartment, where he saw a huge, orange-colored light in the sky over Bayan. He knew immediately what had happened, but walked over to a light switch and flipped it on to confirm his suspicion. The light did not come on.

Moving back to the window, Ali looked out again. To the south another orange-colored light appeared in the night sky. He guessed that the Ahmadi station had just gone up in flames, too.

The loss of commercial power did not paralyze Kuwait as the Iraqis had hoped. What they failed to realize was that most Kuwaiti homes were equipped with emergency generators capable of supplying a limited amount of electricity.

■ ■ ■

Husain, Kareem, and the other prisoners had no idea where they were when the buses stopped inside the prison compound. They had sat in the vehicles for hours, but it was difficult to determine how far they had actually traveled because they had stopped so many times for the air raids. All they knew was that it was nearly dawn, and they had left the juvenile center somewhere around nine o'clock the previous night.

The Kuwaitis were ordered off the buses and divided into two groups. Husain and Kareem's group of about 300 was taken to a room that was about twenty feet long and twenty-six feet wide. It had a concrete floor. The cold, early-morning desert air blew freely into the room through high windows whose glass had apparently been shattered by bomb concussions. Once they were all in the room, the door was shut and locked.

Within an hour, a guard unlocked the door and threw a large canvas bag into the room. He shouted, "This is your breakfast...manage it yourselves!"

The prisoners opened the bag to find wormy, cooked rice that had straw mixed in it, and bottles of dirty water. After four days without food, the men downed the foul mixture with, if not relish, then at least the determination that they would not allow the Iraqis to starve them to death.

When they finished eating, they took turns trying to sleep. There was not enough room for all of them to lie down at the same time. There also were not enough blankets to go around. Everyone shivered from the cold as they huddled together for more warmth.

In early afternoon, the prisoners were let out of their room to use the toilet. To their dismay, they discovered there were only four filthy bathrooms for some 1,800 prisoners. As one guard or another walked by the groups of men waiting to use the toilets, bribes would be offered for food by those who had money or other valuables. Sometimes they received their food, but as often as not, the guards took their money and disappeared.

The air raids continued throughout the day, and the prisoners watched a military barracks across the road go up in flames. They were amazed that not one bomb landed in the prison compound. They concluded that either the allies' intelligence and accuracy were extremely precise, or that they, the prisoners, were extremely lucky.

Living the Nightmare

■ ■ ■

After Ali and his family wore themselves out celebrating the beginning of the ground war, they fell into their beds for a few hours' sleep. Around noon, Ali woke and went into the kitchen, where Bedreah was already heating water for tea. She had a radio on. "...Coalition forces are reportedly nearing Kuwait City," the Voice of America announcer was saying.

Ali looked at his mother and grinned. "It won't be long, Mom, and I'll be with Dina and the children!"

Bedreah beamed back at her son.

All day Ali listened to the news as the allies swept through his country. There were constant reports that the Iraqis were fleeing, but Ali was determined not to get his hopes too high. It would kill him if he found out the Iraqis were just playing another trick, and therefore, he was no closer to being with his family than he had been last week.

■ ■ ■

Ali could safely have been celebrating because the Iraqis were, in fact, retreating. As night fell on the second day of the ground war, more and more of Saddam's disintegrating army rushed from southern Kuwait northward to what the invaders hoped would be safety in their own country. Smoke from the oil fires blotted out the moon and stars, and because of the profound darkness, the Iraqis thought it would be easy to slip out from under the allies' net. Once again, the Iraqis were wrong.

Coalition forces were waiting for them all along the roads leading through and out of Kuwait, with equipment that made it possible to see the enemy in the dark. The fleeing Iraqis were picked off like sitting ducks, and the roads leading out of Kuwait became little more than junkyards for destroyed Iraqi equipment and graveyards for dead Iraqi soldiers.

■ ■ ■

About nine o'clock on the night of February 25, Ali and Mohammed went to the roof to see if there were any indication that the Iraqis were leaving, or that the allies were entering Rumaithiya. What they saw amazed them. For miles there was nothing but vehicle lights. On Al-Fahaheel Expressway. On Al-Maghreb Expressway. On both Fifth and Sixth Ring Motorways. On every major road and street they saw headlights.

"It must be the Coalition forces headed into Kuwait City," Mohammed said to Ali.

"No, Mohammed," Ali said. "I think those are Iraqi vehicles headed for Iraq."

Mohammed left the roof and went downstairs. In just minutes, Ali heard the door to the roof reopen. He turned to see his mother standing in the doorway.

Ali's eyes filled with tears. "Mom," he said, "I think they really are pulling out."

"Mohammed said the lights are from allied vehicles," Bedreah said.

"No, Mom. I'm sure they are Iraqi."

Bedreah went back downstairs to report what Ali had said, but he stayed on the roof watching the parade of lights. It never stopped. Suddenly he noticed a flurry of activity across the street at Jassim's school. As he watched, Iraqi soldiers ran out of the building and crawled into trucks. Some didn't make it before the vehicles pulled away from the curb. With panic-stricken faces, the soldiers began running after the trucks, but the drivers never slowed down.

Ahmad had joined him in his vigil and Ali turned to his brother and shouted, "Look at the bastards run! They're scattering like a bunch of mice with a cat after them!"

Ahmad grinned. "They've got lots of cats after them... American cats, British cats, Saudi cats...a whole world full of cats!"

Suddenly the two sobered. Iraqi soldiers were pouring into the yard of the compound. Ahmad and Ali raced downstairs past the front door, which the Iraqis were now pounding on, into the basement where the rest of the family huddled together in the kitchen, fear etched on their faces.

Ali looked at his father. "Do you think we should go to the door?"

Eidan shook his head. "No. If they want in, they will have to break the door down." Then he told his sons and sons-in-law to hide. "If they come in, they won't bother the rest of us, but they will surely arrest you," the old man told them.

"It is all your fault!" Bedreah shrieked hysterically at her husband. As it had only once before in the nearly seven months of living in fear, Bedreah's steely self-control snapped. "From the first day, I said we should leave, but you said, 'no.' Now the Iraqis have come to kill us all!"

Ali and Ahmad rushed to their mother. "Calm down, Mom," Ali said, as they led her to a chair. "Everything is going to be fine. The Iraqis will leave soon."

At that moment a loud burst of rifle and machine-gun fire pierced the air. The women screamed, the children began crying, and the men looked at each other, wondering what to do.

"Maybe it's the allies," a white-faced Mohammed said to no one in particular.

"I don't know," Ali said, "but I'm going back to the roof to see what's going on." He raced for the stairs, Ahmad on his heels, his mother's hysterical cries of "No, no!" ringing in his ears.

They barely had time to look out over Rumaithiya after they got to the roof when a terrific explosion knocked them to their knees. Then the gunfire stopped. They crawled to the wall and looked down into the courtyard. There wasn't an Iraqi to be seen anywhere. Out on the major thoroughfares, the parade of lights continued northward.

The two men went back downstairs and told the family to relax. "We will just have to wait until daylight to be sure," Ali said, "but I think they are all gone. The best thing we can do now is get a little rest."

At dawn they woke to the sound of silence. There were no rolling, reverberating explosions, sharp cracks of small arms fire, or chatter of machine guns—sounds they had lived with since August 2.

Ali rose from his mattress and climbed the stairs to the roof. Hassan was already there with a radio in his hand.

"Tell me the news," Ali said to his brother-in-law.

"There has been nothing new on yet," Hassan sighed. "They're still saying that the Iraqis are fleeing, but there has been nothing said about anything secured by the allies."

Ali saw a movement a few blocks away and grabbed his binoculars to take a closer look. It was a teenage boy walking toward the neighborhood high school. The youngster entered the building and Ali held his breath, afraid he would hear the sound of an Iraqi rifle. But all remained quiet, and in a few minutes, the youth walked out of the building and continued his lonely trek up the street.

It was now 7:00 and Hassan turned the radio up, hoping to hear new information. BBC Radio announced that the Iraqis had pulled out of Kuwait City during the night and that the Kuwaiti flag was once again flying over the city. The two looked at each other, praying that the news was correct.

Somewhere down the street a door slammed, and Ali and Hassan looked down to see a couple of neighborhood children going out into their yard. In a few moments, they were joined by several more children and a few adults. Then the men heard the sound of horns honking and looked toward Naser Al-Mubarak Street to see another parade of vehicles—only this time it was made up of cars full of jubilant Kuwaitis, shouting and waving their country's flag.

Ali smiled broadly and clapped his brother-in-law on the back. "Let's go!" he shouted.

The two brothers ran headlong down the stairs and out into the street where Ali managed to stop one of the vehicles. He asked the driver what was going on.

"The Iraqis are gone!" the man shouted in glee. "Kuwait is free!"

Ali slumped down on the curb and covered his face with his hands. Tears of relief trickled through his fingers.

■ ■ ■

Chills ran down Dina's spine as she watched scenes of liberation unfolding before her on the television screen. As she watched the Kuwaiti flag being raised in Kuwait City and heard the familiar strains of the Kuwaiti national anthem, she cried tears of gratitude and silently thanked those who had risked their lives to fight for her adopted country.

She had been on her way to take the children to a McDonald's restaurant for a late supper when the car radio blasted the news that the ground war had begun. She turned around and headed back to Gina's, where she planted herself in front of the television. She had been there since, watching the progress of Desert Storm. She had not slept, nor had she eaten. She had barely spoken to the children or her sister.

Now that Kuwait City had been declared secure, she looked for a familiar face in the happy crowd of Kuwaitis welcoming the liberators. A smile danced across her face as she watched a man in a U.S. Marine uniform hug and kiss a man in a *distasha*. The television reporter was explaining that the Marine was a Kuwaiti who had been in America at the time of the invasion. He had begged to join the Marines so he could help liberate his country. Incredibly, he had just been reunited with one of his brothers, who had been standing in the Kuwait City crowd.

Dina wondered if she, too, would be reunited with her loved ones. Bedreah had said that when the liberation came, she would be one of the first to dance in the streets. "Watch for me on television," she had told Dina before she left Kuwait. "I'll be the one with a Kuwaiti flag and a picture of George Bush!" Dina watched television until her eyes crossed, but she couldn't find her mother-in-law, or her husband, or anyone she knew.

It's over! she sobbed silently as she watched the jubilation. *It's finally over.* But, of all the emotions she was feeling, she couldn't feel relief. Kuwait was free, but was Ali alive to see it?

She waited twenty-four hours to find out. The day after the liberation, she received a phone call from London. It was Masuma reporting that one of her cousins had driven to Bahrain to call her and tell her that Bedreah and Eidan's family was alive and unharmed.

For Dina, the war was now over. She could now turn off the television set and sleep.

CHAPTER 16

On February 26, Ali sat outside the courtyard watching the liberation celebration in his neighborhood. There was joy in his heart, but it was still a sad heart. He would have been more excited if Dina and the children had been there to celebrate with him. They had been separated for so long now that it was sometimes hard for him to picture their faces in his mind.

It was a dark, cold, rainy day, and while the weather reflected Ali's mood, it did not dampen his neighbors' spirits. Their faces, hands, and clothes turned black from the oil and soot that had come down with the rain since Saddam had fired the oil wells, but that didn't deter the Kuwaitis in their revelry.

The men and boys had gone to the neighborhood schools in hopes of finding weapons the Iraqis had left behind. They had found an abundance, and now they were firing the guns into the air in glee. Several people waved Kuwaiti and American flags, and many knelt on the soggy ground, chanting Islamic prayers. As Ali watched the celebration he thought: *It took the bitterness of entrapment to make us realize how very sweet freedom tastes.*

Ali had been on the steps about half an hour when he saw Arafat hurrying up the street.

"Arafat!" Ali hailed. "Where are you going in such a hurry?"

"To the police station to look for my brother," Arafat answered. "He was one of those picked up the day before the invasion."

Ali had not heard about that, but then he'd barely stuck his nose out of the house for a week—ever since Kareem and his wife had come to visit. He had taken the warning from the resistance seriously.

"Ali!" a voice called. He stood up and waved as Abass crossed the street and walked toward him.

"Let's go to Farouk's," Abass said. "I want to find out what the resistance plans to do now."

The two men walked down the street and pounded on Farouk's door.

"Looks like the bastards are gone," Ali said when his neighbor opened the door.

"Yes," Farouk nodded somberly, "Most of them, anyway." He stepped aside and motioned Ali and Abass into the apartment. "Come help us organize to protect the neighborhood," he added. As Ali and Abass walked into the living room, their eyes nearly popped out of their heads. The room looked like an arsenal.

"Where did you get all of those guns?" Abass finally asked, after staring at the weapons for several seconds.

"You didn't think I used water pistols to fight the Iraqis, did you?" Farouk laughed.

Farouk's brother Noori and a man Ali did not know were sitting on the floor, intent on cleaning the weapons.

"You said something about organizing to protect the neighborhood," Ali said to Farouk, "but you agreed that the Iraqis have pulled out."

"I said *most* of them are gone," the resistance fighter reiterated. "You can bet there were some left behind to do sabotage work. And what about the collaborators? Will you feel safe with them running around free until the government can get organized and back in control?"

Ali and Abass sat on the couch, quietly listening to Farouk and the others as they listed the reasons for instigating self-protection in the neighborhood. The arguments made sense, the two decided. There would be no one else to protect their families until things returned to normal.

"We hope you will join us," Farouk said when he was done with his "pitch" to his two neighbors.

Ali and Abass exchanged looks, stood up, and walked over to where Farouk stood. "You didn't leave us much room to refuse," Abass said as he shook hands with Farouk. "You guys put up a pretty convincing argument."

"This should mean I'm eligible for a gun now," Ali grinned.

Farouk laughed and slapped Ali on the back. "Go home and change clothes and I'll have one with your name on it ready when you get back."

■ ■ ■

Husain and Kareem heard about the liberation over a radio that one of the prisoners had obtained by bribing a guard. As soon as they heard the news, the prisoners began shouting in elation. Almost immediately an intelligence officer, backed by several armed guards, appeared at the door.

"You all seem so happy," the officer said. "Tell me, have you heard something that makes you joyful?"

No one answered.

"I know someone in here has a radio!" the officer shouted. "If he turns it over immediately, he will not be harmed!"

No one moved.

The officer kicked the door frame in frustration. "All of you out!" he shrieked. "We will find the radio ourselves!"

The search turned up nothing. The man with the radio slipped it into his *distasha* pocket before he left the room. The Iraqis didn't think to search the prisoners themselves.

After the prisoners had been herded back into the room, the officer screamed, "If whoever had the radio doesn't bring it and its batteries to me in ten minutes, all of you will find out what intelligence people can do when they get angry!"

"We have heard important news," one of the prisoners pointed out after the officer and soldiers stomped away from the building. "We know the country has been liberated, so what use is the radio now? All we can do with, or without it, is sit here and wait to be released."

Others who were afraid of the officer's wrath began to plead with the owner of the radio. "It's not worth all of us getting killed over," one man said.

The man was finally persuaded to turn the radio in, and surprisingly, the officer was true to his word. The prisoner was not harmed.

■ ■ ■

Ali rushed home from Farouk's and exchanged his *distasha* for a sweat suit and sneakers. As he was heading for the door to go back to Farouk's, he ran into Mohammed.

"You're not going out," Mohammed said in surprise. "It's still too dangerous to be out on the streets."

"I'm only going to Farouk's."

"You should wait a couple of days," Mohammed said. "We don't know that all of the Iraqis are gone."

Exactly, Ali thought. He ignored his brother-in-law and left the house.

Farouk and several other men were waiting outside Ali's fence. The freedom fighter handed Ali a machine gun. "That should be big enough for you," Farouk grinned.

The gun weighed heavily in Ali's hands. He had only hefted a pistol a couple of times and the power of what he now held sent a chill down his spine.

"This is the plan," Farouk continued. "We will create our own checkpoints throughout the neighborhood and check the IDs of people coming through. This way we will know if there are suspicious people around." He added, "Once there are more of us, we will then go after the collaborators."

Ali nearly dropped his gun. "No," he said in surprise. "That wasn't part of the bargain. I agree we should keep strangers out of the neighborhood, but we should let the government take care of the collaborators."

A strange, and almost evil look came over Farouk's face as Ali spoke. "I know people who informed on me," Farouk said, through clenched teeth, "and I'm going to kill the sons of bitches!"

Ali cringed at Farouk's vehemence. This was a side of his friend that he did not know.

Suddenly they heard the roar of motors and turned and saw two Iraqi trucks with several men in them hurtling down the street. Farouk, never bothering to take cover, aimed his machine gun and opened fire. "I told you there would be some left behind for sabotage," he shrieked.

Luckily, the Iraqis didn't take time from their mad dash to wherever they were going to fire back.

Ali, Abass, and a couple of the other neighbors who had agreed to help Farouk stood in shock, staring at him.

"This is damned stupid," Ali finally blurted out. "If the Iraqis had started shooting, we'd all be dead. Where's your brain, man? If you're going to pick a fight, at least protect yourself!"

That said, he handed his gun back to Farouk. "I'm not ready to die yet!" he shouted. "And I damn sure won't die stupidly!"

Farouk's eyes shot hot sparks at Ali. Then he turned around and stomped off without saying a word. Farouk's brother, the stranger, and a few of the neighbors were at his heels.

Ali and those left behind returned to their homes. Later, Ali found out that Farouk had captured several collaborators but had not harmed them. He took them to the police station, which the resistance had taken over immediately after the Iraqis vacated it, to be held for trial.

■ ■ ■

After Ali and Farouk parted company, Ali decided to go to Jassim's school to see how much damage the Iraqis had caused.

When he entered the front hall, the smell of urine and feces nearly choked him. He followed the odor to the gymnasium, where he found that the soldiers had used it as a bathroom. Human waste covered the floor and walls of the huge room. In the classrooms, pornographic pictures had been drawn on the walls and blackboards. What textbooks hadn't been stolen had been fouled with vulgar drawings and obscenities. A chill went down his spine when he discovered a huge map of Rumaithiya on one of the walls. Every house in the town was on the map, complete with the names of those who lived there. Some houses had been circled and the words *resistance* or *suspected resistance* were written in the circles. Several houses in his neighborhood were marked, including Farouk's, but excluding his own.

When Ali told Ahmad that night about the condition of Jassim's school, his brother told him he also had seen the mess. Then Ahmad added that he'd gone to Nadia's school where there was similar vandalism.

"I found out what the gunfire and loud explosions were while the Iraqis were pounding on our front door that night," Ahmad told Ali. "The Iraqis had stored ammunition in two of the classrooms at Nadia's school," he continued, "and before they left town that night, they blew it all up."

"I bet the sound of the gunfire and explosions scared the bunch of Iraqis at our door, and that's why they left," Ali grinned.

"I bet you're right, brother!" Ahmad laughed.

■ ■ ■

The morning after the Kuwaiti flag went back up in Kuwait City, Ali and Hassan sat in the yard discussing how to get their wives and children home. Ali was still worried about being hobbled with no passport. He was afraid his own country's officials would be reluctant to let him leave Kuwait without one.

Suddenly the two began to hear the sounds of clapping and cheering, which seemed to grow closer and louder each second. Then there came a rumble that sounded like tanks. They walked outside the compound fence but saw nothing, so they decided to go up on the roof.

When they looked out over the main thoroughfares they saw the cause for the noise. The first group of liberators, which was made up of Kuwaiti soldiers who had fled to Saudi Arabia during the invasion, was moving into the town.

■ ■ ■

At Al-Bakoba prison camp, Abdul-Samad and the other air force prisoners took the news of the liberation in stride. They seemed to know it would come quickly after the allies entered the country. Their main concern was how much longer they would have to stay in the miserable camp before they would be liberated.

The day after the liberators entered Kuwait City, rumors began circulating in the camp that the Red Cross was on its way to free the prisoners.

"We will soon be free," Abdul-Samad said to one of his friends. "They say we will be released as soon as the Red

Cross arrives! In a day or two, we will be with our families again!"

The prisoners would wait much longer than a day or two to regain their freedom.

■ ■ ■

After watching Kuwaiti and Saudi soldiers parade down the streets of Rumaithiya for a short time, Ali and Hassan returned to the yard. Before long a neighbor passed by and told them that the neighborhood gas station had reopened. Ali decided to take his car and get if filled up. When he arrived at the station, much to his surprise, he found Abass about to pass out. Abass had been the one to open the station by hooking up a generator capable of pumping the gas out of its underground storage tanks.

Ali asked the white-faced Abass if he needed help.

"I sure do," Abass nodded. "These fumes have about got to me!"

Ali took over. He began filling tanks on cars and the buckets some people brought to haul away extra fuel. There were many cars and people were becoming impatient. Arguments and shoving matches developed.

Ali finally became angry with the crowd. "Get in line and stay there!" he shouted. "There will be no pushing or shoving, or I will take the generator and go home!"

The crowd quieted for a while, but soon he heard another commotion. Glancing up he saw his brother Ahmad and another Kuwaiti in a shoving match over their position in the line. To Ali's horror, he watched as his brother drew a knife from the pocket of his *distasha*. "Stop!" Ali shouted, dropping the nozzle and rushing toward the two men. "Put that knife away!"

"I'll kill him!" Ahmad screamed.

One of the men in line grabbed Ahmad from behind and held him while Ali grabbed the other man, slapped him, and gave him a shove toward his car. "Get the hell out of here!" Ali said to the stranger. Ali turned and took the knife from his brother's hand. "Go home!" he ordered.

Ahmad, his rage spent, got into his car and left. Ali remained at the station until sunset and then returned the next day for the last time.

About four o'clock that day, a group of resistance members with machine guns walked up to Ali and Abass.

"You guys have to quit this right now," one of the men said.

"We're not doing any harm," Ali said. "We're just trying to help our neighbors out. Who the hell do you think you are, anyway?"

"I'm just a good guy giving you some good advice, that's who I am," the man said. "There are still many Iraqis around here, and they wouldn't even need to use guns. One cigarette tossed out a car window, and you and 300 or 400 other people could be blown to hell!"

Ali looked at Abass. "He's right," Ali said.

Abass shook his head. "No, I think it's worth the risk. Our people deserve to have gas now that the occupation is over. We can set up lookouts to watch for Iraqis."

"It's too dangerous," Ali insisted. "What good would all the gas in the world do for these people if they get blown up filling their tanks!" With those words he unhooked the generator, picked it up, and walked away, leaving Abass staring after him.

"You've got a lot of gall!" Abass shouted at Ali's back. "That's my generator, you know!"

Ali just kept walking to his car and after a few minutes, Abass threw up his hands and started walking toward his car. He was tired of being a gas station operator, anyway.

■ ■ ■

Living the Nightmare

One hundred hours after the ground war began, U.S. President Bush ordered a cessation of hostilities.

After the smoke settled over the battlefields, the cost of the war in human lives began to be tallied. The final estimate revealed that some 100,000 Iraqis had been killed, 300,000 were wounded and another 100,000 taken prisoner. Allied losses were reported at 138 killed, 432 wounded, and 57 missing. Kuwait set its losses at 2,000 to 3,000 dead, with some 3,000 missing. A total of 10,000 to 15,000 Kuwaitis had been arrested and imprisoned during the seven-month nightmare.

Some happy stories emerged in the days following the liberation. Many Rumaithiyans learned their loved ones who had been arrested and hauled away by the Iraqis were safe.

One of the happy endings involved Arafat's brother. Arafat did not find him at the police station that day and the family spent several more anxious days before the missing man appeared. He told his family that, even though the Iraqis were retreating from the allies the afternoon of the day the ground war started, he and a busload of prisoners were taken from the Rumaithiya Police Station to a camp near Basra.

Another happy ending came for a friend of Abass, a thirty-five-year-old resistance fighter named Naser. He had been captured at his home in Ardiya at the end of January. Everyone had given him up for dead, but he survived his torture and confinement in an Ardiya jail cell and became a free man on liberation day.

All of the men arrested at Farouk's sister's house in November were found alive in their jail cells after the Iraqis fled from the Al-Jabriya Police Station. However, his sister has never found out her son's fate. He is one of those 3,000 men, women, and children who disappeared and have never been heard from.

■ ■ ■

On the last day of February, Ali drove his mother to Ardiya to see her brother Khalil and to Al-Sulaibikhat to visit her sister Miriam. Bedreah was anxious to find out how her relatives had fared during Operation Desert Storm.

Mobs of people were still celebrating in the streets of every town they drove through and they saw thousands of soldiers in tanks and other vehicles from all over the world. When they arrived at Khalil's house, they were in for a shock.

"Can you believe," Khalil said to his sister, "that Husain and Kareem are still missing?"

"*What*? *Missing*?" Bedreah said. "What are you talking about? Kareem was just at my house a few days before the allies came."

"Yes," Khalil said, "and the day after he was there, he was arrested. The Iraqis picked him, Husain, and Rasul up at a checkpoint in the afternoon. Rasul was later released, but no one has seen or heard from Husain or Kareem since."

Bedreah sat in stunned silence for a few minutes, tears streaming down her cheeks. "I must go to Miriam," she finally said, getting up from the couch.

Ali followed her to the car and drove her to her sister's house. When they arrived, the only one they found was Rasul, who had been making daily trips from his home to check on his parents. The moment he opened the door and saw his aunt, tears came to his eyes.

"It is true, then?" Bedreah sobbed.

"Yes. We do not know if they are dead or alive," Rasul nodded.

Bedreah and Ali waited for Miriam for about an hour and then gave up. "Tell your mother I will try to come back tomorrow," Bedreah told Rasul.

When they got to the car, Ali told his mother he wanted to drive up the Al-Mutla Express Road toward Iraq to see the trail of retreat. Radio stations had been reporting that the roads leading out of Kuwait were lined with bombed and burned-out vehicles, and Ali wanted to see if the reports were true. He also thought the drive might take his mother's mind off her nephews.

It didn't take them long to discover that the radio reports were accurate. The road was not only lined with destroyed vehicles, the bodies of dead Iraqi soldiers were scattered all over the landscape. After Ali had driven about fifteen miles, he turned around. Both he and his mother were becoming ill from the sight.

■ ■ ■

When Ali and Bedreah returned to Rumaithiya, Ali dropped his mother off at the compound and then drove to the American Embassy. He had decided that he was going to try to find a way to call Dina, and he figured her embassy would be a good starting point.

It didn't take him long to find out it wasn't. A woman at the reception desk told him there was only one phone line out of the country and it could only be used in an emergency by the ambassador, who had already returned to Kuwait.

Dejected, Ali went home where Hassan was waiting with more bad news. He told Ali that he had talked to a Kuwaiti soldier who said that word from government officials was that no one would be allowed to leave the country for at least three months.

Now Ali was really depressed. "Damn it!" he roared. "We risked our lives staying here during the whole stinking occupation because they said it was the patriotic thing to do. Big talk! Their asses were all safe in Saudi Arabia the whole time. Now they're back and they're telling us we can't leave and go to our families! Bullshit!"

"Calm down, Ali," Hassan said. "We'll figure something out."

"I'm figuring right now that I'm going to go talk to Khalid. He always seems to come up with a solution to a problem when there doesn't seem to be one."

Ali slammed out the door and crossed the street to his neighbor's house.

"Khalid, I need some help to try to get to America to see my family," he blurted out when Khalid opened the door. "Hassan just told me no one is going to be allowed to leave the country for three months. I can't wait that long to see them!"

Khalid took Ali by the arm and led him to a chair. "I have one friend, Michel Abdul, who might be able to help you," he said. "He is a government employee and is related to the royal family. I will take you to see him tomorrow."

"No," Ali said. "Now! Take me to him now!"

"It's nearly dark," a surprised Khalid said. "Now whose bats are working overtime in his belfry? You know it's still not safe to be out after dark!"

"Please," Ali begged. "I've got to get to America!"

Khalid listened to Ali's pleas for a short time, and then gave in and agreed to make the trip. They left about seven thirty.

When they arrived at Khalid's friend's house, he wasn't home. Michel Abdul's wife told Khalid that he should try to contact him the next day at his office.

The next day, the first day of March, Ali and Khalid went to the man's office. They waited for nearly two hours before they found out from his assistant that he wasn't there. He told them to come back at 4:30, which they did, only to discover that Michel Abdul, had on the spur of the moment left for Saudi Arabia for two weeks.

Ali sank into a chair, disappointment settling over his face. Khalid felt so sorry for his friend that he decided to explain their mission to the assistant. When he finished, the assistant asked if it would help Ali to phone his wife.

Ali's face brightened. "Oh, yes!" he said. "Is that possible?"

The assistant told him there was a generator-operated satellite phone in the building and led him down a hall to another room. There were about a dozen people in the room, all waiting to use the phone. Ali waited impatiently for nearly two hours, and when his turn came, the generator went dead.

Ali wanted to scream. *Why me? Every damned piece of bad luck happens to me!* He was so angry, he stomped out of the building without thanking the assistant.

The next day Ahmad announced that the telephone center in the nearby town of Mushrif was back in operation. "Go," Ahmad told his brother. "You might have to wait a few hours, but you will be able to talk to Dina."

Ali, who was in one of the foulest moods he'd ever been in in his whole life, refused to go. "I could stand there for twelve hours and still not get to talk to her," he growled at his brother. "It would be just like yesterday. Something would go wrong when it was my turn to make the damned call."

Hassan and Bedreah jumped at the chance to call England and America. After only a couple of hours of waiting, Hassan reached Masuma, and when he finished talking, Bedreah spoke with Dina.

When his mother told him she had talked to his wife, Ali felt very sheepish. "Go tomorrow," Bedreah encouraged her son, "and talk to her. She is very worried about you."

Ali got up early on the morning of March 3 and drove to Mushrif. He got through to Dina after a short wait, and he almost cried when he heard her voice.

Her first question was, "When are you coming to America?"

Ali explained the government order saying no one would be allowed to leave for three months, but told her he was working on a way to leave before then. She told him she also had been trying to find someone in the States who could help get him out of Kuwait.

Talking to his wife lifted Ali out of his stormy mood, but it made him even more anxious and desperate to get to America.

■ ■ ■

A few days after Ali found out that he would be getting no immediate help from Khalid's friend he went back to the American Embassy, hoping that Dina's countrymen could figure out a way to help him get to the States. He found no hope. The woman he talked to told him the embassy had been asked not to help Kuwaitis leave the country for the next three months.

"Our hands are tied," she told Ali, with some measure of sympathy.

"I don't know where to go next," Ali said to Hassan that night. "I'm beginning to believe there isn't anyone who can help us."

"How about the Saudi Embassy?" Hassan suggested. "Maybe if we tell somebody there that we know that Kuwait records were smuggled to the embassy in Riyadh during the occupation and that we have to get there to finish renewing your passport, they will let us go."

"It's worth a try," Ali grinned. "Anything's worth a try now."

The next morning they stood outside the Saudi Arabian Embassy at 8:00 waiting for it to open. A Kuwaiti man standing in line behind them struck up a conversation and asked why they were in line. They told him they were going to try to get permission to enter Saudi Arabia.

"You want to leave Kuwait?"

"Yes," Ali said, and then explained their reason.

"Oh, well," the man said, "you will have to get permission from the Kuwaiti government first."

"But the government says it won't let anyone leave the country for three months and I can't wait that long," Ali said.

Taking a piece of paper out of his pocket, the man said, "Go to Ardiya. There's a government office there that will grant you permission to go to Saudi."

Ali and Hassan looked the paper over carefully. It certainly seemed to be an official document.

"Once you get this in Ardiya," the man continued, "you have to bring it here to the Saudi Embassy for them to approve. That's why I'm here now."

Ali and Hassan left the man listening to his own words in their rush to get to their car. They drove home to get the papers the man said they would need. Then Ali sped down Fifth Ring to Ardiya as fast as he dared go with all the military vehicles on the road.

Two days later, on March 10, Ali and Hassan were on their way to Saudi.

CHAPTER 17

While Ali was signing papers in Ardiya that would allow him to go to Saudi Arabia, one of his cousins was still in a prison camp, but two others were on the road to freedom.

The Red Cross had not arrived as expected at Abdul-Samad's camp and the prisoners were becoming more dejected with each passing day. Many expressed the fear that they would be kept an Iraqi prisoner for as long as some Iranian soldiers had been held. Living conditions were deteriorating rapidly at Al-Bakoba. There had been little water since the day the ground war began, and the already scarce food supply had dwindled even further.

At Husain and Kareem's camp, things moved a bit more quickly. Their camp was located near an area where intense fighting had broken out between Iraqi revolutionaries and contingents of troops loyal to Saddam. Not only did the prisoners want out of the area, so did their guards.

On March 7, the camp's commanding officer decided to contact the governor of Saddam's "nineteenth province" to find out if the camp was going to be dissolved, and if so, when. A day after he spoke with the governor by telephone, several cars full of Republican Guards came to the camp and took the commander away. The prisoners wondered if he had fallen into disfavor in Baghdad because he had dared to question the camp's fate. Later that evening, however, he returned to the camp and announced that the governor would decide what to do with the prisoners by morning.

It seemed to the prisoners that morning would never come, but the sun finally chased the darkness away. As it became light, the prisoners saw that large groups of Republican Guards had moved into the camp during the night. They were afraid the appearance of these soldiers, Saddam's most loyal, meant that the governor's decision was to execute them.

Noon came and there still was no announcement. The prisoners were sick with worry. Then about twelve-thirty they heard the sound of trucks pulling into the compound. About the same time, guards began unlocking the prisoners' quarters and ushering them out into the yard. Husain, Kareem, and the others wondered if there were machine guns in the back of the trucks. *Was this to be the end?*

As the Kuwaitis stood anxiously awaiting their fate, the tailgates on the trucks began dropping down. Inside the vehicles were not machine guns but fresh tomatoes, bowls of rice, and chicken! The most, and certainly the best, food they had seen since their capture. The hungry prisoners ran to the trucks, but Husain held back.

"Come on," Kareem shouted, grabbing his brother by the arm.

"No," Husain said, "I'm afraid the food is poisoned."

Kareem laughed and asked Husain why the Iraqis would poison food they needed so badly in their own country and then give it to prisoners when all they would have to do was shoot them if they wanted them dead. He finally convinced his brother that the food was safe to eat.

As they were eating, the prisoners noticed a change in the guards' attitudes. They were all trying to be friendly toward the Kuwaitis, laughing and talking with them and passing out cigarettes. Something had to be up.

"I bet the revolution is over and Saddam lost," Kareem guessed, "or he is dead, and they are getting ready to release us!"

As Kareem spoke to Husain, several empty buses, accompanied by Jeeps filled with more Republican Guards, pulled into the prison yard. The prisoners stared uneasily at the vehicles. Obviously the governor had made a decision, but what was it?

An officer holding a sheaf of papers in one hand jumped out of one of the Jeeps, almost before the vehicle came to a full stop. Facing the prisoners, he commanded, "When I call your name, get on the nearest bus!"

The prisoners shuffled their feet nervously, but no one panicked and bolted. As their names were called, they walked reluctantly to a bus. When they went through the door, each was handed a fresh biscuit and a jar of clean water. They had nearly forgotten what unpolluted water tasted like.

When the buses were full, they pulled out of the prison yard, led and followed by Jeeps full of Republican Guards. Each prisoner wondered if he was being taken to Baghdad (which is where they were told they would eventually be interned when they first arrived at the camp), to a death camp, or was he on his way home?

They were heading in a southwesterly direction, which gave them some measure of hope that they might be going to Kuwait.

After only a couple of hours of driving, the buses stopped. To their alarm, the prisoners looked out the windows to discover that they were at the gates of an area they had heard was where Saddam's "execution regiment" was housed.

■ ■ ■

Living the Nightmare

Ali and Hassan were surrounded by the wreckage of war as they roared down the highway, bound for the Saudi border station of Khafji. The highway was lined with burned-out Iraqi vehicles and Hassan, who was driving Ali's car, dodged potholes in the road caused by allied bombs.

I am seeing the results of what happens when all of the means devised by man to tear both men and machines apart are used, Ali thought as he stared out his window.

He was angry with Hassan for refusing to take his wife's brand new car. Ali's vehicle was a 1986 model, and he felt, much less reliable for the grueling trip through the desert. Hassan retaliated against Ali's anger by driving like a maniac. Neither had uttered a word to the other since they left the family compound.

It had been 10:00 A.M. when they left Rumaithiya under skies that were still darkened by the oil well fires. Both had been nervous about the trip, afraid that what had happened at the Iraqi checkpoint when they tried to flee the country in November might again happen at a Saudi or American roadblock. But they had passed through each one they came to with no problem.

The farther into Saudi Arabia they drove, the more soldiers they saw. They drove by camp after camp where thousands of men and women, mostly Americans, were standing around looking weary and bored.

They don't want to be here, Ali thought. *They're missing their families just as I am.* He swore, and once again damned Saddam to hell for causing so much misery.

When Ali and Hsssan arrived at Al-Damman, Saudi Arabia, they stopped for gas and food. It lifted their spirits to see fresh milk, yogurt, candy, and other items they had not seen for months. They had very little money between them, so they couldn't buy as much as they would have liked. Besides, they would have felt guilty gorging themselves while everyone in Kuwait was still bound to a meager diet.

After nearly twelve hours of driving, they arrived in Riyadh, *distashas* and *gutras* filthy from the oil smoke they had driven through on much of their trip. They quickly found their embassy, only to be told that passports were no longer being issued.

"I will not stand for this," Ali told Hassan. "I'm going to get a passport if I have to steal one!" He decided he would try to find the Kuwaiti ambassador, Sheik Mohammed al-Sabah, to see if he would help him.

The ambassador was in the building, even though it was very late, and consented to see Ali. Tears came to al-Sabah's eyes as Ali told him how he had weathered the occupation, just as his government had asked, and how desperate he was now to be reunited with his family.

Ali had his passport within twenty minutes of talking to the ambassador. He and Hassan were also given enough money for a hotel room, food, and cigarettes.

■ ■ ■

On the morning of March 9, Dina was watching the news on CNN. Suddenly she jumped up from her chair and ran closer to the television set.

Gina looked at her sister in surprise. "What's the matter? Did you see someone you know?"

"Oh, yes!" Dina shouted. "Ali's cousins, Husain and Kareem!" Sure enough—there they were—grinning from ear to ear as they waved wildly from the window of their bus.

The stop at the "execution regiment" camp had not meant what the prisoners had feared. It just happened to be the place where the prison camp buses and a contingent of Red Cross workers coming from Saudi Arabia to get the prisoners met each other. The Red Cross had taken charge of the prisoners at that camp and now they were at a checkpoint near the Iraqi-Kuwaiti border on the last leg of their journey home. CNN and CBS camera crews were at the checkpoint when the buses passed through and had filmed the event.

Ali had not thought to tell Dina that the two had been arrested, and now, by a weird coincidence, she was the first in the family to know they had survived their ordeal.

■ ■ ■

As Continental Airlines flight 35 settled into a cruising altitude of 30,000 feet, Ali pushed his seat in row 38 back in the reclining position. It was March 15. The plane had taken off from Gatwick International Airport at 1:45 P.M., London time, for a ten-hour flight to the United States. As he reached into his pocket for a cigarette, Ali heaved a deep sigh of relief. He was finally on his way to see Dina and the children.

A smile flickered across Ali's face as he thought about how surprised they were going to be. He had planned very carefully to surprise them. He had called Dina from the United Arab Emirates before he boarded a plane for London but had fibbed to her when she asked when he was coming to America.

"They are still saying we can't leave for three months," Ali had said, sighing dramatically into the phone and nearly choking as he suppressed a giggle.

Lighting the cigarette, he stared out the window at the midday sky. Off in the distance, lightning played around the edges of a bank of ominously dark clouds. He wondered if the plane would encounter the storm and the turbulence generated by it. He was not an avid flier and dreaded the possibility of a rough flight. Then he chuckled to himself. *How could anything be rougher than what I'd lived through the past seven months?*

A stray beam of sunlight winked hypnotically on the plane's wing, making Ali drowsy. Stubbing out the cigarette, he closed his eyes. *Am I really on my way to the States? Or am I just dreaming.* Even after he had finally gotten his passport in

Riyadh, Ali had run into stumbling blocks that had delayed his flight to America.

He and Hassan had decided they would go to the Emirates to get a plane to England because Ali's brother Reda and his family were there. Reda had left England for the Emirates shortly after the invasion so that his family would be closer to home when Kuwait was free. Reda had managed to get a letter smuggled into Rumaithiya telling the family where he was. Ali and Hassan figured Reda would be able to help them find a way to obtain plane fare and tickets.

Ali and Hassan left Riyadh the morning of March 11, expecting to be in the Emirates that evening. However, they got lost and wound up in Bahrain, 200 miles out of their way. Then as they began retracing their steps, Ali's car blew a water pump. There they sat in the middle of the desert with a broken-down automobile. Ali shut the motor off and spent the next fifteen minutes berating his brother-in-law for not having driven Masuma's new car.

After he got his temper under control, Ali started the engine again and they limped to a checkpoint where they were told by a Saudi guard that they were approximately 120 miles in either direction to a garage that would be capable of fixing Ali's Chrysler.

"Now what are we going to do, you jackass!" Ali growled at Hassan.

The guard overheard him and said, "Just wait a few minutes, someone will be by and you can hitch a ride with them."

Sure enough, about fifteen minutes later, a Kuwaiti family drove up and after hearing Ali's story, offered to take him and Hassan to the Emirates. At 3:00 the next morning, Ali and Hassan were knocking on Reda's apartment door in the town of Dubi. It had taken them four days to obtain a loan at the Kuwaiti Consulate in Dubi and get passage on a plane bound for England.

■ ■ ■

Living the Nightmare

Abdul-Samad awoke on the morning of March 15 and saw an angel standing in the doorway of his prison cell. It was actually a member of the Red Cross, but to Abdul-Samad and the other prisoners, all of the Red Cross members who arrived at Al-Bakoba that day looked like angels.

"God Gracious, I am free!" Abdul-Samad shouted as he jumped up from the hard floor. *"I have survived being a prisoner of war!"*

Through the long days and nights of waiting for the Red Cross, Abdul-Samad had grown to feel his chances of survival were becoming smaller and smaller. Sometimes he had almost felt like he was choking in his confinement. He had begun to wonder if the feeling that God was going to allow him to survive imprisonment as He had survived the storm at sea had been a false one.

But now, as Abdul-Samad looked into the faces of the Red Cross workers, all the worry and fear that had burdened him since August 2 disappeared. He was going home—back to his country and his loved ones.

The air force prisoners from Al-Bakoba were transported to Saudi Arabia for their official release. When they arrived in Saudi, they were taken to a building where there were real beds with mattresses, pillows, and blankets. They were given a meal of chicken, cola, chocolate, and fresh fruit. They were even issued clean clothes and shoes. Abdul-Samad decided he now knew what paradise would be like.

It took a couple of days to complete the paperwork, but finally Abdul-Samad boarded a plane bound for Kuwait. His family had been notified when he would arrive and a big crowd was waiting for him when he landed at Kuwait International Airport. He was nearly swept off his feet as everyone raced to him with arms outstretched and tears streaming down their cheeks.

He smiled as he watched them coming towards him. *This is home*, he sighed happily. *This is love.*

But as he hugged each one individually, an uneasy feeling came over him. Glancing around, he noticed there was one person missing—his father. *Where is my father?* He began to panic. Why was his father not here? Had something happened to him? It wouldn't be fair for him to come home alive only to find that his father had not survived the occupation.

Frantically he looked over the heads of those gathered around him, searching for his father's face. His eyes probed many faces, and then suddenly, they fell on a familiar, beloved one. He took a deep breath and disengaged himself from the crowd. As if in a dream, he walked toward his father and folded the tearful old man in his arms.

Now Abdul-Samad was truly home.

■ ■ ■

Ali's plane had been on time when it landed in Denver, and now, after a three-and-one-half hour layover, he was on a United Airlines plane headed for Lincoln. It was only an hour's flight. He would be there by nine-thirty.

Ali stretched and smiled at his seat partner, to whom he had just told the circumstances of his trip, and said, "I think I will take a nap. It will make the time go more quickly." Leaning back in his seat, he shut his eyes and soon dozed off, but as happened so many times, what started as a peaceful slumber was interrupted by a nightmare.

"No! No! Jassim!...They've got Jassim!...Help Jassim!"

He awoke with his seat mate holding onto his flailing arms. "Don't!" Ali screeched at the man. "Don't! I've been shot in the leg...." Then reality struck him. He was on an airplane headed for Nebraska, not running away from the Iraqis with his son.

"I'm sorry," Ali said as the man relaxed his grip on his arms. "I must have been dreaming."

"*Some dream,*" a woman across the aisle said. "I'd say it was more like a nightmare."

Living the Nightmare

Ali grinned feebly. "You're right. It was a bad dream. Please accept my apologies," he added as he wiped sweat from his face.

Within minutes the pilot's voice came over the intercom asking the flight attendants to prepare the cabin for landing. Ali looked out the window and saw snowflakes coming down. He had hoped he would see snow in Lincoln, even though it was getting a little late in the season for it. He had liked the snow when he was in college and hadn't seen it since he'd taken Dina, Jassim, and Nadia back to Kuwait to live. When they came to the States, it was always in the middle of the summer.

As soon as the plane braked to a stop at the gate, Ali was on his feet and in the aisle. It seemed like hours before it was his turn to go through the door into the terminal and the baggage claim area. While he was waiting for his bags to arrive, he went outside and hailed a cab.

During the half-hour ride to his sister-in-law's house in southeast Lincoln, all Ali could think of was how lucky he was to be in that taxi. He had come so close to becoming a casualty of the occupation so many times. He squirmed uncomfortably as flashback after flashback shot through his mind. The secret police officer and the French franc. The forged papers in his *distasha* pocket. The night the stray bullet nearly hit him on his own front step. The big man and his soldiers at the Saudi border station. Farouk firing at the fleeing Iraqis. The exploding missiles ripping through the neighborhood. Yes, there had been many times that he could just as easily have died as survived.

Why has God brought me through the nightmare alive and unharmed? Why has He protected me from torture and/or death?

Tears came to his eyes as he thought of his friend, Talal, of Maithem and Jafer, Essa's young and innocent nephews, of the proud and brave young women like Asrar, of Farouk's sister and her relentless and futile search for her son...of all of those who suffered while he was spared.

A prayer of gratitude escaped his lips as the taxi pulled into Gina's driveway. Somehow, Ali knew, he had to make an effort to be worthy of being saved. Somehow he had to find a way to pay tribute to those who had not been.

He wiped his eyes and glanced at his watch. It was 10:30. All of the house lights were on. *They are still awake*, he thought as he slid out of the cab. Light snow was still falling and Ali drew in a deep breath of the fresh, cold air. It smelled so good compared to the sickening smell of burning oil.

Quickly he walked up the sidewalk leading to the front porch and pushed the doorbell. The living room drapes parted slightly, and he saw Gina peering out, a puzzled look on her face. Then her look changed to one of recognition, and Ali heard her scream.

"It's Ali!" as she raced to the door.

The door flew open and Ali was nearly bowled over as his sister-in-law grabbed and hugged him. Returning her hug, he looked over her shoulder to see Dina standing in the kitchen doorway, her face pale with shock and disbelief.

"I told you that you'd find me on your doorstep one day," he said as she walked hesitantly toward him, "and this just happens to be the day."

The sound of Ali's voice assured her that this wasn't a dream, as she had feared when she first saw his face. "Oh, Ali," she shrieked with joy, now moving towards him at a run. "It is you! You are really here!" She flung her arms around his neck and kissed him. Then Ali picked her up and carried her to the sofa, sinking down on it with her in his lap.

"Yes, I am here," he smiled, taking her hand in his. He had dreamed every night of holding her hand since that day in October when it had been torn from his as Mike's car left the driveway. He would die before he ever let that happen again, he vowed to himself."

"Hey, Dad!" Jassim shouted as he threw open the basement door. "I thought I heard your voice, but I was afraid I was dreaming!" The youngster rushed to the sofa and grabbed his father in a bear hug. "Where's the catcher's mitt?"

Ali laughed. "Tomorrow, Jassim," he said. "I'll buy you one tomorrow." *What a precious word tomorrow is*, he thought. There had been so many days after the nightmare had begun that he'd wondered if there would ever be a tomorrow.

Now, Ali knew as he hugged his wife and firstborn, there would be many tomorrows.

EPILOGUE

We returned to Kuwait on July 22, 1991. A certain sadness greeted us when we arrived. It could be felt in the air and seen in people's eyes. The aura of security and trust that I had witnessed for so many years was no longer present. Kuwaitis will always be looking over their shoulder, waiting for another "ally" to stab them in the back. I felt that never again will the people of Kuwait feel totally safe. Their innocence is gone. This is the legacy left by a ruthless, land-worshipping dictator.

But, despite the negative vibrations, I feel a certain optimism in the country, even though nearly everyone has been touched by one type of horror or another. Some Kuwaitis suffered physically during Saddam's seven-month reign of terror; all suffered psychologically.

Despite the suffering and mistrust, however, I am confident that my adopted country will emerge stronger than it was on August 2, 1990. Kuwaitis are survivors. Survival was bred in them by their desert ancestors. They will not let a Saddam Hussein extinguish their spirit.

Since our return, our family has grown with the birth of our sixth child and second daughter, Iman. She is our symbol of the rebirth of a proud nation.

—Dina

Publisher's note:

In 1998, as we go to press, the family in Kuwait tries to live a "normal" life—"at least as normal as any family with six children," says Dina. All are taking karate lessons. Jassim has received his black belt.

Dina is now teaching kindergarten in an American bilingual school system. Ali is a librarian at the local high school. Jassim is a freshman at Kuwait University majoring in computer engineering. Nadia is a freshman in high school; Zade is in eighth grade; Yacoub, seventh grade; Hussain fourth grade and Iman is in second grade.

ABOUT THE AUTHOR

Karen Kirk Huffman was born in 1937 in the small town of Neligh, Nebraska, to a farm couple, Orville and DaNolda Kirk. She met her husband Richard Huffman while a senior at

Karen Kirk Huffman

Neligh High school and the couple married in May of 1956. They had two children, a daughter Debra, who died in 1987 of malignant melanoma, and a son Rick, a former television reporter, currently Director of Community Relations for Southeastern Behavioral Healthcare in Sioux Falls, South Dakota.

This was the author's first attempt at writing a book, although she spent twenty-five years as a reporter and humor columnist for a chain of four suburban Omaha, Nebraska, newspapers.

A personal friend of the book's main characters, Dina and Ali, Huffman felt the need to write their story after learning the details of the nightmare they lived after the Iraqi invasion.

Karen Kirk Huffman died from cancer on February 17, 1996 without seeing her work in print.